Solving the Samaritan Riddle

Solving the Samaritan Riddle

Peter's Kingdom Keys Explain Early Spirit Baptism

KERMIT ZARLEY

WIPF & STOCK · Eugene, Oregon

SOLVING THE SAMARITAN RIDDLE
Peter's Kingdom Keys Explain Early Spirit Baptism

Copyright © 2015 Kermit Zarley. All rights reserved. Except for brief quotations in critical publications or reviews, no part of this book may be reproduced in any manner without prior written permission from the publisher. Write: Permissions, Wipf and Stock Publishers, 199 W. 8th Ave., Suite 3, Eugene, OR 97401.

Wipf & Stock
An Imprint of Wipf and Stock Publishers
199 W. 8th Ave., Suite 3
Eugene, OR 97401

www.wipfandstock.com

ISBN 13: 978-1-4982-2528-1

Manufactured in the U.S.A.   08/28/2015

A portion of the material in this book is quoted from the book by James D. G. Dunn entitled *Baptism in the Holy Spirit: A Re-examination of the New Testament Teaching on the Gift of the Spirit in relation to Pentecostalism today*, and it is reproduced here with permission from the publisher.

Unless otherwise noted, all Scripture quotations contained herein are from New Revised Standard Version Bible, copyright © 1989 National Council of the Churches of Christ in the United States of America. Used by permission. All rights reserved.

Scripture quotations marked (NIV) are taken from the Holy Bible, New International Version®, NIV®. Copyright © 1973, 1978, 1984, 2011 by Biblica, Inc.™ Used by permission of Zondervan. All rights reserved worldwide. www.zondervan.com The "NIV" and "New International Version" are trademarks registered in the United States Patent and Trademark Office by Biblica, Inc.™

Scripture quotations marked (NASB) are taken from the New American Standard Bible®, Copyright © 1960, 1962, 1963, 1968, 1971, 1972, 1973, 1975, 1977, 1995 by The Lockman Foundation. Used by permission. www.Lockman.org

Scripture quotations marked (ESV) are from the ESV® Bible (The Holy Bible, English Standard Version®), copyright © 2001 by Crossway, a publishing ministry of Good News Publishers. Used by permission. All rights reserved.

Contents

Preface | vii
Abbreviations | xiii

CHAPTER 1
The Holy Ghost Visits Pop | 1

CHAPTER 2
The Holy Spirit Visits Me | 15

CHAPTER 3
Jesus' Life and Teaching Regarding the Holy Spirit | 34

CHAPTER 4
The Apostle Peter's Keys of the Kingdom of Heaven | 51

CHAPTER 5
Spirit Baptism on the Day of Pentecost (Acts 2) | 72

CHAPTER 6
Spirit Baptism on the Samaritans (Acts 8) | 96

CHAPTER 7
Spirit Baptism on the Apostle Paul (Acts 9) | 119

CHAPTER 8
Spirit Baptism on the Cornelius Household (Acts 10) | 131

CHAPTER 9
Spirit Baptism on the Ephesians (Acts 19) | 142

CHAPTER 10
Paul's Teaching on the Holy Spirit and Spiritual Gifts | 155

CHAPTER 11
Roman Catholicism | 178

CHAPTER 12
Conclusions | 195

Works Cited | 211
Index of Authors | 211
Index of Subjects and Names | 211
Index of Scripture and Other Ancient Documents | 211

Preface

I met Dr. Scot McKnight in 1992. It was my first year as a professional golfer on the PGA Senior Tour (now Champions Tour). Scot was a New Testament (NT) professor at Trinity Evangelical Divinity School near Chicago, and he was a good golfer. Since I was competing in our Ameritech Senior Open tournament in the Chicago area that summer, I invited Scot to attend it. We became close friends after that, and we remain so to this day.

Scot was an answer to prayer. I was asking God to give me a friendship with a theological professor with whom I could learn and discuss the Bible and theology. With Scot, God answered that prayer beyond my wildest imagination. Scot is very bright, friendly, and he writes many theological books. So, he knows lots of people in his profession. Through Dr. Scot McKnight, I now have many theological professor friends.

During the late 1990s, Scot changed employment to North Park University in Chicago. He then invited me to be the sole donor for a new, two-day lecture series for NPU students that he was thinking of creating and directing. It would be an annual affair that would feature a different, renowned Bible scholar as the only guest lecturer each year. Scot said that if I became the donor, the school wanted to use my name as the title for it. I eventually agreed to do it.

The first Kermit Zarley Lectures were held in 2000. The guest lecturer was Dr. James D. G. Dunn. He was Scot McKnight's dissertation supervisor when Scot earned his PhD at Nottingham University in Nottingham, England. Dr. Dunn, whom friends call "Jimmy," had become one of the most distinguished NT scholars in the world.[1] And his many theological

---

1. Dunn was born in 1939 and retired in 2009 as Lightfoot Professor Emeritus of Divinity at the University of Durham, England. He is a Fellow of the British Academy.

Preface

books were being widely read. Jimmy is very cordial, so I enjoyed hearing him speak and getting to know him. Some of us had dinner with him that first evening.

Scot also persuaded me that year to join the Society of Biblical Literature (SBL) even though most of its 8,000 members are professors with PhDs. He said I would benefit from it due to my interest in Bible studies and theology. Founded in 1880, SBL is the oldest and largest society in the world that critically examines the Bible from multiple disciplines. So, after the lectures in 2000, Jimmy, Scot, and I flew to Nashville to attend SBL's five-day annual meeting. Its two main features are religious publishers offering their discounted books for sale in a large hall and hundreds of SBL study groups meeting for two-to-three hour sessions wherein members present papers that are then discussed by attendees.

I was still competing on the Champions Tour fulltime and doing well financially. So, Scot also asked me if I wanted to attend and fund the "Dunn dinner" there in Nashville. Held every year at SBL's annual meeting, it consists of Jimmy having dinner with his PhD students at a fine restaurant. I was excited to do that, too, and had a wonderful time. And I attended it two more times after that.

The next year, in 2001, SBL's annual meeting was held in Denver. I was privileged to room with Scot, John Lunde, and Jimmy Dunn. It was quite an experience getting to know Jimmy more and asking him questions.

After first meeting Dr. Dunn, I began adding many of his books to my theological library and reading most of them. I had his first book, *Baptism in the Holy Spirit*,[2] which was his PhD dissertation. But I had not read it. Published in 1970, it is the first scholarly book that thoroughly examines the Bible in an attempt to refute the Pentecostals' "doctrine of subsequence" as they call it. This means that Christians experience the baptism with the Holy Spirit mentioned in the NT *subsequent to*, that is, *after* their conversion to faith in Jesus as Savior. Classical Pentecostals also insist that recipients

---

Dunn also has been a minister in the Church of Scotland and a Methodist local preacher.

2. The subtitle of this book is *A Re-examination of the New Testament Teaching on the Gift of the Spirit in Relation to Pentecostalism Today*. The publisher produced a second edition of it in 2010 upon the book's fortieth anniversary. The only difference in the second edition is an added, twelve-page, second preface. Dunn's primary periodical articles on this subject include "Baptism in the Spirit: A Response to Pentecostal Scholarship in Luke-Acts," "Baptism in the Holy Spirit: Yet Once More," and "Baptism in the Holy Spirit: Yet Once More—Again." Dunn treats this issue partially in his books *Jesus and the Spirit*, *The Acts of the Apostles*, and *The Christ and the Spirit: Volume 2: Pneumatology*, which has a collection of these periodical articles.

Preface

must "speak in tongues" as incontrovertible, initial evidence of this Spirit baptism. Thus, these Pentecostals say if you don't speak in tongues you have not been baptized with the Holy Spirit. This "doctrine of separability and subsequence" is still the primary feature that distinguishes Pentecostals from other Christians.

In *Baptism in the Holy Spirit* (=*Baptism*), Dunn contends that the Apostle Paul's NT letters indicate people are baptized in the Holy Spirit simultaneously at conversion so that there is no separation ("separability") in time between these two events.[3] Jimmy has adhered to this position ever since. Other prominent scholars who later wrote books about this subject from the same viewpoint have included Professor Frederick Dale Bruner of Fuller Theological Seminary, Reformed systematic theologian Anthony A. Hoekema, and John R. W. Stott, who was the UK's leading Evangelical theologian.[4]

The foremost Pentecostal scholars who have written books advocating subsequence are former Professor Howard M. Ervin and current Professor James B. Shelton of Oral Roberts University, Professor Roger J. Stronstad of Summit Pacific College in British Columbia, and Robert P. Menzies, an American scholar-missionary to Asia.[5] Pentecostal scholar Gordon D. Fee and ex-Pentecostal Max Turner have written on this subject and sided with Dunn.[6]

Dunn's *Baptism* unexpectedly helped propel Pentecostals into the academic arena that their tradition formerly rejected. It caused a firestorm of books authored by new, Pentecostal scholars who tried to rebut Dunn's book.[7] After forty-five years, what Pentecostals call the Dunn Debate has not dissipated.

---

3. I prefer "separateness" rather than "separability," as used by Pentecostals, since the latter is peculiar to mathematics and law.

4. Bruner, *A Theology of the Holy Spirit*; Hoekema, *Holy Spirit Baptism*; Stott, *Baptism & Fullness*.

5. Ervin, *Conversion-Initiation*; Ervin, *Spirit-Baptism*; Stronstad, *The Charismatic Theology of St. Luke*; Shelton, *Mighty in Word and Deed*; Menzies, *The Development of Early Christian Pneumatology*; Menzies, *Empowered for Witness*.

6. Fee, *Gospel and Spirit*; Fee, *God's Empowering Presence*; Fee, "Baptism in the Holy Spirit: The Issue of Separability and Subsequence;" Turner, *Power from on High*.

7. Steve Hendrickson, founder and past owner of Hendrickson Publishers and Christian Book Distributors, deserves much credit in making this debate happen. Hendrickson Publishers produced many books written by Pentecostal scholars in response to Dunn's *Baptism in the Holy Spirit*.

Preface

Even before Jimmy wrote this book, I was taught as an Evangelical what he claims about Paul's teaching, that people receive the Holy Spirit when they believe in Jesus. And for a long time I believed that what Jesus said to his disciples—that they would be baptized with the Holy Spirit and become his witnesses in Jerusalem, Judea, Samaria, and the ends of the earth (Acts 1:5, 8)—began to be fulfilled in incidents that Luke records early in his book of Acts.

Then one summer day in 2012 I asked myself this question about Matt 16:19: "Does the NT say anything about Peter using 'the keys of the kingdom of heaven' that Jesus promised to give him?" I then said, "If it does, it must be in Luke's book of Acts." Upon further reading of this exciting history of the early church, I concluded that Peter exercised his role with his kingdom keys not only in his preaching Luke mentions in Acts 2 and 10, but also regarding Spirit baptism in those texts and Acts 8. I then wrote a two-page article about this discovery and thought no more of it.

On November 1, 2013, I enlarged this article, titled it "Peter's Kingdom Keys Explain Spirit Baptism," and posted it on my Kermit Zarley Blog hosted at patheos.com. In doing research on it, I noticed that scholars who wrote books about Spirit baptism did not connect it to Jesus' promise in Matt 16:17–19. And I learned that nearly all scholars who write commentaries on the Gospel of Matthew do not identify any of Peter's activities Luke records in his book of Acts as Peter exercising his role in using his kingdom keys. Then I asked Scot McKnight and other professors, including some Pentecostals, to read this post and tell me what they thought of it. All of them said they had not known of my hypothesis, and all but one said they thought it was interesting. Scot suggested it was worthy of a book.

I didn't know about the Dunn Debate until the next month. That's when I read the excellent, small book about it by Pentecostal scholar William P. Atkinson entitled *Baptism in the Spirit: Luke-Acts and the Dunn Debate* (2011). He thinks Pentecostals are right about Spirit baptism, so that Dunn is not right about it. But Atkinson seems to think Pentecostals are not fully persuasive about it since they cannot sufficiently align their distinctive doctrine with Paul's NT epistles. Atkinson concludes, "A convincing alternative to Dunn's view needs to be offered."[8]

That's what I'm trying to do with this book—offer an alternative for possibly solving this debate between Dunn's simultaneity and the Pentecostal's subsequence regarding conversion and Spirit baptism. In so doing,

---

8. Atkinson, *Baptism in the Spirit*, 66.

Preface

I agree and disagree with elements of both positions. I have much respect for my friend Jimmy Dunn. So I feel somewhat reluctant to write a book that focuses a lot on what he has written on this subject and disagree with some of it.

Yes, Scot's suggestion caused me to write this book. I have tried to restrict it mostly to Peter's kingdom keys and Spirit baptism. I only briefly discuss such related topics as the transition between ages, conversion, water baptism, and spiritual gifts such as tongues. I barely treat the OT background of the Holy Spirit or hermeneutics. Although I often interact with NT scholars, I also have attempted to make this book accessible to general readers. To further do so, I set the theological table in chapters 1 and 2 with personal, human-interest stories to help draw general readers into what has been a prominent theological discussion in much of church history, but especially in the past century due to the rise of Pentecostalism.

Abbreviations

GENERAL

CE	Common Era (=AD)
cf.	*confer*, compare
ch(s).	chapter(s)
diss.	dissertation
ed.	editor, edition, edited by
e.g.	*exempli gratia*, for example
esp.	especially
etc.	*et cetera*, and so forth
Ger.	German
Gr.	Greek
ibid.	*ibidem*, in the same place
n	note
n.d.	no date
orig.	original
p., pp.	page, pages
par.	and parallel(s) in other gospel(s)
v., vv.	verse, verses
vol(s).	volume(s)

Abbreviations

BOOKS OF THE BIBLE

Old Testament

Gen	Genesis	Ps	Psalm
Exod	Exodus	Isa	Isaiah
Lev	Leviticus	Jer	Jeremiah
Num	Numbers	Ezek	Ezekiel
Deut	Deuteronomy	Dan	Daniel
Josh	Joshua	Hos	Hosea
1 Kgs	1 Kings	Mic	Micah
2 Kgs	2 Kings	Hag	Haggai
2 Chr	2 Chronicles	Zech	Zechariah
Esth	Esther	Mal	Malachi

New Testament

Matt	Matthew	1 Tim	1 Timothy
Rom	Romans	2 Tim	2 Timothy
1 Cor	1 Corinthians	Heb	Hebrews
2 Cor	2 Corinthians	Jas	James
Gal	Galatians	1 Pet	1 Peter
Eph	Ephesians	2 Pet	2 Peter
Col	Colossians	Rev	Revelation
1 Thess	1 Thessalonians		

BIBLE VERSIONS, REFERENCE WORKS, JOURNALS

AB	Anchor Bible
ANF	*Ante-Nicene Fathers.* Edited by Alexander Roberts, James Donaldson, et al. 1985–1987. 10 vols. Repr., Peabody, Mass.: Hendrickson Publishers, 1994
BAGD	Walter Bauer, W. F. Arndt, F. W. Gingrich, and Frederick W. Danker. *Greek-English Lexicon of the New Testament and Other Early Christian Literature.* 2nd ed. Chicago: University of Chicago Press, 1979

Abbreviations

BECNT	Baker Exegetical Commentary on the New Testament
CJPCC	*Canadian Journal of Pentecostal and Charismatic Christianity*
DDD	*Dictionary of Deities and Demons in the Bible.* Edited by K. van der Toorn, B. Becking, and P. W. van der Horst. Leiden: Brill/Grand Rapids: Eerdmans, 1999. Second ed. Orig. ed. 1995.
EBC	Expositor's Bible Commentary, The, with the NIV. 12 vols.
ESV	The Holy Bible, English Standard Version (2001)
ET	English Translation
Hermeneia	Hermeneia: A Critical and Historical Commentary on the Bible
IBS	*Irish Biblical Studies*
ICC	International Critical Commentary. London: T&T Clark, 1991
JPT	*Journal of Pentecostal Theology*
JEPTA	*The Journal of the European Pentecostal Theological Association*
KJV	King James Version (1611)
LXX	Septuagint (Gr. OT)
NAC	New American Commentary
NASB	New American Standard Bible (1995)
NCE	*New Catholic Encyclopedia.* Edited by W. J. McDonald et al. 15 vols. New York, 1967
NICNT	New International Commentary on the New Testament
NIGTC	New International Greek Testament Commentary
NIV	The Holy Bible, New International Version (2011)
NPNF[1]	*Nicene and Post-Nicene Fathers*, Series 1. Edited by Philip Schaff. 14 vols. Reprint, Peabody, Mass., 1994
NPNF[2]	*Nicene and Post-Nicene Fathers*, Series 2. Edited by Philip Schaff and Henry Wace. 14 vols. Reprint, Peabody, Mass., 1994
NRSV	New Revised Standard Version Bible (1989)
NT	New Testament
NTC	New Testament Commentary

Abbreviations

NTS	*New Testament Studies*
OT	Old Testament
PNTC	Pillar New Testament Commentary
Pneuma	*Pneuma*: The Journal of the Society for Pentecostal Studies
SPS	Sacra Pagina Series
SJT	*Scottish Journal of Theology*
TDNT	*Theological Dictionary of the New Testament.* 10 vols. Edited by Gerhard Kittel and Gerhard Friedrich. Translated by George W. Bromiley. Grand Rapids: Eerdmans, 1964–76.
UBS⁴	*Greek New Testament, The.* 4th edition. United Bible Societies.

CHAPTER 1

The Holy Ghost Visits Pop

(Chapter 1 of Barbara Zarley's unpublished memoirs, with minor editing by her son Kermit)

"Wanna go to a dance Monday night?" Pop asked.

"Monday night?" I echoed. That was strange. We *never* went to a dance *any* night. And on Monday night, no one went dancing. There wasn't any dance.

"Duke Ellington's playin' at the Hippodrome," Pop informed. "It's an off night. He's just passing through town."

My eyes got big and my jaw dropped open. Never did I dream I'd dance to Duke Ellington's band, let alone see and hear the Duke himself. This would truly be a momentous occasion for me—to attend Duke Ellington's only appearance ever in our little vicinity of the world.[1]

I had just met this guy named Kermit that summer, one year after I graduated from high school. I first noticed him at the Triple X Root Beer Drive-In Stand in the city of Yakima, which is located in Eastern Washington. My sister, Giner, pointed him out to me. My eyes bugged out. This guy was *handsome*.

---

1. Duke's "big band" is the best-known orchestra in jazz history. Duke Ellington (1899–1974) wrote over a thousand orchestral compositions that represent the largest, recorded, personal jazz legacy ever. In 1999, he was awarded a Pulitzer Prize for music post-humously.

There he was, dressed in whites and charming some girls hanging all over his car. He wasn't a doctor, an intern, or a male nurse in a medical uniform. No, he was a soda jerk. And he didn't work there at the Triple X. Only girls worked there, serving. They wore brown costumes, the color of root beer, trimmed in yellow and orange.

The Triple X Drive-In was *the place* to gather for us young folks. But my sister and I rarely congregated there. We lived in Selah, four miles away. Some people called it a "hick town." Downtown Selah was only two blocks long. Selah is a town; Yakima is a city. Our town fathers got the name Selah from the Bible.

When we first met I asked, "What's your name?"

"Kermit Zarley," he answered.

What a strange name, I thought. But it didn't stick in my head that first time, neither his first name nor his last name. Maybe I was too googly-eyed over his good looks.

So, reminiscing, I call him "Pop." That's our family name for him. It seems to fit him better now.

I first met Pop out at Eschbaugh Park where he worked selling hot-dogs and sodas. One night I hung around until he gave me a free hot dog and soda. But I wasn't looking for handouts. That wasn't why I was there.

Even though it was the end of the Great Depression, Pop owned a car—an old, black Model-A Ford. He had quit high school early so he could work, make money, and help put food on the table at home. All of my brothers did the same thing.

Monday night arrived. "I hope the Duke shows up," I muttered, "and Kermit, too."

And they did. Out to Selah Pop drove in that rumbling Ford. It rattled to a stop under the large, swaying cottonwood trees hovering beside our house. Those shade trees provided us with some needed respite from the hot summer sun. Eastern Washington is hot and dry in the summertime, unlike its counterpart—Western Washington.

The beautiful Cascade mountain range runs north and south through the middle of our state. Yes, Western Washington is known for its many days of rain, especially in Seattle. But Eastern Washington doesn't have that much moisture. The prevailing winds blow eastward from the Pacific Ocean across the Puget Sound saltwater and then elevate over the Cascades, dropping tons of rain and snow on them. With little moisture left, those same winds continue, descending down the eastern slopes of the Cascade

The Holy Ghost Visits Pop

Mountains. And as they do, they warm significantly. The result is that Eastern Washington is much warmer and drier than Western Washington.

I breathed a sigh of relief. There Kermit stood, smiling with his big, wide grin, his bluish eyes a-twinkle, semi-blond hair combed back in an oily, distinct wave, sparse whiskers on his Burma-shaved chin, and smelling good. He was wearing his only suit—a spiffy, medium-blue pin-stripe with a matching vest jacket.

Kermit helped me into my black, skunk-fur, bolero jacket that ended at the waist. The plush, white sleeves ended at the elbow. That upper outfit was striking, if I say so myself. I never thought I'd own a jacket like that. It cost me a pretty penny.

All dolled up in my best, I was. I had on a red organdy dress that I sewed myself on the treadle sewing machine. The dress was a straight bodice over my skinny bust and a full skirt to below the knees.

We jumped into the Ford and headed to see and hear the Duke and dance the night away.

Time and again, waiting for this big night to come, I had imagined it all—my red skirt billowing out and flowing round-and-round on the dance floor, with Pop leaning forward, his cheek pressed to mine.

We motored off the tarred road of town, behind the city limits and just past the state bank. I sneaked a look in my compact mirror as we chugged along down the narrow, gravelly road stretched out straight ahead.

With summer nearly over, the temperature right, the night growing dark, a full moon out, and many stars shining brightly in the sky, it was the perfect night for a young couple on a date.

The smell of all those apples would soon be in the air. They were making the Yakima Valley sort of famous during the last years of the Depression. Apples would be everywhere on the trees, ripening and waiting to be hand-picked, transported, and stored in warehouses, or to be sent to the vaps. Vap is short for evaporator. That's where they dry apples. Dried apples don't have to be refrigerated, and they are easier and cheaper to ship.

Just outside of Selah, Mt. Jones was scooping up free truckloads of fresh apple peelings and cores at the vap for his pigs. Healthy pigs they were—healthy but smelly.

Not me, I thought, smelling good and feeling garishly beautiful with a willowy wisp of a figure. Colored rouge on my cheeks, thick red lipstick on my lips, a thin dark eyebrow pencil drawn over hard to pluck eyebrows, black mascara applied to painfully curled eyelashes, red-painted nails and hair set in hair-pins, the hair now loosely combed. I did my hair myself. You can get your hair permed at the beauty shop in heavy clasps that hang from cords to an umbrella-like machine hovering over your head. "It's a waste of time and money," I always said.

It's a wonder I didn't go up in smoke. It's painful to be beautiful.

Odd bits of jewelry I wore, including a double strand of pearls I bought at the Five and Ten-Cent Store.

I was ready for an exciting and gala evening. And Pop, I confide, appeared just as excited as I was. Outlandishly confident in his spiffy, mobster-looking suit, a smile all over his face, he laughed and talked smoothly a mile-a-minute, at times out of the side of his mouth so I could hear him over the rattle of his old jollopy.

Laugh wrinkles already, a bit of a golden wave in a curl bouncing on his acne forehead. Acne all over his face. He looked like he'd been squeezing the blackheads out or else he had stayed under the sun lamp too long. His face was uncommonly red.

I still had a little bit of acne myself, but it was clearing up.

Pop said he was my age, but I found out later he was six months younger than me.

"Umm," Pop exclaimed, "you look ravishing, doll. And you smell really good. Yes, you do," as he sniffed the air.

"Thanks," I responded, "it's my Mom's perfume."

He sniffed the air again and again. I sensed something was wrong.

I looked down at the jacket in my lap. Still warm outside, I didn't need a jacket. It was only to show off.

"No," I thought. I couldn't blame the skunk; it's dead. I had poured on too much of that perfume, that's what it was. That stuff is old. Mom got it when Dad used to sell Raleigh goods. How long ago was that? I was a little girl then. "I'm not using perfume ever again," I thought.

The dead hide in my lap seemed to squirm about as we bounced along on the lumpy road.

I smiled at Pop and looked down the road. Desolate country.

I could see the Hippodrome ahead. It's the big, fat, round building all lit up and ready to go. As we got closer to those lights, I got more excited. We could hear the musicians warming up over the rattle of the car. Lots of people were walking in. I was anxious to get out of that bouncy car and join those people for a fun time.

The Holy Ghost Visits Pop

A bridge was in front of us. You take the bridge over the Yakima River and turn right to Playland Park and the Hippodrome Dance Hall, or you turn left into the Riverside Golf Course.

The golf course appeared dark, with a little red flag waving here and there. That's where the rich go to play: dentists and doctors and bankers and the like. My three older brothers used to caddy there for a few cents. They'd find old, beat-up, golf balls and bring them home. We'd cut off their rubber covers and unwind the elastic, rubber string from their insides. When we got finished, the ball was a mess.

We crossed the rickety wooden bridge spanning the Yakima River and came to the turn-in to Playland and the Hippodrome. But we continued straight ahead for the City of Yakima. That was *not* the way to the Hippodrome.

"Where are we going?" I asked with surprise.

Suddenly, Duke Ellington, his orchestra, and the musical sounds of the glorious Hippodrome were vanishing away. Out of sight, out of mind.

I thought things were looking dangerous and that I might need to save my life, let alone the night. Will I wake up dead out in the sagebrush someplace? How do I get out of this situation? "Think," I thought!

"We're going to church," Pop answered matter-of-factly.

My eyes grew big and round again. What for? I wondered. *To get married?*

"There're having a revival meeting at my folks' church," Pop explained. "I promised them we'd come."

"*Revival meeting*," I chirped.

Well, did I ever feel tricked. I didn't know what to say or do. Blow up, tell him to stop the car, get out of the car, walk home alone in my high heels and never see Pop again? I could get sarcastic and say, "Oh, that's what I wanted to do all along." Or should I feign rejoicing and say, "Oh, I'd love to do that?" But none of that was me. Should I go along and make the best of it? I sure thought of walking home. Selah is one mile from the Selah Bridge.

But I was in love.

So, I decided to go along and make the best of it. Seemed like the thing to do.

We headed for the Free Methodist Church. As the car rolled up near the entrance to the church and came to a screeching halt, there stood Pop's folks waiting to greet us.

Grandpa's baldhead glistened in the porch electric light. His brown suit jacket was too tight and his mismatched trousers too baggy. His worn brown shoes turned up at the toes. He grinned from ear to ear, his eyes little and merry. His forehead was wrinkled, and he had big laugh wrinkles on the sides of his face that sported square-shaped jowls. Kermit had gotten his big grin from his dad, Con Zarley. Con was short for Conover.

And there stood Grandma Edna, her smiling face cheery looking and happy, premature white hair contrasting an olive colored skin with her blue-grey eyes bright.

The small church was nearly packed with people, yet it was only Monday night. Folks were tired from working all day, ready to sit down and rest their weary bones. The little church building hummed with conversation. Many of the people had mid-western accents.

It was a hodge-podge of people. Most were dust bowl folks from the Midwest. Many had lost their mortgaged farms to the banks in foreclosure. Then they traveled west to try to find work, eke out a living, and just find a new life. They came from the Great Plains states such as North Texas, Oklahoma, Arkansas, Missouri, Nebraska, Kansas, Iowa, South Dakota, and North Dakota. They settled mostly in the western coastal states, first California, then Oregon, Washington, and some in Idaho.

This colossal migration was caused mostly by two factors. There was the Great Depression that started back east on Wall Street. Then came the drought in the Midwest. It resulted in many desolate, tumbleweed-filled Main Streets. In 1939, John Steinbeck wrote a famous novel about this migration of people—*The Grapes of Wrath*. The next year it became a blockbuster movie starring Henry Fonda.

But the Great Depression of the 1930s wasn't caused only by a decade-long, depressed economy and sparse rainfall. Farmers planted seeds but hardly anything grew due to their European ancestry. They had not known about the necessity of replenishing their rich topsoil with organic matter. They applied European agricultural methods to the drier Great Plains that only received an annual rainfall of twenty inches or less. Neither did they rotate crops or intermittently grow cover crops, such as grasses or alfalfa. And they didn't plow corn stocks and other agricultural refuse back into the soil. All of this reduced the topsoil's moisture content. Plus, they often plowed too deeply, burying the natural topsoil, which was rich in minerals and nutrients, beyond the reach of many plant roots. When drought came and strong winds blew, what topsoil they had just blew away.

The Holy Ghost Visits Pop

That period of time in the Midwest was called the Dirty Thirties. Sometimes, those dark, dust clouds prevented people from seeing more than a few feet away. When it got bad enough, children wore dust masks to school. The dust storms sometimes blew southward, but mostly eastward. The blackened sky could reach all the way to the eastern seaboard. Much of that Great Plains topsoil was actually deposited into the Atlantic Ocean.

Both Kermit and I were born in the Midwest. Both of our families were farmers. They lost their mortgaged farms to the banks and moved west. My family came from Kansas, and Kermit's came from Iowa. This human migration is still the largest within a short period of time in all of U.S. history.

So, at one time many of these church folk had owned a flourishing business or a farm back in their previous home state. But now, they were dirt poor. Why had they moved here to the Yakima Valley? They had gone from the Dust Bowl to the Fruit Bowl. There was no problem with drought here, and men could get work.

Canal irrigation had made this area blossom in the springtime with its many fruit trees. And in those days, there was no mechanical, fruit-picking equipment. Since the fruit had to be handpicked, at least there were plenty of part-time jobs available. But if you were going to try to make a fulltime living at it, you had to become a migrant laborer. Still, most people called fruit-picking pay "starvation wages."

The men were hired out to pick cherries, peaches, pears, and prunes in the summer. The biggest crop—apples—ripened in the fall. Of course, everyone ate some of what they picked, and many of them got diarrhea from it. Most of the women and kids picked hops that were used for brewing beer. Hops were easier to pick since they grew on vines that were lower to the ground. And you didn't have to tenderly handle them to avoid bruising, as with fruit.

As Pop and I walked into the church, those nearby in the pews turned toward us, smiling. People moved over to make room for us to sit on the hard, wooden bench alongside Pop's folks.

There wasn't a touch of make-up on any woman's face in that house of worship. All of the ladies wore non-descript dresses that hung nearly to their ankles. They were clothed in long-sleeved blouses or sweaters to modestly cover their arms. Their worn hands rested in their laps on open hymnbooks, with closed, black Bibles sitting on the bench nearby. And all of them kept their hair long and done up in a knot in the back. And I didn't see any jewelry, not even a wedding band. No luxury or pretense here in this modest looking house of God.

Kermit's mother later told me, sounding intelligent and her grey eyes looking bright, "the Apostle Paul said women must dress modestly. We don't cut our hair short because it is our crowning glory. We don't adorn ourselves with jewelry. I used to have a wedding ring, but I threw it away somewhere. I couldn't find it now if I wanted to."

We energetically sang lots of songs, such as "Love Lifted Me," "Standing on the Promises," "When the Saints Go Marching In," and "Onward Christian Soldiers." They sang forcefully, harmoniously, and sounded well.

They had no piano or musical instruments to accompany their singing. They didn't believe in such worldly things. Musical instruments they deemed the work of the devil. I was told later that most parishioners had forgotten the reason for this excision in their tradition.[2]

The women clearly sang out the loudest, as if venting hidden frustrations, I thought.

The aging evangelist, with the long, graying beard, flailed his thin arms this way and that. A tall, gangly man, he shuffled about the stage, sometimes circling the pulpit. It looked like a strong dust storm could have blown him away. Yet his voice was deep and powerful.

"If you don't have the Lord in your heart, you're going to hell if you don't repent and accept him tonight," the preacher thundered, waving his arms to and fro. "Jesus died on the cross to save us from our sins. By grace we are saved, not by our good works. Now, let's stand up and sing, 'The Old Rugged Cross.' Let heaven hear how you feel about your sins having been removed as far away from you as the east is from the west."

We stood and sang with gusto. I pondered that old rugged cross far away in both time and distance on that little hill called Golgotha. Then we sang, "Whiter than Snow."

"Where do you want to spend eternity, in heaven or hell?" the evangelist forcefully inquired. "If you haven't made that most important decision in life, this may be your last chance. If you died tonight, where would your precious soul spend eternity, in heaven or in hell?"

As he preached, he swayed back and forth and then sideways some more, sometimes with his eyes shut. Then he suddenly threw up his slender

---

2. Three years later, in 1943, the General Conference of the Free Methodist Church voted to allow each of its conferences to decide if they wanted instrumental music in their church meetings.

The Holy Ghost Visits Pop

arms, jerked his head back, looked up at the ceiling, and shouted at the top of his strong voice, "Open your heart to *Jeeee-sus*. He's knocking at the door of your heart to come in."

This preacher of destiny shifted about some more. With a grimaced, serious look on his face he asked us, "What's the worst sin in the whole world anyone can commit?"

Most of us sat on the edge of our seats, necks bent forward toward the pulpit, and our eyes riveted on this man of God. No one dared offer an answer. All mouths were tightly shut. That moment was his and his alone to break the deafening silence.

"To refuse the Holy Ghost when he's knocking at the door of your heart to come in" was his bellowing, self-assured answer. "*That's* the worst sin you can ever commit. Now, all you fine Christian folk who have already answered that heavenly call of the Holy Ghost upon your lives, *please stand up*."

Most people stood up. But Pop and I just sat there as if glued to our seats. We were *so* nervous. We kept our heads down, staring at the floor. I thought we were what these good people might call "outcasts" or "sinners."

The preacher man then gave the beckoning call, "Let all come forward who want to dedicate the remainder of their lives to serve the Lord."

About half of the folks standing walked forward to the altar and knelt to pray. They prayed out loud for themselves, then their kinfolk, their neighbors, the wayward folks in the audience who were still sitting in the pews, like me and Pop, and for sinners everywhere, even for the whole wide world.

Their voices rose in a chorus, first low, and then so loud that anyone outside the church, no doubt blocks away, could hear them crying out with such heartfelt emotion.

"Amen, hallelujah, amen, brothers and sisters," the minister shrieked with joy. With his voice loud and shaky, his head held high, tears began to roll down his cheeks.

The scene was so surreal, as emotionally close to heaven as fallen humans could possibly attain, I thought.

Then Grandpa Con walked over, sat down beside us, and put his arm around Kermit's shoulder. I didn't look up. I kept my eyes fastened on that hardwood floor.

I knew Kermit was in some sort of a bewildering state of mind. I thought I could tell that his body was quivering. There he sat, young at heart in his finest attire, his back bent forward, his head bowed low, and a very strained look on his handsome, ruddy face. Was the Holy Ghost stirring about in his heart and mind?

His muscled body appeared tense. I imagined that if he stood up, his hidden pack of cigarettes in the pocket of his tight shirt might pop out and fly across the altar. But then, maybe he'd give them up along with the cussing, drinking, gambling, card playing, and banging on those colorful pinball machines at the pool hall until late at night.

Then I started thinking about my own life, about my own sins. "No one is perfect, no, not one," I murmured under my breath. "All have sinned and come short of the glory of God," I recalled from somewhere in the Bible. I had a little bit of church in me, too. Still, I sat there pretty scared.

Pop turned to me and said, "Let's go up to the altar." The minister had his hands outstretched right toward the two of us. I thought he was pleading with only us in mind. Now I noticed tears rolling down Grandpa's face, too.

But not mine. My cold, English heart held back. This salvation call was just too much and too soon for me. I couldn't give up my life of dancing, picture shows, card playing with my family, playing the piano, and just letting the good times roll.

I envisioned Pop up there at the pulpit some day, hollerin and preachin like that evangelist. "I tell you folks, *there's a better life*," I imagined him shouting. "Where do you plan to spend eternity?" Then I mused in my mind, "Yeah, us married, with a bunch of kids, and all of us starvin to death."

So, I responded to Kermit silently with pierced lips and barely shaking my head from side to side. I let him know that my answer was firmly "no." So, we stood up, walked out of that pressure-cooker church, got into the Ford, and drove off toward my house.

When we arrived, Pop uttered softly, "Those are the happiest people on earth." His shiny, blue-grey eyes moistened up and glistened in the moonlight. Then he kissed and hugged me as we said goodnight and parted.

But his thoughts seemed to me to be elsewhere. Was he pondering the preacher's words, the spiritual condition of his own soul, and perhaps where *he'd* spend eternity? Maybe. Or was he thinking of some late card game he had lined up with his buddies in some nightclub in Yakima? I was afraid to ask.

The Holy Ghost Visits Pop

I opened the unlocked door of my house and went in. My mother was in bed by now, in the bedroom next to the parlor. She raised herself up on one elbow. "Oh, it's you, baby," she said lovingly. That's what she always called me. "Home early, huh?"

She was usually in bed and sound asleep by nine. But there she was, wide awake, waiting for me to come home. I sat on the edge of her bed beside her. Her large blue eyes appeared quizzical in the light streaming in from the light bulb that was still turned on in the dining room.

"Did you have a good time?"

"We didn't go to the dance."

"You didn't? Where did you go?"

"We went to his folks' church, the Free Methodist Church. They had a revival meeting."

"Well, I do declare. I never heard the like. I thought you were going to the dance."

"I sure wanted to go, and I thought about it all night long. But we didn't go."

"Does he like to dance?"

"I don't think so. He's never learned how. But he seems to have good rhythm."

"What did the people think of your new dress?"

"They didn't say. It's probably not the sort of thing they would wear. They talked to us and were friendly, and his mom and dad gave me a hug."

"I guess they were glad you came."

I knew to say good night so she could get to sleep and be up by five in the morning. She would trot as fast as her short, sturdy legs could carry her four feet, ten inch frame to her little restaurant around the corner and five doors up Main Street. With sixteen stools, she sometimes worked it alone. She opened the place at six in the morning for breakfast and served through lunchtime. I kissed her goodnight and gave her a big hug.

Then, beside the old ironwood and coal-heating stove in the dining room, I took off my party clothes that didn't get to go to the party. I got into my homemade cotton flannel pajamas, unmasked my painted face with Pond's cold cream, and went back to being me again. A month from now the stove will be warm this time of night.

Upstairs in my bed, I lay dreaming the night through. The moon lit up the room in a ghastly, bluish-yellow light. In my dreams, I danced with Pop until morning to the magical sounds of Duke Ellington's piano. We seemed like a good-looking couple together, Pop being five feet and ten plus inches and me at five feet six. We danced cheek-to-cheek right out of the Hippodrome and up to the stars far away. We touched first one star and then another. Duke's music was enchanting.

"Prelude to a Kiss."

"Sophisticated Lady."

"Dancing in the Dark."

Then we kissed the stars goodnight and danced back to the Hippodrome just in time for Duke's orchestra to respectfully stop playing as the dancers gathered 'round to listen to the charming, charismatic Duke tell a few tales and entertain us some more by both sight and sound.

Bent over the keys his long ebony fingers, each a strong hammer, gave throbbing life to the black and white keyboard. Up and down it his fingers raced quickly, gently tapping and then pounding those ivories. Quick and catchy there, slow and mellow and dreamy, here. Now, syncopated rhythm. The melodies were hypnotic.

The next thing I knew, my alarm clock went off, blasting away, right in the middle of "Take the 'A' Train." I was so disappointed that my dreaming was over. It was time to go to work.

I jumped out of bed and into my clothes lying next to the cold heating stove downstairs. I placed my wrinkled, damp pajamas on a chair to dry. I guess I sweated in my sleep, being emotionally strung-out due to the unusual evening.

Before getting out the door to work, I kinda got in an argument with my sister. Younger than I, she was now a junior at Selah high school.

"How was Duke Ellington?" she queried, her brown eyes flashing, and her uncombed, brown, shiny hair in a bit of a crook-wave circling above her bright face.

"I'll tell you later," I grumbled. "Gotta go now."

"Think you're smart, don'cha, getting to see and hear the Duke. I wanted to go, too. I play the drums, ya' know. How come you got to go and I didn't?"

"See you later," I muttered, and was quickly out the door.

On my way up Main Street I popped into the Bright Spot Café for a grilled cheese sandwich that Mom already had for me to eat on my way to the bus stop up on the corner.

The Holy Ghost Visits Pop

Town is one block long, including some vacant lots here and there. The buildings are all wooden and small, one-story high with extra-tall, false fronts. Half the stores are vacant.

Just then, Mr. Alvord came through on his wagon pulled by a team of unmatched horses. Mr. Alford is thin, and his horses are thinner. None of them get fed too well.

Hard times they were. It wasn't easy for hardly any man to make a living for his family. But a man did the best he could.

We waved.

"Good morning," Mr. Alvord said, smiling and nodding, his old, worn straw hat pulled down in a slouch over his head. He was on his way early to haul things for people, I guessed.

It seemed to me that he went by like a ghost from the past. Still misty out, the sun was nowhere to be seen. It hadn't peeped out through the crisp, early morning air yet.

As I went along at nearly the same pace, Mr. Alvord and his entourage provided a harmonious, yet clackity-looking, scene. The horses snorted, blowing vapors through their nostrils into the cool morning air. Their heads bobbed up and down as if they had something to say. Their hooves sounded a heavy clop-clop on the black-tarred road, with their leather harness giving and slapping and pulling and swaying here and there in a heavy, tinkling rhythm. The wheels turned and creaked. The wagon hummed noisily as Mr. Alvord appeared to sing along. At least his mouth and lips were moving.

The rickety bus was at the corner, ready to take off just as I jumped onboard. Away we went down the road, bumping along. The bus jiggled and rolled across the planks of the narrow, swaying Selah Bridge. It spanned the now mud-colored, swollen, and fast-flowing Yakima River that was full of recent rains. And when we arrived in the City of Yakima, we all got off the bus. I hurriedly strolled past the Red Light District on First Street and over the railroad tracks until I reached the Union Apple Warehouse.

There at my office job—from eight in the morning until six at night, except for an hour's break for lunch—I added, subtracted, multiplied, and divided on the little manual comptometer machine. Still, I kept thinking about last night. Was Pop right? Were those church people—all poor, simple, and plain-looking—really rich in a way I knew not of?

I believed in Jesus Christ in my heart, just like they did. And with my family I attended the Christian Church located a block from our house going the other way from Selah on Wenas Road. And I loved to sing the old hymns in church. But I didn't broadcast my spiritual beliefs like some people do. I kept them to myself.

By my refusal last night, did I keep Pop out of heaven? And what about me?

But more immediate, and also very important to me, will I hear from Pop again?

Only time will tell.

CHAPTER 2

The Holy Spirit Visits Me

CONVERSION, COLLEGE, AND CHURCH*

It happened! My father and mother were married in Yakima, Washington, in 1941. They soon moved to Seattle. And yes, I'm a junior. I was the first-born and have two sisters. We grew up in West Seattle.

Our family was not religious. But both of our parents were from church-going families. So, our parents respected Christians and the church. My mother's Thompson family attended the Christian Church. My Zarley grandparents were members of the Free Methodist Church.

Also, on the paternal side of my family I had two uncles who were pastors in the Church of the Nazarene denomination. For two years my Uncle Glenn Butler pastored the West Seattle Church of the Nazarene.[1]

Partly due to my Uncle Glenn, when I was six years old my mother got me going to Sunday school at that church. My two sisters eventually joined me. We attended Sunday school there regularly for several years.

In 1949, when I was seven years old, I accompanied my mother in attending the Billy Graham Crusade in Seattle. As Mr. Graham preached,

---

* Scripture quotations herein are taken from the New Revised Standard Version (NRSV) unless otherwise noted.

1. Many years later, my uncle Glenn taught Sunday school for several years at the First Church of the Nazarene in Pasadena, California. When Dr. James Dobson was about 18–20 years old, he regularly attended my uncle's class.

my mother cried. I rarely saw her do that. It caused me to think to myself right then, "When I grow up, I want to learn what that man says that makes my mother cry."

When I was thirteen years old I had a Sunday school teacher who was a golfer and student at the University of Washington. He led me in private prayer to receive Jesus into my life.[2] That's when I was born again, like Jesus told Nicodemus in the Bible (John 3:3–5). So, the Holy Ghost visited me on that blessed day of my life. Walking home, I felt "the joy of the Lord" in my heart. But nowadays, we say Holy Spirit, not Holy Ghost. It's not as scary.

My dad was in the restaurant business. He did it all: owner, manager, and chef. I grew up working for him, starting at age twelve. I first swept and washed the floors. Then I became a dishwasher. Eventually, I was a cook and learning to become a chef. But by then it was time for me to go to college.

My passion was golf. I had won some local junior golf tournaments. In 1958, I won the National Hearst Junior Golf Championship in Baltimore, Maryland. That gave me some national recognition that caused the University of Houston's Golf Coach Dave Williams to recruit me. So, in 1959 I went far away from home to college in Houston, Texas, on a partial golf scholarship. If you were a successful junior golfer who was aspiring to become a PGA Tour player, as I was, that was the place to go to college.[3]

The University of Houston was becoming the powerhouse in collegiate golf. Coach Dave Williams' golf teams had won the NCAA Team Championship the past four years, from 1956 to 1959. It was the beginning of a dynasty that would become unparalleled in all of American collegiate sports to this day. During the thirty-one year coaching career of Dave Williams, his golf teams at the University of Houston won sixteen men's NCAA Team Golf Championships, finished second four times, and third four times. And beginning in 1956, his teams won the Team Championship an astounding twelve out of the next fifteen years.

During my freshman year I roomed in the athletic dormitory on campus. Some of those athletes were meeting for prayer and Bible study, so I joined them. Sometimes, I also attended Campus Crusade for Christ's College Life meetings held every Friday night.

---

2. Gordy had us memorize ten Bible verses. I asked him about Eph 2:8–9. Then I stayed after class as we discussed them and prayed.

3. In 1962, I won the NCAA Individual Golf Championship and led my team to victory for the team title.

The Holy Spirit Visits Me

Most of all, I often attended Berachah Church, located next to the very successful Galleria shopping mall.[4] It was an independent Bible church loosely associated with Dallas Theological Seminary (DTS). You could say that I began my theological education at this church, which I describe as "a mini-seminary." Pastor Robert B. Thieme Jr. (1918–2009) had graduated with honors from DTS. For decades he taught the Bible six days per week for one hour and fifteen minutes per session. He taught from the Hebrew Old Testament and the Greek New Testament. Thieme was a very confident, brilliant, indefatigable student and teacher of the Bible. I still regard his method of writing with an overhead projector flashed unto a huge, white screen as the best teaching method I've seen. From Thieme I gained a strong appreciation for the Bible that would lead me to become a serious Bible student. I was enthusiastic about what I was learning at Berachah. In college, sometimes I talked to my non-Christian friends about Jesus.

During the holidays break of my freshman year at college, I went home to Seattle. My mother gave me her Bible she had gotten while attending a ladies Bible study during WWII. It was the Scofield Reference Bible in the King James Version (KJV). At the time, that was the Bible that almost everyone used at Berachah Church. For the next ten years I wore out that Scofield Bible. And the ten years after that I wore out a New Scofield Reference Bible in the KJV. They were full of my notes. Those two Bibles popularized the theological system Dispensationalism more than any other publications ever did. This theological exposure I was getting was somewhat different from that of my youth. But in attending Sunday school back then, I learned Bible stories rather than theology.

DISCUSSING THEOLOGY WITH MY GRANDMOTHER ZARLEY

My Zarley grandparents were devout, church-going Christians. They were Methodists back in Iowa. But after moving west they became Free Methodists the rest of their lives. My Grandmother Edna was involved in the Holiness Movement from which the Free Methodist Church emerged. I didn't know anything about either of them. What I knew was that she never

---

4. "Berachah" is a Hebrew word meaning "blessing." Charles Swindoll and Hal Lindsey came from this church. Both were graduates of DTS. Swindoll was its president from 1994 to 2001 and still is its chancellor. Lindsey's mega-selling, eschatological book, *The Late Great Planet Earth* (1970), has reportedly sold about forty million copies.

allowed her children, thus my dad, to do things such as play cards, see "picture shows" (movie theater), or go to dances and pool halls. When my dad got into his later teens, he quit being the leader of his Sunday school class and started making up for lost time by doing some of those things. During my college years I asked him, "With your background, why aren't you a Christian?" He replied, "I couldn't live the life."

After my first year of college, in 1959–1960, I came home for the summer. I soon drove a car to Portland, Oregon, and stayed with my Grandma Zarley in her home for a week while I competed in the Oregon State Open Golf Tournament. I bogeyed the last hole and finished second, losing by two strokes. I had been looking forward to talking with my grandma about the Lord, which I had never done. So, I shared with her what I was learning.

One of the main things I had learned at my new church was a verse in the Bible—1 John 1:9. In my King James Bible this verse says of God, "If we confess our sins, he is faithful and just to forgive us our sins, and to cleanse us from all unrighteousness." I applied this to myself as a Christian, since that is what my church taught. But when I shared it with my grandmother she said, "Oh, that verse is not for Christians; it's for non-Christians." Then she showed me two other verses in that epistle. One reads in the KJV, "He that committeth sin is of the devil" (3:8, cf. v. 6). And the next verse says, "Whosoever is born of God doth not commit sin; for his seed remaineth in him: and he cannot sin, because he is born of God" (v. 9; cf. 5:18).

I didn't know about those two verses, so I was surprised. They seemed to say Christians don't sin, just as my grandmother explained them. I later learned that the Greek text does support those two KJV translations. Yet most English Bible versions published after that year, 1960, translate those texts differently, such as "practices sin" (NASB, ESV similarly) or "continue to sin" (NIV). The NRSV, which is preferred by most Bible scholars, is like the KJV in rendering them "commits sin." So, the words in the Greek text can be translated either way.

My Grandmother Zarley and I then had an extended discussion about this matter. I told her I still sinned sometimes and that if I believed what she said, and what those verses in our KJV Bibles say, I would have to conclude that I had *lost my salvation*. I told her my church taught that born again Christians *cannot lose their salvation* because we are "eternally secure." So, I asked her if she ever sins. She said, "Sometimes I make mistakes, but I wouldn't call that sin."[5] She spoke of "entire sanctification," calling it

---

5. John Wesley authored a tract that begins, "What is Christian Perfection?" In it he

"Christian perfection," "the second blessing," and "a second work of grace." She said it was an instantaneous, post-conversion experience with the Holy Spirit that every Christian should strive to have. By now, I was feeling confused and discouraged.

THE WESLEYAN-HOLINESS MOVEMENT

The Church of the Nazarene and the Free Methodist Church are very similar. Both were birthed in the Holiness movement and are Arminian-Wesleyan in theology.[6] This reform movement started in the U.S. in the mid-1800s to recover the "holiness teaching" of England's John Wesley (1703–1791), the founder of Methodism. This movement was a reaction to the depersonalization of religion due to creeds and liturgy in Roman Catholicism and Anglicanism, and the viewpoint that a holy life is only for monastics and clergy.

John Wesley called his most distinctive teaching "Christian perfection" and "entire sanctification." He was greatly influenced by two books written by William Law entitled *A Practical Treatise on Christian Perfection* (1726) and *A Serious Call to a Devout and Holy Life* (1729). Thus, Wesley's first and most popular book is entitled *A Plain Account of Christian Perfection*.[7] In it, he teaches that a Christian can, and should, live without willfully sinning by being filled or anointed with the Holy Spirit. Wesley's favorite description of Christians living a life of sanctification was that it is a state of "perfect love." The two foremost Bible texts he cited for support were Jesus saying, "Be perfect, therefore, as your heavenly Father is perfect" (Matt 5:48), and 1 John 1:7 which reads, "if we walk in the light . . . the blood of Jesus Christ cleanses us from all sin." That last verse, of course, is only two verses away from 1 John 1:9 that brought comfort to me. Some scholars have called John Wesley "the theologian of 1 John" because it was his favorite portion in the Bible.

---

states, "all men are liable to mistake, and that in practice as well as in judgment. But . . . this is not sin, if love is the sole principle of action."

6. For a history of the Holiness movement see Smith, *Revivalism and Social Reform in Mid-Nineteenth Century-America*.

7. This book, called "a tract," consisted of 80–90 pages. It seems to have been published in 1726. But it underwent several editions, due to revising each time by Wesley, with the added subtitle, "As Believed and Taught by The Rev. Mr. John Wesley, From the year 1725, to the year 1777."

Yet John Wesley never taught sinless perfection as some have alleged. Rather, he insisted that all believers still have "inbred sin" inherited from fallen Adam, making them subject to "imperfect judgment."

John Wesley also taught that conversion and sanctification are two separate experiences. He claimed, and rightly so I believe, that Christian conversion occurs when a person believes in Jesus as Savior and Lord and thus has his or her sins forgiven. Wesley also seems to have said sanctification occurs gradually after conversion, but it preferably can happen instantaneously. Yet many years later, the Methodist Church taught firmly that sanctification is a gradual process, thereby intending to deemphasize that it could be an instantaneous event. People in the Holiness Movement believed they adhered more closely to Wesley's teaching, that sanctification is an instantaneous, post-conversion experience.

Wesley's doctrine of sanctification as "a second work of grace" recalls the Puritans, who strongly influenced Wesley. Many of them were the early settlers in North America during the seventeenth century. They were Protestants who sought to reform, and thereby purify (from which they derive their name), the Church of England. They believed, somewhat differently, in having a post-conversion experience regarding "the assurance of salvation." Some Puritans equated this assurance with baptism in the Holy Spirit.

Some Holiness Teachers also referred to their belief in an instantaneous, post-conversion experience of sanctification as "the baptism of/in the Holy Spirit." Foremost was John Fletcher, Wesley's closest advisor. While Wesley disagreed with him on this point, he designated Fletcher as his successor to the Methodist societies. Breakaway groups, such as the Free Methodists and Nazarenes, relied much on Fletcher for his explanations of Wesley's teaching.

Vinson Synan, a Holiness and Pentecostal historian, states, "By 1840 perfectionism was becoming one of the central themes of American social, intellectual, and religious life. And from the ground of perfectionist teaching sprang the many reform movements intended to perfect American social life—women's rights, the abolition of slavery, anti-masonry, and the various temperance campaigns."[8]

So, many holiness-social organizations and church denominations were established in the U.S. during the second half of the nineteenth century. The Free Methodist Church was created in 1860. It happened because the U.S. Methodist Episcopal Church excluded some of its members for

---

8. Synan, *The Holiness-Pentecostal Tradition*, 17.

too strongly advocating Wesleyan-Methodist traditions. Today, the Free Methodist Church is the second largest holiness church denomination in the world, with 880,000 members worldwide. The National Holiness Association was established in 1867 at a camp meeting in Vineland, New Jersey. The Salvation Army was founded in 1878. The Church of the Nazarene began in Los Angeles, California, in 1895.[9] It is the largest of the holiness church denominations, with 1.8 million members worldwide. The differences between these two holiness church denominations regard mostly practice and polity.

My mother reveals in chapter 1 of this book that during the Depression my dad's family migrated from Iowa to Washington state. Vinson Synan says that by 1895, Iowa "had been a major holiness stronghold for at least two decades."[10] Indeed, the Iowa Holiness Association began in 1879 as the first such group west of the Mississippi River. Synan cites two historians who affirm, "Many of the more radical doctrines that later influenced the rise of Pentecostalism had their beginnings in Iowa."[11]

Benjamin Hardin Irwin of Lincoln, Nebraska, was a member of the Iowa Holiness Association. At Lincoln, he founded the Fire-Baptized Holiness Church. Due to his own life experiences, he distinguished conversion, entire sanctification, and "baptism with the Holy Ghost with fire" as three separate acts. This triple distinction gained much attention, yet the Holiness Movement at-large soon denounced it. Synan says, "It is probable that Charles F. Parham, the man who initiated the Pentecostal revival in Topeka, Kansas, in 1901, received from Irwin the basic idea of a separate baptism of the Holy Ghost following sanctification . . . In a social, doctrinal, and intellectual sense, the Fire-Baptized Holiness Church was a direct precursor of the modern Pentecostal movement in North America."[12]

REVIVALISM AND FUNDAMENTALISM

The heartbeat of the Holiness and the Pentecostal movements was revivalism. These so-called "revivals" were conducted over a period of days, usually a week or a weekend. They were held in church buildings or outdoors in campgrounds. (Large tents were used later.) Clergymen often preached

---

9. For its history see Smith, *Called Unto Holiness*.
10. Synan, *The Holiness-Pentecostal Tradition*, 51.
11. Ibid., 51.
12. Synan, *The Holiness-Pentecostal Tradition*, 59.

emotional, fire-and-brimstone sermons. Attendants sometimes exhibited shouting, jerking, dancing, and uncontrollable laughter. During the second half of the twentieth century, the largest revival gatherings also were called "crusades." Billy Graham and Oral Roberts held the largest crusades in North America. Revivals held in the U.S. by Pentecostals who were healing evangelists increasingly declined in attendance beginning in the 1970s, except for Benny Hinn. Yet they had much success in other regions, especially Africa.[13]

The first revival camp meeting in the U.S. was conducted in 1801 at Cane Ridge, Kentucky. Barton Stone led it. He and Alexander Campbell eventually teamed up and co-founded the Christian Restoration Movement. Later, it mostly became the Christian Church.

Charles G. Finney (1792–1875) was a lawyer who became America's preeminent evangelist of the nineteenth century. He regularly conducted revival meetings. Although he was a Presbyterian minister, and thus largely a Calvinist in theology, Finney was an advocate of John Wesley's "Christian perfectionism."

Finney was converted in a moment in 1821 at age twenty-nine. He said that hours later, while alone in his law office, "I received a mighty baptism of the Holy Spirit. Without any expectation of it, without ever having the thought in my mind that there was any such thing for me, without any recollection that I had ever heard the thing mentioned by any person in the world, the Holy Spirit descended upon me in a manner that seemed to go through me, body and soul. I could feel the impression, like a wave of electricity . . . No words can express the wonderful love that was shed abroad in my heart. I wept aloud with joy and love."[14] Many Pentecostals cite this much-quoted statement to support their doctrine of subsequence.

But Pentecostals usually don't cite Finney's extreme teaching on perfectionism. In his *Systematic Theology* he wrote, "Present evangelical faith implies a state of present sinlessness . . . This, and nothing short of this, is evangelical faith." He also called it "perfect, instantaneous, perpetual holiness."[15]

Following Wesley and Finney, the next non-Pentecostal preacher-evangelist who Pentecostals cite most for their belief that Spirit baptism happens instantaneously and after conversion is R. A. Torrey (1856–1928).

---

13. Synan, *The Century of the Holy Spirit*, 325–46.
14. Finney, *Memoirs of Rev. Charles G. Finney*, 20. See also pp. 21, 55, 65.
15. Finney, *Lectures on Systematic Theology*.

He is called "the father of Christian Fundamentalism." Torrey was one of three editors of the twelve-volume series entitled *The Fundamentals*.[16] It became the guide for Fundamentalism and much of Evangelicalism in the USA. Torrey wrote, "*The Baptism with the Holy Spirit is a work of the Holy Spirit separate and distinct from His regenerating work.*" Torrey cites Scriptures and concludes, "From this it is evident that regeneration is one thing, and that the baptism with the Holy Spirit is something different, something additional. One may be regenerated and still not yet be baptized with the Holy Ghost."[17] He further explains, as do many Pentecostals, "the Baptism with the Holy Spirit is not for the purpose of cleansing from sin, but for the purpose of empowering for service."[18]

The Holiness and early Pentecostal movements consisted mostly of poor, uneducated people. Like Christian Fundamentalists, early Pentecostals opposed higher education for theological study or ministry. That began to change when the Charismatic Movement emerged in the 1960s. Yet both Holiness and Pentecostal folk were known for earnestly seeking God and his power for life and ministry.

Yet there is much precedent for such lack in the Bible. Among NT gospel writers, only Luke tells of the Magnificat—which became a liturgy sung often in church services—and Jesus' reading from Isaiah the Prophet. Both tell of God especially caring for the poor and lowly in society (Luke 1:47–53; 4:18; cf. Isa 61:1). Plus, Jesus' Jewish antagonists had said of him, "How does this man have such learning, when he has never been taught?" (John 6:15). And the religious authorities at Jerusalem "saw the boldness of Peter and John, and realized that they were uneducated and ordinary men" (Acts 4:13).

In 1907, the Association of Pentecostal Churches of America merged with the Church of the Nazarene and renamed it the Pentecostal Church of the Nazarene. In the ensuing years, other Holiness and Pentecostal church denominations were merged into it. In 1919, "Pentecostal" was withdrawn, thereby returning to its original name—the Church of the Nazarene. It occurred due to a disagreement with Pentecostals, who insisted Spirit baptism must be evidenced by speaking in tongues. The Nazarenes most distinctive doctrine has remained "entire sanctification." It means the evidence of

---

16. These 90 essays were published from 1910 to 1915 by The Bible Institute of Los Angeles, now named BIOLA.

17. Torrey, *The Baptism with the Holy Spirit*, 12. Emphasis his.

18. Ibid., 14.

Spirit baptism is a righteous life lived by the filling of the Holy Spirit (cf. Gal 5:22–23), thus not speaking in the tongues as Pentecostals claimed.

So, due to my having been a Nazarene during my youth, and my Zarley grandparents being Free Methodists, my early spiritual roots are embedded in Methodism. Yet throughout all of my adult life I have been an Evangelical Christian in the independent Bible church movement.

MEETING BILLY GRAHAM AND ORAL ROBERTS

In 1965, my second year on the PGA Tour, Jim Hiskey imparted an idea to me and his brother Babe, also a Tour player and my close friend, to start a Bible study on the Tour. We did, and we named it the PGA Tour Bible Study.

Because of this Christian fellowship, I achieved one of my lifetime goals in meeting and getting to know evangelist Billy Graham. It was because he liked to play golf. Sometimes, Billy participated in pro-ams at PGA Tour tournaments, especially Atlanta and Charlotte. He lived near Charlotte, in Montreat, North Carolina. Because of this, Billy spoke to our fellowship group three times. Another year, our group sponsored a dinner at the Hyatt Hotel in Atlanta that was only for Tour players and their wives, and Billy was the keynote speaker. Years later I felt very honored that Billy Graham endorsed my first book, *The Gospels Interwoven* (1987).

Back when I was a teenager, I sometimes watched Oral Roberts conduct his televised, healing crusades. I was skeptical that he could heal people. But I must say I also found it rather entertaining. He typically would put his hand(s) on the forehead of some volunteer in the audience and loudly shout the word "heal." This sort of activity, including tongues-speaking, caused the Christian community to somewhat marginalize Pentecostals.

In 1970, I met Oral Roberts in Tulsa, Oklahoma, where he lived. It was because the PGA Championship was held that year at Southern Hills Country Club in Tulsa. I had begun to have neck pain. Two days after I arrived at Tulsa I considered withdrawing from the tournament due to this pain. That evening I attended the Tour Bible Study. Jim Hiskey had arranged for it to be held at the home of Oral Roberts and his lovely wife Evelyn. They were gracious hosts. During the meeting, Oral made brief remarks and introduced the main speaker as the best professor at Oral Roberts University. I don't recall for sure, but I think he was Howard M. Ervin whom I quote

The Holy Spirit Visits Me

several times in this book. Dr. Ervin served on the ORU faculty for forty years.

Jim Hiskey was there that evening, and he was concerned about my neck pain. So, when the meeting ended he gathered Oral Roberts and I together and told Oral about my problem. Oral nonchalantly put his hand on the back of my neck as we talked for a while. Later, when my wife Marilyn and I were driving back to our hotel, I said, "my neck pain is gone." And I didn't have neck pain in that tournament. The trouble was I needed Oral to be my regular caddy so he could occasionally lay hands on my neck the succeeding weeks and years!

During that time I was trying to decide what I thought of Pentecostals and their teaching on Spirit baptism and speaking in tongues. I didn't want to rely on my pastor to tell me what to believe about it. So, one time I asked Billy Graham, "What do you think of Oral Roberts?" Billy replied, "When I go to India, I see so much human suffering and sickness that is partly due to poverty. Then I always wish I was Oral Roberts." Billy added, "I've shed tears over how some of our Christian leaders have mistreated, or ill-spoken, of Oral." That pretty much answered my question. And in my research for this book, I learned that in 1967 Billy gave the commencement address at the dedication of Oral Roberts University.

I have had relatives who were Pentecostal or Charismatic. My younger sister, Linda, became a Charismatic Christian in her mid-twenties and still is to this day. For several decades she has been saying to me, "Kerm, if you would just get the baptism of the Holy Spirit with tongues, you would have the joy of the Lord." The first time she said that I laughed and replied, "Well, I guess you don't think I have the joy of the Lord."

Recently, I was talking about Linda and her tongues-speaking to our sister, Pam, who is also a Christian. She said, "I don't think Linda speaks in tongues anymore." I responded, "I don't think you've got that right." So, Pam then phoned Linda and asked her about it. Linda said, "When you get the gift of tongues, it never goes away." Pam asked her, "Then why don't you talk about it anymore?" Linda answered, "I don't talk about my gift of tongues much to people who don't believe in it." Ha! That ended that conversation.

SOLVING THE SAMARITAN RIDDLE

MORE ABOUT BERACHAH CHURCH AND PASTOR BOB THIEME

My pastor at Berachah Church in Houston, where I attended regularly from 1959 to 1970, taught that the "supernatural gifts"—which he identified as miracles, healings, prophecy, and tongues—ceased at the end of the first century when all of the books and letters of the New Testament had been written. About the only biblical text he cited to support this was what the Apostle Paul wrote in 1 Cor 13:8–10. It reads in the NRSV, "Love never ends. But as for prophecies, they will come to an end; as for tongues, they will cease; as for knowledge, it will come to an end. For we know only in part, and we prophesy only in part, but when the complete comes, the partial will come to an end." My pastor taught, as he had learned at DTS, that Paul's expression here, "when the complete comes," refers to the completed Bible. Some say it is the completed apostolic era. Both occurred about the same time.

After I had been in Berachah Church for about six years, this "cessationism" was the first of Bob Thieme's teachings that I jettisoned. It became obvious to me, solely through my own personal Bible reading, that in 1 Cor 13:8–10, Paul is not referring to a completed Bible or apostolic era but to Jesus' future return with his "complete" (consummated) kingdom.[19] For Paul adds, "For now we see in a mirror, dimly, but then we will see face to face. Now I know only in part; then I will know fully, even as I have been fully known" (v. 12). This refers to Jesus' second coming and the simultaneous resurrection of the dead. Thieme also taught that the practice of speaking in tongues by Pentecostals and Charismatics was either psychosomatically induced or the work of the devil.

In the next few years, I became troubled by other teachings of Pastor Thieme. I thought he taught too much of an intellectual religion. "Knowledge of Bible doctrine" was his mantra. I also decided he was becoming a little antinomian by teaching a libertarian faith that some Christian leaders would call "easy believism" and/or "cheap grace." So, my wife and I departed Berachah Church and attended another Bible church for the next twenty years.

---

19. See D. A. Carson, *Showing the Spirit*, 67–72.

The Holy Spirit Visits Me

MEETING MRS. AND MR. GORDON FEE

Way back when I turned sixteen years of age, I was glad to get my driver's license and begin driving a car to the municipal, city-owned West Seattle Golf Course. I had started playing golf there when I was ten years old. But from now on, I wouldn't have to ride my bicycle there or get my mom to drive me.

A few months later, in early 1958, I was driving my car from my home to the golf course. There was no auto traffic. Less than one mile from the course, I saw a car in the oncoming lane that had slowed to a stop, as if to turn left. I was driving about the speed limit of thirty-five miles per hour as I approached it. Its driver didn't see my approaching car and turned left. There was no way for me to avoid a collision. It was my first auto accident.

When we drivers got out of our cars, both of us were thankful we had not incurred any injuries. The lady driver was worried about her baby daughter who had been sitting in the front passenger seat. There were no infant car seats then or seat belts. The collision caused the baby to be thrown forward, perhaps hitting her head against the dashboard. We were glad to discover that she appeared all right. An accident report was filed, and the lady's insurance company paid most of the damages. I never recalled her name, and that was the end of the matter.

Almost fifty years later, as a member of the Society of Biblical Literature, I attended its five-day Annual Meeting. Many of the world's most renowned Bible scholars attend this large conference every year. So, you never know whom you will see there, and perhaps meet. In biblical scholarship, meeting Dr. N. T. Wright or Dr. James D. G. Dunn is like meeting Jack Nicklaus or Arnold Palmer in my golf profession. My friend, Dr. Scot McKnight, invited me to go with him to a dinner hosted by the Christian book publisher Zondervan. We sat at one of the large, round tables in the room. I noticed that sitting across the table from me was a man having a nametag that read "Dr. Gordon Fee."

Gordon Fee, whom I quote several times in this book, had been a leading, world-renowned NT scholar for decades. Expert M. W. Mittelstadt says Fee is "the first world-class Pentecostal scholar to experience substantial acceptance within the academic world."[20] Fee also distinguished himself as a textual critic and a member of the translation committee for the New International Version of the Holy Bible that Zondervan distributes

---

20. Mittelstadt, *Reading Luke*, 49.

exclusively in the U.S. In my home library, I had a copy of Dr. Fee's commentary on 1 Corinthians, and it is very good.

Sitting next to Dr. Fee was a lady who appeared to be his wife. And sitting next to her, I thought, might be their daughter. I soon detected that Mrs. Fee was looking rather curiously at me, probably because she noticed my nametag. She asked me from across the table, "Are you the pro golfer?" I answered, "Yes." Then she inquired, "Do you remember a lady crashing her car into your car in West Seattle during the late 1950s?" I replied, "Oh my goodness; you must be her." We both laughed. And that was their daughter sitting next to her who was in the crash. She is now Dr. Cherith Fee Nordling, a professor at Northern Seminary near Chicago and a colleague of my friend Scot McKnight. I have wondered ever since if this whole affair was a coincidence or divine intervention.

Until that moment at SBL, I did not know anything about Gordon Fee or his background, only that he was an esteemed Bible scholar. In the late 1950s, he and his family lived in West Seattle, where I grew up. Gordon had been on the pastoral staff of the West Seattle Assembly of God Church located a mile from my house. In 1959, he was ordained in the Assemblies of God church denomination. In 1966, he became the first Pentecostal in the world to achieve a PhD in either theology or biblical studies. He earned it at Seattle Pacific University, a Free Methodist school. Gordon Fee eventually had a profound influence on neo-Pentecostalism.

THE PENTECOSTAL-CHARISMATIC MOVEMENT

The Pentecostal-Charismatic Movement is an offshoot of the Holiness Movement. In fact, it is the fastest-growing sect of Christianity in the world, consisting of over 600 million people worldwide. That is over one-fourth of the approximately 2.4 billion professing Christians in the world. Yet this movement only began a little over a century ago. Both the Holiness and Pentecostal-Charismatic movements have been very evangelistic and therefore missionary-oriented. Historians now recognize three primary movements in the history of Christianity: Catholicism, Protestantism, and Pentecostalism.

The Pentecostal Movement began at the Azuza Street Revival in Los Angeles, California, on April 9, 1906. It almost never quit, lasting until 1915. Its attendance was quite racially mixed, partly because William J. Seymour led this revival. He was a one-eyed African-American preacher who had moved there from his home in Houston, Texas, where I later lived for nearly forty years. In Houston, Seymour had heard Parham preach about Spirit baptism and tongues. So, the so-called "miraculous" or "supernatural" gifts of the spirit purportedly were quite prevalent in the Azusa Street worship services, especially speaking in tongues. Emotional, ecstatic behavior was common there. Critics described it as "fanaticism" or "enthusiasm." Seymour's earliest sermons were about tongues-speaking as the evidence of Spirit baptism. The meetings grew and had a widespread, yet controversial, impact.

Pentecostalism has been a diverse movement. Its largest group is still the Assemblies of God (AOG) church denomination, founded in 1914. Worldwide, the AOG now consists of over sixty-six million members.

Due to theological controversies in early Pentecostalism, in 1916 the AOG drafted what it calls "The Assemblies of God Statement of Fundamental Truths." Much of its Article 7 still reads to this day: "All believers are entitled to and should ardently expect and earnestly seek the promise of the Father, the baptism in the Holy Spirit and fire, according to the command of our Lord Jesus Christ. This was the normal experience of all in the early Christian Church . . . This experience is distinct from and subsequent to the experience of the new birth (Acts 8:12–17; 10:44–46; 11:14–16; 15:7–9)." Accordingly, Spirit baptism occurs sometime after conversion.

Most of Article 8 of the AOG's Fundamental Truths states, "The baptism of believers in the Holy Spirit is witnessed by the initial physical sign of speaking with other tongues as the Spirit of God gives them utterance (Acts 2:4)." This concept is sometimes called "the doctrine of initial/evidential tongues."

These AOG Articles 7 and 8 have caused much discussion and controversy in Christianity. And they comprise the most distinctive doctrines of the AOG church as well as most other Pentecostal church denominations compared to all non-Pentecostal churches. The AOG calls this Pentecostal belief in Spirit baptism occurring *after* conversion "the doctrine of subsequence" or "the doctrine of separability and subsequence." In 1991, the General Conference of the AOG-USA reaffirmed Articles 7 and 8 by declaring that Spirit baptism is an experience "distinct from and subsequent to conversion" and that speaking in tongues is the "initial physical evidence" of it. These two doctrines of Pentecostalism are most succinctly stated as *post-conversion Spirit baptism evidenced by tongues*.

Article 9 of the AOG's Fundamental Truths is entitled "Sanctification." It states, "By the power of the Holy Spirit we are able to obey the command: 'Be ye holy, for I am holy.'" This quotation is of God in Lev 11:44 (cf. Lev 20:7; 1 Pet 1:16). But this AOG article does not say anything about the relation of "the baptism in the Holy Spirit" with "the power of the Holy Spirit" in the two previous articles. Thus, it raises the question of whether or not Christians who have never spoken in tongues can experience the power of the Holy Spirit to obey this command to be holy. If the AOG means they can't, as it seems, then these three AOG articles allege that Pentecostals are able to be holy but non-Pentecostal Christians are not. That fosters an elitist mentality, a super-spiritual attitude of which Pentecostals have been accused.

Gordon Fee is a lifetime member of the AOG, and his father was a lifetime AOG pastor. Early in Gordon's academic career he questioned its Articles 7 and 8. He has disagreed with them ever since.[21] This stance put him at odds with some of his fellow AOG brethren. Due to Dr. Fee's unusual accomplishments as both a NT textual critic and exegete, he may be the most able defender, as well as critic, of Pentecostalism in the world. In 1985, he made the following observations about the AOG's Article 7:

> The theological sentiment expressed in this statement, it should be noted, is not unique to Pentecostalism. Rather, it reflects a classical view of many pietistic groups, reaching at least as far back as early Methodism, and found subsequently in various holiness and deeper life movements, namely that there is for all believers a "baptism in the Holy Spirit," which is separate from and sequential to the initial experience of conversion. Indeed two of the best known defenses of this position were written by none other than the first president of Moody Bible Institute, R. A. Torrey, and one of the founders of Gordon-Conwell Theological Seminary, A. J. Gordon. The uniquely Pentecostal contribution to this theological construct was to insist on the gift of tongues as the evidential sign that such baptism had indeed taken place, and to insist on the empowering-for-service dimension of the experience. . . .
> . . . they tend to make the *timing* of the experience of equal significance to the experience itself.[22]

The World Assemblies of God Fellowship was formed in 1988. It is a loose federation of 140 national church groupings that form the largest

---

21. E.g., see Fee, "Baptism in the Holy Spirit," 87–99; Fee, *Gospel and Spirit*, 105–19.
22. Fee, "Baptism in the Holy Spirit" 87. Emphasis his.

Pentecostal church denomination in the world. It has over 300,000 ministers and, as stated above, over sixty-six million congregants. It is the sixth largest church denomination in the world. Surprisingly, each AOG national church branch is free to formulate its own creedal statement. The Assemblies of God USA adopts the Statement of Fundamental Truths.

THE THREE PHASES OF PENTECOSTALISM

So, Pentecostalism began with the distinctive belief in a post-conversion Spirit baptism accompanied by tongues-speaking. Most Charismatics accepted this doctrine of "subsequence," but many rejected tongues-speaking as the necessary evidence of Spirit baptism.

Historians now divide the Pentecostal-Charismatic movement into three phases that most call "waves." Its first wave or phase is classical Pentecostalism that began in 1906. The second phase is the Charismatic Movement that began in the late 1950s and the 1960s.[23] It emerged only in non-Pentecostal, mainline, denominational and independent churches. The third phase is The Third Wave, also called the Signs and Wonders Movement. It emerged among Evangelicals in the 1980s. Third Wavers reject both subsequence and evidential tongues.

Early, prominent Third Wave leaders included C. Peter Wagner, thirty years a professor of church growth at Fuller Theological Seminary and an authority on spiritual warfare, John Wimber (1934–1997), founder of the Vineyard church movement, and Chuck Smith (1927–2013), founder of the Calvary Chapel church movement.[24]

All three of these divisions of the Pentecostal-Charismatic Movement have emphasized miraculous gifts such as healing, miracles, prophecy, and *glossolalia*. Adherents are called "continualists" since they believe these gifts have continued throughout the church age. In contrast, Protestants have relegated them to the apostolic age only. So, Protestants are called "cessationists" since they believe these gifts ceased when the apostolic era ended.

---

23. The word "charismatic" derives from the Greek word *charisma*, meaning "gift." The Greek word *charis* means "favor" or "grace." The Charismatic and Third Wave movements are renewal efforts emphasizing initial conversion, use of spiritual gifts, and practice of miracles, signs, and wonders, all under the direction of the Holy Spirit.

24. For a few years during the 1980s, during the week of the PGA Tour's Los Angeles Open golf tournament, the PGA Tour Bible Study met in the home of Pat and Shirley Boone. Either one or two of those years, Chuck Smith was the keynote speaker.

SOLVING THE SAMARITAN RIDDLE

Third Wavers challenge Pentecostals on subsequence. Third Wave theologian C. Samuel Storms says Third Wavers believe in Spirit baptism at conversion mostly due to 1 Cor 12:13. He explains,

> The context of 1 Corinthians 12 militates against the doctrine of subsequence. The apostle stresses that all, regardless of their gift, belong to the body as co-equal and interdependent members. The idea of a Spirit-baptized elite would have played directly into the hands of those who were causing division in Corinth. Paul emphasizes here the *common* experience of the Holy Spirit for everyone, not what one group has that another does not (note the emphatic "we all") . . . Therefore, evangelicals are right in affirming that all Christians have experienced Spirit-baptism at conversion, . . . In summary, there is one Spirit-baptism, but multiple fillings. In no New Testament text is there an appeal or a command to be baptized in the Holy Spirit. On the other hand, we *are* commanded in Ephesians 5:18 to "be filled with the Spirit."[25]

CONCLUSION

In sum, my early church experience was on both sides of the spectrum regarding sanctification and Spirit baptism. Although I have never spoken in tongues, I think God still gives that gift today. As for sanctification, I view it is as a lifetime process of God working in his people by means of his Holy Spirit to conform us to the image of his Son, our Lord Jesus Christ. Nevertheless, many people have dramatic experiences that greatly affect the remainder of their lives. So it can be for life with God and his Spirit. As with surges in physical growth, a Christian can have a profound religious experience that results in an instant surge of spiritual growth just as some people have a dramatic change of life after they are truly converted to faith in Jesus as Savior and Lord.

In the following chapters, we will examine the Bible to see what the baptism with the Holy Spirit has to do with conversion, sanctification, mission, and world evangelization. Also, we will examine how the Apostle Peter used his keys of the kingdom of heaven to ignite an explosion of this spiritual activity that is still burning brightly and continuing to spread around the world nearly two-thousand years later.

---

25. Storms, "A Third Wave View," 177, 179, 180. Emphasis his.

The Holy Spirit Visits Me

Both of my parents eventually turned back to God. After twenty-four years of marriage, my dad left my mom for another woman. My mother was devastated, turned to God, and went back to church. She then attended the West Seattle Christian Church regularly for decades. She loved to sing in the choir, participate in church plays, and was well known and loved by all in that congregation. A few years ago, she moved into an assisted-living facility. At ninety-five years of age, she presently attends a Methodist church every Sunday for its worship service.

My mom had always said that my dad would be like the thief on the cross—turn back to God near the end of his life. She was right. He had a debilitating stroke during heart surgery. While still in the hospital he phoned a local, Baptist pastor friend of his. The man visited my dad and led him in prayer to receive Christ. I immediately flew on an airplane from my home in Houston, Texas, to see "Pop" in that Yakima hospital. He had always been sort of a tough guy, and I had never seen him cry. He shed tears of joy as he told me about accepting Jesus into his life.

CHAPTER 3

Jesus' Life and Teaching Regarding the Holy Spirit

THE HOLY SPIRIT EMPOWERS THE LIFE OF JESUS[1]

Jesus' earthly life, from beginning to end, was completely immersed in the Holy Spirit. First, his supernatural conception was accomplished by the power of the Holy Spirit (Matt 1:18, 20; Luke 1:35). Second, at his baptism at the Jordan River the Holy Spirit "descended upon him" (Matt 3:16 par.). Prior to that blessed event, the Holy Spirit no doubt greatly influenced Jesus' life. But it is doubtful he ever performed any miraculous deeds until after his water baptism at about age thirty.[2] The NT makes it clear that the Spirit-anointing of Jesus at his water baptism was something quite new and pivotal in his life, and that it was necessary for his imminent, God-given mission.[3] Third, "Jesus, full of the Holy Spirit, returned from the Jordan and

---

1. The next two subheads and their text are from my book, *The Restitution of Jesus Christ*, with minor editing.

2. It is doubtful Jesus performed miracles prior to the Spirit-anointing at his baptism. Some non-canonical, spurious writings assert otherwise. Satan tempting Jesus to turn stones into bread suggests Jesus may have been able to do so due to past experiences. The Fourth Evangelist says when Jesus turned water into wine it was "the first of his signs" (John 2:11). Does this mean it was the first miracle Jesus ever did or the first recorded in this gospel?

3. Dunn, *Jesus and the Spirit*, 65.

Jesus' Life and Teaching Regarding the Holy Spirit

was led by the Spirit in the wilderness, where for forty days he was tempted by the devil" (Luke 4:1–2). Fourth, "Then Jesus, filled with the power of the Spirit, returned to Galilee" (v. 14). Fifth, Jesus "came to Nazareth, where he had been brought up" (v. 16), and at its synagogue he quoted from Isaiah, "The Spirit of the Lord is upon me, because he has anointed me" (v. 18; cf. Isa 61.1), thus applying it to himself (v. 21). Sixth, after Jesus died he was resurrected by the power of God's Spirit (John 6:63). Eduard Schweizer concludes, "The Spirit of God presides over the whole life of Jesus."[4]

That is what people thought about Jesus, at least those who knew him best, especially the Apostle Peter. Soon after Jesus' death, resurrection, and ascension into heaven, Peter preached to thousands of people on the next day of Pentecost. He said, "You that are Israelites, listen to what I have to say: Jesus of Nazareth, a man attested to you by God with deeds of power, wonders, and signs that God did through him among you, . . . " (Acts 2:22). Another time Peter told about "how God anointed Jesus of Nazareth with the Holy Spirit and with power; how he went about doing good and healing all who were oppressed by the devil, for God was with him" (10:38).

Some leading NT scholars conclude that the fullness of the Holy Spirit in Jesus' life is what made him so unique. Eduard Schweizer says the NT church "community had ascribed to the Spirit that which distinguished Jesus from all other men, even the greatest of the prophets."[5] Jimmy Dunn says of the NT gospels, "*Jesus is presented consistently as a man of the Spirit during his life and ministry.*"[6] Scholars label this phenomenon Spirit Christology.[7]

Despite the Apostle Peter's bold and important proclamations in the book of Acts about the Holy Spirit having worked in Jesus' life, in the year 1900 Abraham Kuyper made the insightful and profound observation, "the church has never sufficiently confessed the influence of the Holy Spirit exerted upon the work of Christ."[8] Why?

The idea of the Holy Spirit empowering Jesus to do his mighty works does not accord well with traditional belief that he is God. Church father

---

4. Schweizer, *The Holy Spirit*, 56. In an interview at http://frankviola.org/2012/06/25/jamesdgdunn/, Dunn says Schweizer is among six scholars who most influenced his understanding of the NT. Accessed March 25, 2015.

5. Ibid., 57.

6. Dunn, *Christology in the Making*, 141. Emphasis his.

7. See esp. Lampe, *God as Spirit*.

8. Kuyper, *The Work of the Holy Spirit*, 97. Cited by Hawthorne, *The Presence and the Power*, 2–3.

Athanasius asserted that Jesus' miracle-working power originated from his deity as the Logos-Son, thus not from the Spirit.[9]

But the NT does not confirm this. Instead, Dunn well remarks, "If we spell out Jesus' own religious experience, his experience of God, solely in terms of sonship, we misunderstand Jesus almost totally. Jesus' experience was also of God as Spirit."[10]

Church father Justin Martyr put in the mouth of the fictional Trypho the Jew the question of how Jesus could be preexistent God, yet Isa 61:1 says the Spirit of God would rest on him "as if He were in lack."[11] This suggests it was a prominent question then, in the second century. To defend his Christology, Justin flatly denied that Jesus "needed" the Holy Spirit.[12]

On the contrary, *the power of the Holy Spirit is what enabled Jesus to accomplish his many miracles.* Gerald Hawthorne explains, "the Spirit so fully motivated Jesus' speech and actions that the miracles he performed and the words he spoke he spoke and performed, not by virtue of his own power, the power of his own divine personality, but by virtue of the power of the Holy Spirit at work within him and through him." Hawthorne assents that although Jesus was "divine," he needed the Holy Spirit.[13]

So, *Jesus' reliance upon the Holy Spirit indicated his need of the Holy Spirit.* But classical theism argues that God, being totally self-sufficient, does *not need* anything; otherwise, he would not be God. In fact, the very OT name for God—YHWH—means "the self-sufficient One." In contrast, the Johannine Jesus said of himself, "the Son can do nothing on his own" (John 5:19; cf. v. 30), suggesting his need of the Holy Spirit.

Whatever impact the incarnation had on Jesus, that is, the Logos (Word) taking flesh to become the man Jesus (John 1:14), it must not have satisfied his need of empowerment by the Holy Spirit in order to accomplish his earthly mission. For instance, Isaiah says of the Davidic Messiah, "The spirit of the LORD shall rest on him" (Isa 11:2). Isaiah also says on behalf of God about his servant Jesus, "I have put my spirit upon him" (42:1; cf. Matt 12:18).

---

9. E.g., Athanasius, *Orations against the Arians* in NPNF², 3.31.

10. Dunn, *Jesus and the Spirit*, 89.

11. Justin Martyr, *Dialogue with Trypho* in ANF, 87.2.

12. E.g., Justin Martyr, *Dialogue with Trypho* in ANF, 87.4; 88.1, 4.

13. Hawthorne, *The Presence and the Power*, 145–46, cf. 148, 154–55, 160, 162. See Dunn, *Jesus and the Spirit*, 87.

Jesus' Life and Teaching Regarding the Holy Spirit

Jesus' miracle-working power therefore was not intrinsic to himself. This is most evident from Jesus' reply to his opponents' accusations that he did miracles in the power of Satan. He said, "Whoever speaks a word against the Son of Man will be forgiven, but whoever speaks against the Holy Spirit will not be forgiven" (Matt 12:32). Herein, Jesus clearly attributes all of his mighty works to the Holy Spirit working in and through him. And he distinguishes this power from himself as the Son of Man. So, if Jesus' miracle-working power was essential to his nature, then, to speak against this power would be to speak against him rather than against some entity other than him, such as the Holy Spirit.

Surprisingly, the Synoptic Evangelists do not furnish much information about the Holy Spirit empowering Jesus. And they rarely report that he acknowledged the Holy Spirit as the source of his miraculous power. They seem to have presumed it by what all of them earlier relate concerning his water baptism. Eduard Schweizer explains, "there can be no doubt that the three evangelists are trying to tell us that the Holy Spirit which descended upon Jesus [at his baptism] will be manifested in all his life to come."[14]

Was Jesus reluctant to talk about the Holy Spirit's presence and empowerment in his life? If so, one reason could have been that the Prophet Joel had predicted that the Holy Spirit would be poured out on all of God's people as the principal sign of the in-breaking of the glorious messianic age (Joel 2:28–29). It seems Jesus wanted to avoid unnecessarily causing his disciples to think that blessed time was imminent (cf. Acts 1:6–7).[15] Schweizer offers a pragmatic reason, saying, "the best way to teach about the Holy Spirit is simply to . . . let the Spirit permeate one's life."[16] Indeed, and Jesus certainly did that.

Apparently, *the idea of the Holy Spirit indwelling and empowering Jesus is synonymous with God being in him.* For Jesus said, "Do you not believe that I am in the Father and the Father is in me? The words that I say to you I do not speak on my own; but the Father who dwells in me does his works" (John 14:10). In other words, God the Father indwelt the earthly Jesus by means of the Father's Spirit. Friedrich Schleiermacher states, "the existence

---

14. Schweizer, *The Holy Spirit*, 52.

15. Contra Albert Schweitzer (*The Quest of the Historical Jesus*, 1906) and many modern scholars who postulate that Jesus preached an imminent, eschatological kingdom and that subsequent history proved him wrong. Jesus said he did not know that time (Matt 24:36/Mark 13:32).

16. Schweizer, *The Holy Spirit*, 50.

of God in the Redeemer is posited as the innermost fundamental power in Him."[17]

SOME ACTS OF THE HOLY SPIRIT IN THE LIFE OF JESUS

A few synoptic gospel incidents indicate that Jesus constantly depended on being led by the Holy Spirit. For example, immediately following Jesus' water baptism the Spirit "led" him forth so that he thereafter accomplished all of his healings, other miracles, and exorcisms in the power of the Holy Spirit (Matt 4:1 par.; 12:28 par.). We saw above that Jesus affirmed this early in his ministry when he attended synagogue in his hometown of Nazareth and read to the people from Isa 61:1, "The Spirit of the Lord is upon me, because he has anointed me to bring good news to the poor . . . and recovery of sight to the blind" (Luke 4:18). Then he explained, "Today this scripture has been fulfilled in your hearing" (v. 21). So, he applied this text to himself to mean that he did his mighty deeds by God's Spirit.

Occasionally, Jesus spoke implicitly of his dependence upon the Holy Spirit. When the imprisoned John the Baptist questioned whether Jesus was the Promised One of the OT, Jesus sent word of assurance to his imprisoned cousin. He indirectly told John he was indeed that Promised One by drawing John's attention to his miracles and quoting some of Isa 61:1 as being fulfilled in himself (Matt 11:2–5; Luke 7:18–22; cf. Isa 35:5–6).

Another time was when Jesus healed a deaf and dumb man by casting a demon out of him (Luke 11:14). Some witnesses alleged, "He casts out demons by Beelzebul, the ruler of the demons" (v. 15). Luke says Jesus retorted, "It is by the finger of God that I cast out the demons" (v. 20). Matthew records this saying by substituting Luke's metaphor, "finger of God," with "Spirit of God" (Matt 12:28). So, Jesus said he casts out demons by the power of God's Spirit. Dunn says of it, "This was evidently Jesus' own explanation for his success as a healer."[18]

Of course, Jesus was not the only one who did miracles in the power of God's Spirit. According to the OT and other Judaic traditions as indicated by those who accused Jesus, some prior prophets performed miracles. But the extent to which the Holy Spirit impacted Jesus was far greater than it was with them. In OT times, the Spirit came upon select individuals in Israel, such as prophets or kings, only temporarily and, assumedly, partially.

---

17. Schleiermacher, *The Christian Faith*, 397.

18. Dunn, *Christology in the Making*, 137.

Jesus' Life and Teaching Regarding the Holy Spirit

And it is questionable if the Spirit ever permanently indwelt anyone prior to Jesus' Spirit-anointing at the Jordan.

In contrast, during the Christian era the Holy Spirit indwells all believers (e.g., John 7:38–39; Rom 8:9). But still, the current, universal, and constant indwelling of the Holy Spirit in God's people is only partial and thus not the same as it was with Jesus (despite Eph 3:19). God gave his Spirit to Jesus "without measure," so that "the fullness of God" dwelt most uniquely in him (John 1:16; 3:34; Col 1:19; cf. 2:9).

To sum, the Synoptic Gospels imply that Jesus could only have accomplished his mission by means of the Holy Spirit. So, Jesus' *need* of supernatural power—a power he acquired through God's Spirit to perform his divinely-ordained mission—shows that such power *did not* reside intrinsically in Jesus as a part of his nature. *Jesus' uniqueness as a miracle-worker can be explained only by his extraordinary, filial relationship with God, resulting in his empowerment by God's Holy Spirit.*

BEING BORN AGAIN BY THE HOLY SPIRIT

Soon after Jesus began his public ministry, a member of the Sanhedrin, which was the religious council at Jerusalem, came to him. Only the Fourth Evangelist reports this narrative, and it begins as follows:

> 1Now there was a Pharisee named Nicodemus, a leader of the Jews. 2He came to Jesus by night and said to him, "Rabbi, we know that you are a teacher who has come from God; for no one can do these signs that you do apart from the presence of God." 3Jesus answered him, "Very truly, I tell you, no one can see the kingdom of God without being born from above. . . . without being born of water and Spirit. 6What is born of the flesh is flesh, and what is born of the Spirit is spirit. 7Do not be astonished that I said to you, 'You must be born from above.' 8The wind blows where it chooses, and you hear the sound of it, but you do not know where it comes from or where it goes. So it is with everyone who is born of the Spirit." 9Nicodemus said to him, "How can these things be?" 10Jesus answered him, "Are you a teacher of Israel, and yet you do not understand these things?" (John 3:1–3, 5–10)

Jesus' expression here, "born from above," renders *gennethe anothen* in the Greek text. It also can be translated "born again" (NASB, NIV, ESV) or "born anew." Jesus' mention of "the Spirit" refers to the Holy Spirit. This translation from the NRSV has Jesus calling Nicodemus "a leader" and "a teacher." But the Greek text has the article, thus *ho didaskalos*, which means "the teacher" (NASB, ESV, similarly NIV). Accordingly, Nicodemus must have been a leading Torah teacher even though it cannot be confirmed from other ancient, Jewish literature.

Christians have always explained this concept of being "born again" as spiritual regeneration. Many of them have thought that Jesus telling Nicodemus he needed to be "born again" was a new teaching. And most have thought the clause, "being born of water and the Spirit," refers to Christian baptism. Dunn rightly rejects this latter view of John 3:5 as do most Pentecostals.[19] Yet I don't think Jimmy is right in saying of it, "the experience of the new birth and new creation was possible only after the sin-bearing death of the Lamb of God and his resurrection."[20] That would mean Jesus' faithful apostles and many other disciples were not born again during Jesus' ministry. Dunn also says of Jesus' disciples, "It was only at Pentecost that the one hundred and twenty became Christians."[21] Dunn refers to the 120 disciples in Acts 1:15 who were gathered together on the day of Pentecost when the Spirit came.

I think Pentecostal scholars who write books arguing with Dunn about Spirit baptism, such as Roger J. Stronstad, James B. Shelton, and Robert P. Menzies, are right in saying Jesus' true disciples were born again, thus regenerated, prior to their Spirit baptism at Pentecost since they already had believed Jesus was the Messiah.

For instance, at the beginning of Jesus' mission, Andrew found Simon Peter, his brother, and told him, "We have found the Messiah" (John 1:41). Also at that time Nathanael (Apostle Bartholomew?) said to Jesus, "Rabbi, you are the Son of God! You are the King of Israel!" meaning King Messiah/Christ (v. 49). And when Jesus later asked his disciples who they thought he was, Peter declared, "You are the Messiah, the Son of the living God" (Matt 16:16 par.). Further on in the NT we read, "Everyone who believes that Jesus is the Christ has been born of God" (1 John 5:1). In fact, the word "Christian" means "Christ-follower" or "relating to Christ."

Jesus' questioning of Nicodemus in John 3:10 means that Nicodemus, by being "the teacher in Israel," should have understood what Jesus was saying—that Nicodemus needed to be born again. How so? It's in the Torah

---

19. Dunn, *Baptism in the Holy Spirit*, 189.
20. Ibid., 181.
21. Ibid., 53.

Jesus' Life and Teaching Regarding the Holy Spirit

and the prophets. So, Jesus wasn't saying anything new, but only in a new way. He didn't mean Nicodemus had to wait until after Jesus' death and resurrection before he could believe these things and be born again. Jesus meant Nicodemus needed to be born again *right now* to become a true child of God.

As we should expect, Moses is the first to tell about it—in the Torah. It concerns God's covenant he made with Israel that was symbolized by male circumcision. In that context, Moses said to the men of Israel, "The LORD set his heart in love on your ancestors alone and chose you, their descendants after them, out of all the peoples, as it is today. Circumcise, then, the foreskin of your heart, and do not be stubborn any longer" (Deut 10:15–16). So, this covenant is applied corporately (to Israel) and personally (individually). Even under this old covenant, God expected his people to get new hearts. That is what Jesus meant by being born again—to get a new heart.

Some of the prophets echo Moses in this and add more. Ezekiel says to Israel, "Repent and turn from all your transgressions; otherwise iniquity will be your ruin. . . . Get yourselves a new heart and a new spirit" (Ezek 18:30–31). He later adds on behalf of God, "I will sprinkle clean water upon you, and you shall be clean from all your uncleannesses, . . . A new heart I will give you, and a new spirit I will put within you" (36:25–26). Jeremiah proclaims likewise, "Circumcise yourselves to the LORD, remove the foreskin of your hearts" (Jer 4:4). He adds on behalf of God, "I will make a new covenant with the house of Israel. . . . I will put my law within them, and I will write it on their hearts" (31:31, 33). Christians reflect this concept with their Old and New Testaments, with testament meaning "covenant."

So, even though salvation history proceeds chronologically according to God's plan—to include Jesus' death, resurrection, ascension, and heavenly exaltation—the necessity to be born again existed for all Jews in OT times. Thus, being "born again" is not exclusively a Christian phenomenon. Plus, many NT texts can be cited to verify that people were spiritually regenerated during Jesus' public ministry.

Put another way, the Holy Spirit has always been active in bringing about spiritual regeneration during old covenant times. So, the later, universal gift of the Holy Spirit to God's people, which is the baptism with the Holy Spirit, was going to be something *in addition to* the Spirit's involvement in a person being "born again." Robert P. Menzies is right in saying, "Luke does not view the gift of the Spirit as a necessary element in conversion."[22] In contrast, Dunn says, "the one thing which makes a man a Christian is the gift of the Spirit."[23]

So, Jesus' words "born again" refer to spiritual conversion. This truth will become very important when we consider the relationship of this new birth to Spirit baptism.

In Dunn's *Baptism* book, he often uses the expression "conversion-initiation." Years later he calls it "my hybrid formulation," indicating that he coined it.[24] He explains in *Baptism* that he uses "'initiation' to describe the ritual, external acts" and "'conversion' when we are thinking of that inner transformation as distinct from, or rather without including the ritual acts. The total event of becoming a Christian embraces both 'conversion' and 'initiation,' and so we shall call it 'conversion-initiation.'"[25]

I don't use this expression since I think it suggests baptismal regeneration. Initiation means "admittance into a group." In this case, initiation refers to spiritual entrance into the church or God's kingdom. So, in my view, conversion automatically results in initiation into Christ, thus into his church. I therefore regard the rite of Christian baptism as only a symbol, thus an outward expression of this initiation. And I use the words "regeneration" and "conversion" interchangeably. In this book, I sometimes refer briefly to baptismal regeneration; but it is complex, involves church history, and many books have been written on it.

THE PROMISE THAT JESUS WILL BAPTIZE WITH THE HOLY SPIRIT

John the Baptist was the first to prophesy that Jesus would baptize with the Holy Spirit. Before John water-baptized Jesus, he said to the many people coming to him for baptism, "I baptize you with water for repentance, but one who is more powerful than I is coming after me; I am not worthy to carry his sandals. He will baptize you with the Holy Spirit and fire. His winnowing fork is in his hand, and he will clear his threshing floor and will gather his wheat into the granary; but the chaff he will burn with unquenchable fire" (Matt 3:11–12; cf. Mark 1:7–8; Luke 3:16–17).

---

22. Menzies, *Empowered for Witness*, 224.
23. Dunn, *Baptism in the Holy Spirit*, 93.
24. Dunn, *The Christ and the Spirit*, 223.
25. Dunn, *Baptism in the Holy Spirit*, 7.

Jesus' Life and Teaching Regarding the Holy Spirit

The Fourth Evangelist reports that, apparently, soon after John baptized Jesus,

> 29he saw Jesus coming toward him and declared, "Here is the Lamb of God who takes away the sin of the world! 30This is he of whom I said, 'After me comes a man who ranks ahead of me because he was before me.' 31I myself did not know him; but I came baptizing with water for this reason, that he might be revealed to Israel." 32And John testified, "I saw the Spirit descending from heaven like a dove, and it remained on him. 33I myself did not know him, but the one who sent me to baptize with water said to me, 'He on whom you see the Spirit descend and remain is the one who baptizes with the Holy Spirit.' 34And I myself have seen and have testified that this is the Son of God." (John 1:29–34)

Luke informs in his gospel that just before the risen Jesus took his disciples up on the Mount of Olives and he ascended to heaven, he said concerning the Holy Spirit and Jerusalem, "I am sending upon you what my Father promised; so stay here in the city until you have been clothed with power from on high" (Luke 24:49).

Luke also writes in Acts regarding the risen Jesus and his disciples at this same time, "While staying with them, he ordered them not to leave Jerusalem, but to wait there for the promise of the Father. 'This,' he said, 'is what you have heard from me; for John baptized with water, but you will be baptized with the Holy Spirit not many days from now'" (Acts 1:4–5).

Luke also informs in Acts about an incident Peter reported to the apostles at Jerusalem that we will consider later. It caused Peter to say to them about Jesus, "I remembered the word of the Lord, how he had said, 'John baptized with water, but you will be baptized with the Holy Spirit'" (Acts 11:16). Peter referred to the baptism with the Holy Spirit on the day of Pentecost (Acts 2), which we will examine in chapter 5.

Jesus' teaching about the Holy Spirit is mostly in the Gospel of John. The author says after the Nicodemus incident that Jesus led his disciples from Jerusalem through Samaria to Galilee (John 4:3–4). On the way they stopped at Jacob's well near the Samaritan city of Sychar, and the disciples went to buy food (vv. 5–8). We read, "A Samaritan woman came to draw water, and Jesus said to her, 'Give me a drink'" (v. 7). A conversation ensued between them. Jesus told her, "Everyone who drinks of this water will be thirsty again, but those who drink of the water that I will give them will never be thirsty. The water that I will give will become in them a spring of water gushing up to eternal life" (vv. 13–14).

Herein, Jesus may have alluded to what the Prophet Jeremiah said on behalf of God to Israel, "My people have . . . forsaken me, the fountain of living water" (Jer 2:13). Since everything God does with people is through his Spirit, Jeremiah must mean God is a fountain of living water to his people through his Spirit.

Neither Jeremiah, nor Jesus at the well, said precisely that the water refers figuratively to the Holy Spirit. Yet that is what the Johannine Jesus indicated later. For, the Fourth Evangelist says of the Feast of Tabernacles at the temple in Jerusalem, "On the last day of the festival, the great day, while Jesus was standing there, he cried out, 'Let anyone who is thirsty come to me, and let the one who believes in me drink. As the scripture has said, "Out of the believer's heart shall flow rivers of living water."' Now he said this about the Spirit, which believers in him were to receive; for as yet there was no Spirit, because Jesus was not yet glorified" (John 7:37–39). Maybe Jesus said this by drawing upon some or all of what Isaiah says in Isa 44:3; 55:1; 58:11. But what did the Fourth Evangelist mean by saying, "Jesus was not yet glorified?"

JESUS PROMISES THE HOLY SPIRIT AS AN ADVOCATE

At the Last Supper, Jesus told his disciples he was going to leave them (John 13:31—14:3). He added, "I will ask the Father, and he will give you another Advocate, to be with you forever. This is the Spirit of truth, . . . the Advocate, the Holy Spirit" (14:16–17, 26; cf. 15:26; 16:7). The word in the Greek text here translated "advocate" is *paracletos*. Scholars often render it "paraclete." English Bibles usually translate it "comforter."

When was the Father going to give the Holy Spirit to the disciples as an advocate or a comforter? Jesus implied it would be after he left to "go" to his "Father's house" in heaven (John 14:2–3), thus his ascension. Anticipating his disciples' disappointment at his impending departure, Jesus said explicitly, "But because I have said these things to you, sorrow has filled your hearts. Nevertheless I tell you the truth: it is to your advantage that I go away, for if I do not go away, the Advocate will not come to you; but if I go, I will send him to you" (16:6–7).

It seems this sending of the Holy Spirit to be an advocate for the disciples will fulfill Jesus' declaration at the Feast of Tabernacles about the

Jesus' Life and Teaching Regarding the Holy Spirit

Holy Spirit, "Out of the believer's heart shall flow rivers of living water" (John 7:38; cf. 4:13–14). He had prefaced this remark with the metaphor of drinking. His disciples would drink in the Holy Spirit and out of them would flow blessing. But it would not happen until after Jesus departs and is glorified (7:39).

JESUS BREATHES THE HOLY SPIRIT ON HIS DISCIPLES

On the first Easter evening, Jesus' disciples were gathered together in a house with locked doors (John 20:19). They must have included all of the apostles except Thomas and the deceased Judas Iscariot (v. 24). We read, "Jesus came and stood among them and said, 'Peace be with you. . . . As the Father has sent me, so I send you.' When he had said this, he breathed on them and said to them, 'Receive the Holy Spirit. If you forgive the sins of any, they are forgiven them; if you retain the sins of any, they are retained'" (vv. 19, 21–23). It seems that right then Jesus imparted the Holy Spirit to his disciples. This instruction about forgiving or not forgiving people is similar to what Jesus earlier told them in Matt 18:18.

This transfer of the Spirit from Jesus to his disciples is reminiscent of Moses and Israel's seventy elders. Moses had complained to God about the responsibility he had given him of bearing the burden in leading the Israelites to the promised land despite their grumblings (Num 11:1–15). So, God told Moses to choose "seventy of the elders of Israel" (v. 16). When he did, "the LORD came down in the cloud and spoke to him, and took some of the spirit that was on him and put it on the seventy elders; and when the spirit rested upon them, they prophesied. But they did not do so again" (v. 25). Then Joshua, Moses' assistant, told Moses two others in the camp were doing likewise. Joshua said, "'My lord Moses, stop them!' But Moses said to him, 'Are you jealous for my sake? Would that all the LORD's people were prophets, and that the LORD would put his spirit on them!'" (vv. 28–29). In chapter 5, we will see that Joel later prophesied that this will happen in the eschaton (Joel 2:28–29). Notice that "his spirit" refers to God's Spirit, which is the Holy Spirit, but the NRSV does not capitalize it here.

Some scholars assert that Jesus' disciples who accompanied him during his itinerant ministry were not regenerated, that is, not born again, until Easter evening when Jesus breathed on them the Holy Spirit or even afterwards, on the day of Pentecost. Pentecostal Howard Ervin says of John 20:22, "The disciples of Jesus were born again on the evening of the resurrection day when He breathed on them and said, 'Receive the Holy Spirit.'"[26]

Jimmy Dunn says, "The decisive act of salvation is not complete until the Son of Man has ascended and bestowed the Spirit."[27] And he says of John 3:5, "It is probable that . . . the new birth by the Spirit was not possible till after the resurrection."[28]

So, these scholars say there was no spiritual regeneration of the disciples until after Jesus' death and resurrection. As stated above, I differ with this view of salvation history.

Right before Jesus breathed the Spirit on the disciples he said to them, "As the Father has sent me, so I send you" (John 20:21). He referred to their imminent mission of world evangelism in which they would continue Jesus' ministry and extend it. Surely, Jesus would not have said this if his disciples had not been spiritually born again. For, he earlier told those apostles-to-be, who were commercial fishermen, "Follow me, and I will make you fishers of men" (Matt 4:19 KJV). There was a prerequisite to the disciples undertaking their God-given mission—following Jesus that would immediately lead to their believing in him (e.g., John 1:35–49).

On the surface, Jesus' breathing of the Spirit on his disciples seems to conflict with their Spirit baptism at Pentecost weeks later. Did they receive the Spirit two different times—at Easter and Pentecost? If so, was there a difference in the measure of the Spirit given? Some scholars refer to John 20:22 as the "Johannine Pentecost" and Acts 2:1–4 as the "Lukan Pentecost." Historical-critical scholars usually allege that these texts conflict.

Dunn says, "We could therefore say that in [John] 20.22 John records the disciples' baptism in the Spirit."[29] But this seems to conflict with what the risen Jesus later told these disciples, "You will be baptized with the Holy Spirit not many days from now" (Acts 1:5), that is, at Pentecost. Does Dunn think they were Spirit baptized twice? No. He says, "The way to view the relation between John 20.22 and Acts 2 is as alternative ways of telling the same story, not as two parts of the one story."[30]

So, Dunn joins historical-critical scholars in saying John 20:22 and Acts 2:1–4 refer to the same incident. It is because these scholars deem it

---

26. Ervin, *Spirit-Baptism*, 68–69.
27. Dunn, *Baptism in the Holy Spirit*, 174.
28. Ibid., 175.
29. Ibid., 176.
30. Dunn, *Baptism in the Holy Spirit*, 2nd ed., xvii.

Jesus' Life and Teaching Regarding the Holy Spirit

impossible to harmonize these accounts as two separate events. They think this problem is amplified by Thomas' absence Easter evening.

Admittedly, this is a difficult issue. Both authors have located their narrative on Spirit reception in different chronological schemes. For most Christians, treating John 20:19–23 and Acts 2:1–4 as the same event impugns the historical integrity of the NT. If you go down that dirt road—questioning the historical reliability of the NT—how do you decide where to draw the line beyond which you will not go?

We have just seen that at the Festival of Booths Jesus made a declaration about "rivers of living water." The Fourth Evangelist explains, "Now he said this about the Spirit, which believers in him were to receive; for as yet there was no Spirit, because Jesus was not yet glorified" (John 7:39). "No Spirit" likely means the Holy Spirit had not yet been given, not that the Holy Spirit did not exist. Then, when would Jesus be glorified?

Jesus' glory is a major theme in the Gospel of John. It presents ascending levels of Jesus being glorified by using the imagery of literally being "lifted up." The first level was his being lifted up on the cross.[31] The second level was God raising him from the dead. The third level was Jesus being "lifted up" to heaven and exalted there by God inviting him to sit with him on his throne (Acts 1:9; 2:33; 5:31), called "the session." The Fourth Evangelist seems to refer to this third level when he says, "Jesus was not yet glorified" (John 7:39).

Thus, the risen Jesus had not yet ascended to heaven to be glorified there when he breathed on his disciples and said, "Receive the Holy Spirit" (John 20:22). If the Evangelist meant the third level of Jesus' glorification in John 7:39, to not contradict himself he also must have meant that Jesus' breathing of the Spirit on the disciples was inferior to their subsequent Spirit baptism at Pentecost. Raymond E. Brown says of John 20:22, "Many exegetes have been disturbed by the problem of reconciling John's dating of this event on Easter night with the picture in Acts ii . . . Most think that the Spirit was truly given on Easter but in a way different from the Pentecostal giving. Some make a qualitative distinction."[32] Maybe Jesus breathed the Spirit on the disciples Easter evening to sustain them spiritually *until* Pentecost, thereby preparing them to receive that later, greater measure of the Spirit.

---

31. John 3:14; 8:28; 12:32, 34; 13:31–32; 17:1.
32. Brown, *The Gospel According to John (xiii–xxi)*, 1038.

Pentecostal John Christopher Thomas well explains John 20:22 as follows:

> As with each of the synoptic gospels it appears that the promise that Jesus will baptize with the Holy Spirit is not fulfilled within the gospel [of John], but rather the narrative leaves the readers with the expectation that such a baptism is to take place outside the narrative. Such a reading would appear to coincide with Jesus' anticipated work as Spirit Baptizer (1.33), the coming of the Paraclete after Jesus' departure (16.7), and the anticipated activities of the disciples after the Paraclete arrives (14–16; 20.21–23). From the standpoint of narrative analysis, such an understanding of John 20.22 is less problematic than views that see an immediate and forthright reception of the Spirit in this verse.[33]

WHEN DID THE HOLY SPIRIT BEGIN TO INDWELL JESUS' DISCIPLES?

John 14:16–17 may be crucial to resolving this apparent conflict between John 20:22 and Acts 2:1–4. We have considered the first part of John 14:16–17, in which Jesus told his disciples that after his departure, "I will ask the Father, and he will give you another Advocate," that is, "the Holy Spirit" (John 14:16, 26). He added, "You know him, because he abides with you, and he will be in you" (v. 17b). Jesus meant the Spirit was *among* them but would come to *indwell* each of them at Pentecost. If the Spirit had indwelt them then, that would have conflicted with what Jesus said about the Spirit being "another Advocate" to replace him after his departure.

John Christopher Thomas, however, quotes John 14:17b regarding the Holy Spirit as follows, "You know him, because he remains among you and is in you."[34] Notice the difference between his "is in you" and the NRSV's "will be in you." This difference is due to manuscript variance concerning the second verb *eimi* in this verse in the Greek text. Raymond E. Brown says of it, "The textual witnesses are divided on whether to read a present or a future form of the verb," and Brown prefers the present tense.[35] The present

---

33. Thomas, "A Celebration of and Engagement with James D. G. Dunn's *Baptism*," 22–23.

34. Thomas, "A Celebration of and Engagement with James D. G. Dunn's *Baptism*," 22.

35. Brown, *The Gospel According to John (xiii–xxi)*, 637, 640.

Jesus' Life and Teaching Regarding the Holy Spirit

indicative of *eimi* is *esti(n)*, and its future indicative is *estai*. So, Brown and Thomas prefer *estin*, translated "is in you." But again, that nullifies the purpose of the Spirit as a substitute Advocate after Jesus' ascension.

In John 14:17b, both preeminent Greek NTs—the 27th edition of Nestle and the 4th edition of the United Bible Societies—have *estai*, thus the future form, which renders the text "will be in you." English versions that agree include NASB, NRSV, NIV, ESV, and similarly the KJV. Also, the Committee for the *UBS*[4] Greek NT preferred *estai* yet gave it a D rating ("a very high degree of doubt"). Plus, Committee member Bruce M. Metzger, in his commentary on the *UBS*[4], lists a substantial number of early Greek manuscripts that support *estai*. He relates, "A majority of the Committee interpreted the sense of the passage as requiring the future *estai*."[36] Indeed, for Jesus to say that the Advocate (Holy Spirit) "abides with you," and then add the more important concept, "is in you," seems to render the former irrelevant.

The initial baptizing with the Holy Spirit on the day of Pentecost is when the Spirit first came to indwell people permanently. It is also described as being "filled with the Holy Spirit" (2:4), indicating the Spirit resides in people and fills them as rivers of living water. Yet the baptizing of the Spirit at Pentecost was a one-time event when the Spirit came to indwell those recipients. All subsequent experiences that these people had with the Holy Spirit are properly called "filled with/filling of the Holy Spirit" (e.g., Acts 4:8, 31; 13:9, 52). A large majority of Evangelicals and some Pentecostals agree by saying, "one baptism, many fillings."

MORE PREPARATION OF THE DISCIPLES FOR THE DAY OF PENTECOST

Luke informs in his gospel that the risen Jesus appeared to his disciples gathered at Jerusalem and said to them, "Thus it is written, that the Messiah is to suffer and to rise from the dead on the third day, and that repentance and forgiveness of sins is to be proclaimed in his name to all nations, beginning from Jerusalem. You are witnesses of these things. And see, I am sending upon you what my Father promised; so stay here in the city until you have been clothed with power from on high" (Luke 24:46–49).

Luke also writes in Acts 1:4–9 about the risen Jesus and some of his disciples saying,

---

36. Metzger, *A Textual Commentary*, 245.

> 4While staying with them, he ordered them not to leave Jerusalem, but to wait there for the promise of the Father. "This," he said, "is what you have heard from me; 5for John baptized with water, but you will be baptized with the Holy Spirit not many days from now."
>
> 6So when they had come together, they asked him, "Lord, is this the time when you will restore the kingdom to Israel?" 7He replied, "It is not for you to know the times or periods that the Father has set by his own authority. 8But you will receive power when the Holy Spirit has come upon you, and you will be my witnesses in Jerusalem, in all Judea and Samaria, and to the ends of the earth." 9When he had said this, as they were watching, he was lifted up, and a cloud took him out of their sight.

So, Luke says that between Jesus' resurrection and ascension he gave "instructions through the Holy Spirit to the apostles whom he had chosen" (Acts 1:2). This is one of the few NT texts that show Jesus depending on the Holy Spirit in word and/or deed. But the main thing to learn from such texts is that Jesus was preparing his disciples for something dramatic that was going to happen that would empower them to evangelize the world.

CHAPTER 4

The Apostle Peter's Keys of the Kingdom of Heaven

THE SPIRIT OF GOD IN THE BIBLE

The Bible begins by saying, "In the beginning God created the heavens and the earth. Now the earth was formless and empty, darkness was over the surface of the deep, and the Spirit of God was hovering over the waters" (Gen 1:1–2 NIV). So, the Bible begins by telling how "God" and "the Spirit of God" created the universe, but especially the earth.

The Christian Bible consists of two parts: OT and NT. The OT is the Jewish Bible. It originally was written in the Hebrew language thousands of years ago over a period of hundreds of years. English versions of the OT mention "the Spirit of God" twelve times, and they mean God's Spirit. The NT mentions "the Spirit of God" eleven times. The OT mentions "the Spirit of the LORD" twenty-four times. "The Spirit of the LORD" and "the Spirit of God" are equivalent. Six times in the OT, God speaks of "my Spirit."

In English versions of the OT, "LORD" (in small capitals) is the customary translation for God's name. In the Hebrew Bible, God's name is YHWH or YHVH, depending on whether the sixth letter of the Hebrew alphabet is a *waw* or *vav*. Ancient Hebrew had only consonants, thus no vowels. When Hebrew became a "dead" language due to persecution of Jews, it was uncertain how God's name should be pronounced and written. It could be

Yahweh, Yahveh, Yehwah, or Yehvah. Most Jewish scholars prefer Yehvah, and most Gentile scholars favor Yahweh.

The Bible also mentions "(the) Holy Spirit." The OT has "Holy Spirit," thus without the article in the Hebrew text, only three times. The original books and letters of the Hebrew OT and Greek NT did not have lower and upper case. Thus, capitalizing "Holy Spirit" has to do with a translator's theology. Christians capitalize Holy Spirit and add the article, but Jews do neither.[1]

The NT mentions "the Holy Spirit" eighty-nine times. Thirteen of these are in the Gospel of Luke, and forty are in the Acts of the Apostles. Luke likely wrote both. So, fifty-three out of eighty-nine occurrences of "the Holy Spirit" in the NT are in Luke-Acts. That is sixty percent even though Luke-Acts represents only twenty-six per cent of the NT. Also, "the Holy Spirit" occurs sixteen times in the Apostle Paul's letters. So, Luke and Paul—who were associates on some of Paul's missionary journeys—mention "the Holy Spirit" in their NT writings seventy-eight per cent of all such occurrences in the NT. This shows why the NT writings of Luke and Paul are so important in understanding what the Bible says about the Holy Spirit in relation to people. And it shows why Pentecostals, who focus on the Holy Spirit far more than any other Christians do, emphasize Luke-Acts so much in relation to the rest of the NT.

Everything God does with human beings he does by means of his Spirit, except when he sends angels to do it. This has always been true, irrespective of ages in history. For instance, God created the universe by means of his Spirit and his word.[2] When corruption became rampant among humans he said, "My Spirit will not contend with man forever" (Gen 6:3 NIV). In the era of the Hebrew prophets, God's Spirit often fell upon them and they spoke "the word of God/LORD," often convicting the Hebrew people of their sins. Stephen, the first Christian martyr, explained it well. He delivered a lengthy speech to the council of religious leaders at Jerusalem and concluded, "You stiff-necked people, uncircumcised in heart and ears, you are forever opposing the Holy Spirit, just as your ancestors used to do. Which of the prophets did your ancestors not persecute?" (Acts 7:51–52).

---

1. Some NT scholars, e.g., Trinitarian N. T. Wright, think "holy spirit" is a better Bible translation than "Holy Spirit."

2. See "Spirit" or "wind" in Gen 1:2. And "God said," in v. 3, indicates God's spoken "word."

In chapter 3, we learned that during the Last Supper, Jesus told his disciples he would send them "the Holy Spirit" as "another Advocate," that is, "the Spirit of truth whom the world cannot receive" (John 14:16–17, 26). He said this Spirit "will prove the world wrong about sin and righteousness and judgment" (16:8). The first disciple through whom the Spirit would do this was Peter, not Stephen. So, after Jesus' departure, the Spirit would bring great blessing and comfort to God's people while proving the world wrong, and it all would begin with Peter.

JOHN AND JESUS AS BAPTIZERS

So, Jesus was going to send the Holy Spirit to come upon his disciples for blessing. We first learn from John the Baptist, Jesus' slightly older cousin, about "baptism with/in the Holy Spirit."[3] John was baptizing people in the Jordan River, nearly twenty miles east of Jerusalem. The Gospel of Mark says, "John the baptizer appeared in the wilderness, proclaiming a baptism of repentance for the forgiveness of sins. And people from the whole Judean countryside and all of the people of Jerusalem were going out to him, and were baptized by him in the river Jordan, confessing their sins. . . . He proclaimed, 'The one who is more powerful than I is coming after me; I am not worthy to stoop down and untie the thong of his sandals. I have baptized you with water; but he will baptize you with the Holy Spirit'" (Mark 1:4–5, 7–8).

The Gospel of John says of John the Baptist, "the Jews sent priests and Levites from Jerusalem to ask him, 'Who are you?' He confessed and did not deny it, but confessed, 'I am not the Messiah.' . . . Then they said to him, 'Who are you? Let us have an answer for those who sent us. What do you say about yourself?' He said, 'I am the voice of one crying out in the wilderness, "Make straight the way of the Lord,"' as the prophet Isaiah said. . . . They asked him, 'Why then are you baptizing?' . . . John answered them, 'I baptize with water. Among you stands one whom you do not know, the one who is coming after me; I am not worthy to untie the thong of his sandal'" (John 1:19–20, 22–23, 25–27). John was speaking of Jesus.

The Gospel of Matthew relates, "Jesus came from Galilee to John at the Jordan, to be baptized by him. John would have prevented him, saying, 'I need to be baptized by you, and do you come to me?' But Jesus answered

---

3. "Baptism with/in/of the Holy Spirit" does not appear in the NT, but "baptized with/in the Holy Spirit" does.

him, 'Let it be so now; for it is proper for us in this way to fulfill all righteousness.' Then he consented. And when Jesus had been baptized, just as he came up from the water, suddenly the heavens were opened to him and he saw the Spirit of God descending like a dove and alighting on him. And a voice from heaven said, 'This is my Son, the Beloved, with whom I am well pleased'" (Matt 3:13–17; cf. Mark 1:9–11; Luke 3:21–22).

Matthew further reports, "Then Jesus was led up by the Spirit into the wilderness to be tempted by the devil" (Matt 4:1). But first, Jesus "fasted forty days and forty nights" (v. 2). Then Satan, that diabolical deceiver, came and solicited Jesus with three mighty temptations (vv. 3–11). But Jesus resisted triumphantly. Then he went forth to conduct his itinerant ministry of preaching, teaching, healing, and exorcizing demons—mostly in Galilee, but occasionally in Judea during the appointed feasts—all for a total of about three years. His message was the same as that of his cousin John: "Repent, for the kingdom of heaven has come near" (Matt 3:2; 4:17).

QUESTIONING JESUS' IDENTITY

During Jesus' ministry, thousands of people saw him do miracles, heal people, and cast out demons. They were awestruck. So, they often asked among themselves who he was.

The question of Jesus' identity is a prominent theme in the Gospel of John. For instance, when Jesus spoke prophetically to the Samaritan woman at the well, she told her town folk about him and asked, "He cannot be the Messiah can he?" (John 4:29). Later, at the Sea of Galilee, Jesus multiplied food for a large crowd that said, "This is indeed the prophet who is to come into the world" (6:14). They referred to Moses' prediction, "The LORD your God will raise up for you a prophet like me" (Deut 18:15). On another occasion, people said of Jesus, "'Can it be that the [religious] authorities really know that this is the Messiah?' . . . Yet many in the crowd believed in him and were saying, 'When the Messiah comes, will he do more signs than this man has done?'" (John 7:26, 31). Sometime afterwards, "some in the crowd said, 'This is really the prophet.' Others said, 'This is the Messiah.' But some asked, 'Surely the Messiah does not come from Galilee, does he?'" (vv. 40–41). They did not understand that Isaiah said of Jesus that God "will honor Galilee of the Gentiles by the way of the sea along the Jordan—the people walking in darkness have seen a great light" (Isa 9:1–2 NIV). Thus, Jesus said repeatedly, "I am the light of the world" (John 8:12; 9:5; cf. 12:46).

The Apostle Peter's Keys of the Kingdom of Heaven

Sometimes, people asked Jesus himself who he was.[4] Once, a group of Pharisees asked him, "Who are you?" (John 8:25). They asked again, "Who do you claim to be?" (v. 53). Later, "the Jews" asked Jesus more specifically, "How long will you keep us in suspense? If you are the Messiah, tell us plainly" (10:24).

JESUS—"WHO DO YOU SAY THAT I AM?"

All three synoptists tell about Jesus taking "his/the disciples" into the region of Caesarea Philippi (Matt 16:13 par.). They likely were his twelve apostles. Caesarea Philippi was a Roman city located twenty-five miles north of the Sea of Galilee at the base of Mount Hermon in the present Golan Heights. There, Jesus asked his disciples two important questions about his identity. It was a pivotal event in Jesus' career. Matthew provides a fuller account in his gospel, in Matt 16:13–20, as follows:

> 13 Now when Jesus came into the district of Caesarea Philippi, he asked his disciples, "Who do people say that the Son of Man is?" 14 And they said, "Some say John the Baptist, but others Elijah, and still others Jeremiah or one of the prophets." 15 He said to them, "But who do you say that I am?" 16 Simon Peter answered, "You are the Messiah, the Son of the living God." 17 And Jesus answered him, "Blessed are you, Simon son of Jonah! For flesh and blood has not revealed this to you, but my Father in heaven. 18 And I tell you, you are Peter, and on this rock I will build my church, and the gates of Hades will not prevail against it. 19 I will give you the keys of the kingdom of heaven, and whatever you bind on earth will be bound in heaven, and whatever you loose on earth will be loosed in heaven." 20 Then he sternly ordered the disciples not to tell anyone that he was the Messiah.

The disciples' answer to Jesus' first question reveals that during antiquity, it was common to believe that dead heroes might reappear as visionary, spirit-like, or even fleshly humans. Matthew reports, "Herod the ruler heard reports about Jesus, and he said to his servants, 'This is John the Baptist; he has been raised from the dead, and for this reason these powers are at work in him'" (Matt 14:1–2). Herod had imprisoned John, and to keep his foolish promise he unwillingly had him beheaded (vv. 3–12). Mark

---

4. E.g., Matt 21:10; Luke 5:21; 7:49; 9:9; John 12:34.

and Luke differ somewhat in their account of the details of this incident recorded in Mark 8:27–29 and Luke 9:18–20.

First, Mark and Luke say Jesus' first question was, "Who do people/the crowds say that I am?" So, they have Jesus saying "I," but Matthew says he said "the Son of Man." This difference is not important except that, during the mid-twentieth century, Rudolf Bultmann and other NT, historical-critical scholars alleged that Jesus never called himself "the Son of Man;" rather, they claimed whenever he invoked this title, which was often, he referred to some unknown person. But Matthew here indicates otherwise with Jesus asking again, "Who do you say that I am?" This is clear evidence of Jesus claiming to be the Son of Man, alluding to Dan 7:13.

Second, Mark and Luke do not record any of Jesus' reply in Matt 16:17–19. Historical critics tend to deem this logion historically inauthentic since the other synoptists do not confirm it via multiple attestation and Jesus' sole use here of the word "church" (Gr. *ekklesia*). But Matthew was one of the twelve apostles who heard Jesus make this magisterial pronouncement, whereas Mark and Luke did not. For, Jesus said it only to his twelve apostles. Thus, unlike most NT gospel sayings of Jesus, no crowd was present to later recall what he had said. For these reasons, the oral and written sources available to Luke and perhaps Mark, which they surely used in compiling their gospels, likely did not include these words in Matt 16:17–19.

Although Matthew may not have written the gospel that bears his name, many scholars believe his church community did. Many think it was the church at Antioch. So, some think Matthew was most influential in developing Jesus' traditions at Antioch. If true, that would be why Matthew's name was later attached to this gospel.

When Jesus asked his second question, Peter answered. That is what Peter often did, speaking first among the apostles. Thus, Peter has been well regarded as the spokesman for the twelve apostles. He also has been well described among the apostles as "first among equals."

PETER—"YOU ARE THE MESSIAH, THE SON OF THE LIVING GOD"

When Peter answered this question about Jesus' identity, Peter was not saying any more than Matthew reports that the disciples had said earlier. For instance, when Jesus walked on water and Peter left the boat and went to him, both of them afterwards got into the boat. Then, regarding Jesus, "those in the boat worshiped him, saying, 'Truly you are the Son of God'" (Matt 14:33; cf. John 1:34, 40–41, 49; 6:69).

Some Christians claim there is a big difference between identifying Jesus as the Messiah and recognizing him as the Son of God. They mean that Jesus being the Son of God means that he is God, which is far greater than saying he is the Messiah. But sometimes in the Bible both titles are mentioned together, as if meant synonymously. The most prominent OT example is Psalm 2, and in the NT it is the high priest's question to Jesus. Matthew renders it, "tell us if you are the Messiah, the Son of God" (Matt 26:63 par.). They seem to be used interchangeably.

Another example is the Fourth Evangelist's stated purpose for writing his gospel. He says the signs Jesus did "are written so that you may come to believe that Jesus is the Messiah, the Son of God, and that through believing you may have life in his name" (John 20:31).

As for Jesus telling Peter that his confession was revealed to him by the Father, Craig S. Keener explains that it "undoubtedly" included "God's revelation through Jesus' miraculous acts (14:33; cf. 15:22)."[5]

JESUS—"YOU ARE PETER, AND ON THIS ROCK I WILL BUILD MY CHURCH"

Here is an astounding observation. Some historians say *Matt 16:16–19 may be the most discussed and disputed five sentences in human history!* Many admit it has been so among Christians, especially regarding Jesus' words in vv. 18–19.

Recall that Peter's original name was Simon. When Jesus declared to him, "And I tell you, you are Peter," Jesus therein reiterated what had happened when they first met. The Fourth Evangelist tells about "Andrew, Simon Peter's brother," that "he brought Simon to Jesus, who looked at him and said, 'You are Simon son of John. You are to be called Cephas' (which is translated Peter)" (John 1:40, 42).

The Bible often tells about peoples' names being changed. God changed Abram's name to Abraham and Jacob's name to Israel (Gen 17:5; 32:28). Such new names usually had a meaning, and they often characterized the person's future life.

---

5. Keener, *A Commentary on the Gospel of Matthew*, 426.

The name "Peter" is *petros* in the Greek text of Matt 16:18, though Jesus would have spoken in his native language of Aramaic. R. T. France says, "This new name, *Petros*, representing the Aramaic *Kepha*, 'stone' or 'rock,' is otherwise virtually unknown as a personal name in the ancient world, which makes it the more probably that Jesus chose it for Simon with a view to its literal meaning. He is to be a 'Rock.' And one important function of a rock, as [Matt] 7:24–27 has reminded us, is to provide a firm foundation for a building. So on this rock Jesus will build his church."[6] Much ink has been spilled over interpreting a word-play between Peter's name and the word "rock" (Gr. *petra*) in Matt 16:18, including their Aramaic equivalents.

Throughout church history, there have been three main interpretations of "rock" in Matt 16:18. First, the Roman Catholic Church claims *the rock is Peter and his keys make him the vicar of Christ*. In chapter 11, we will consider this interpretation of Peter and his keys as the main scriptural basis of the Catholic papacy.

Second, Augustine and others claimed *the rock is Jesus* largely due to Paul writing of certain experiences the Israelites had in their wanderings in the wilderness prior to entering the promised land. Paul says, "our ancestors were all under the cloud, and all passed through the sea, and all were baptized into Moses in the cloud and in the sea, and all ate the same spiritual food, and all drank the same spiritual drink. For they drank from the spiritual rock that followed them, and the rock was Christ" (1 Cor 10:1–4). So, the last phrase, "the rock was Christ," is made the basis of interpreting the "rock" in Matt 16:18 as Jesus.

Third, Protestants and most other non-Catholics have claimed that the rock in Matt 16:18 is *not* Peter but his confession to Jesus, "You are the Messiah, the Son of the living God."

Surprisingly, recent non-Catholic NT scholars, regardless of church affiliation, have asserted Jesus meant the rock in Matt 16:18 is Peter. They insist that saying the rock is *not* Peter, but his confession, is an over-reaction to the Roman Catholic view of Peter as first pope. Evangelical D. A. Carson says, "If it were not for Protestant reactions against extremes of Roman Catholic interpretation, it is doubtful whether many would have taken 'rock' to be anything or anyone other than Peter. . . . In this passage Jesus is the builder of the church and it would be a strange mixture of metaphors that also sees him within the same clauses as its foundation."[7]

---

6. France, *The Gospel of Matthew*, 620–21.

7. Carson, *Matthew*, 368.

The Apostle Peter's Keys of the Kingdom of Heaven

The idea of referring to someone as a rock has precedent in the Bible. Paul wrote about "the household of God, built upon the foundation of the apostles and prophets, with Christ Jesus himself as the cornerstone" (Eph 2:19–20; cf. 1 Cor 3:10–11). Indeed, Jesus had quoted Ps 118:22 and thereby subtly identified himself as a stone, saying, "The stone that the builders rejected has become the cornerstone" (Matt 21:42 par.; cf. Acts 4:11; Rom 9:33; Isa 28:16; 1 Pet 2:4–8). And the author of Revelation describes "the holy city, the new Jerusalem" as the church which "has twelve foundations, and on them are the twelve names of the twelve apostles of the Lamb" (Rev 21:14). R. T. France says of the church, "In principle all the apostles constituted the foundation, with Jesus as the cornerstone."[8]

Despite objections to the Catholic papacy, interpreting Peter as the rock in Matt 16:18 is most compelling. He likely is the rock upon which Jesus would build his church *because* Peter spoke up and confessed Jesus as the Messiah, the Son of God. This identification of Jesus is the message Peter would preach (Acts 2:36; 3:18–20; 4:10).

PETER AS PREEMINENT AMONG THE TWELVE APOSTLES

In the NT gospels, when Jesus' disciples are gathered together, it is surprising how often Peter speaks up and how rare when the other apostles speak up. In examining this and other data, it is obvious that Peter was the preeminent leader among Jesus' chosen apostles during his public ministry and thereafter as the following texts reveal:

- In all lists of any of the twelve apostles, Peter is mentioned first (Matt 10:2; 17:1; 26:37).
- When the woman touched Jesus' garment to be healed, Peter spoke to Jesus (Luke 8:45).
- Jesus took "Peter, James, and John" into the house to raise a girl from the dead (Mark 5:37).
- As Jesus walked on water, Peter said, "Lord, . . . command me to come to you" (Matt 14:28).
- Only Peter asked Jesus to explain the parable about what defiles a person (Matt 15:15).

---

8. France, *The Gospel of Matthew*, 623.

- Only Peter answered Jesus, "You are the Messiah, the Son of the living God" (Matt 16:15).
- When Jesus predicted he would be killed at Jerusalem, Peter rebuked him (Matt 16:22 par.).
- On the Mt. of Transfiguration, only Peter spoke to Jesus (Matt 17:4 par.).
- The tax collectors asked Peter, "Does your teacher not pay the temple tax?" (Matt 17:24).
- Peter asked Jesus, "Lord, how many times shall I forgive my brother?" (Matt 18:21 NIV).
- Only Peter said to Jesus, "we have left everything and followed you. What then will we have?" (Matt 19:27).
- Peter said to Jesus, "Rabbi, look! The fig tree that you cursed has withered" (Mark 11:21).
- Peter asked Jesus, "Lord, are you telling this parable for us or for everyone" (Luke 12:41).
- Jesus "took with him Peter and the two sons of Zebedee" to pray (Matt 26:37–41).
- An angel told the women, "go, tell his disciples and Peter" that Jesus is risen (Mark 16:7).
- Peter answered Jesus, "Lord, . . . you have the words of eternal life" (John 6:68).
- Peter told Jesus, "We have come to believe . . . you are the Holy One of God" (John 6:69).
- When Jesus washed his disciples' feet, Peter said, "Lord, not my feet only" (John 13:9).
- At Jesus' arrest, Peter "struck the high priest's slave, and cut off his right ear" (John 18:10).
- Mary Magdalene, seeing Jesus' tombstone removed, "went to Simon Peter and the other disciple" (John 20:1–2).
- Peter was the first apostle to enter Jesus' tomb and search for his body (John 20:1–6).

The Apostle Peter's Keys of the Kingdom of Heaven

- Peter said, "'I am going fishing.' They said to him, 'We will go with you'" (John 21:3).

- Peter jumped from the boat into the water and swam ashore to Jesus (John 21:4–8).

- Jesus asked three times, "Simon son of John, do you love me?" (John 21:15–17).

- Jesus told Peter, "Feed my lambs/Tend my sheep/Feed my sheep" (John 21:15–17).

- Peter guided the 120 disciples to fill Judas' office by choosing Matthias (Acts 1:15–26).

Yet Matthew records the following failures of Peter: (1) when Jesus walked on water and Peter did too, but began to sink, Jesus soon said to him, "You of little faith, why did you doubt?" (Matt 14:31); (2) when Jesus told his disciples he must go to Jerusalem and be killed (16:21), Peter objected and Jesus said, "Get behind me, Satan! You are a stumbling block to me" (v. 23); and (3) when the Sanhedrin was interrogating Jesus, three times the fearful Peter denied that he knew Jesus (26:69–74).

W. F. Albright and C. S. Mann well state about Matt 16:18: "In view of the background of vs. 19 [see "the Key of the House of David" below], one must dismiss as confessional interpretation any attempt to see *this* rock as meaning the faith, or the Messianic confession, of Peter. To deny the pre-eminent position of Peter among the disciples or in the early Christian community is a denial of the evidence. Cf. in this gospel x 2, xiv 28–31, xv 15. The interest in Peter's failures and vacillations does not detract from this pre-eminence; rather, it emphasizes it. Had Peter been a lesser figure his behavior would have been of far less consequence."[9]

Notice in Matt 16:17–19 that Jesus spoke of "my church" and "the kingdom of heaven." The Roman Catholic Church interprets these two concepts synonymously whereas many non-Catholic scholars distinguish them. I think it is difficult to decide. The "kingdom of God" may be a larger entity than the church, so that the kingdom includes the church as well as God's angels. This may be indicated in the so-called Lord's Prayer. Therein, Jesus taught us to pray, "Our Father in heaven, . . . Your kingdom come . . . on earth as it is in heaven" (Matt 6:10).

---

9. Albright and Mann, *Matthew*, 195. Emphasis theirs.

What are "the gates of Hades?" The Greek word *Hades* is the equivalent of the Hebrew word *Sheol* that appears sixty-seven times in the Hebrew Bible. During antiquity, most Greeks and Hebrews or Jews believed in an afterlife, and that when people died their souls went to an actual locality called "the place of the dead." Also called "the underworld," it was believed to be located under the earth.[10] So, Jesus spoke of "the gates of Hades" since he lived in Hellenistic times. But King Hezekiah, who lived earlier, spoke of "the gates of Sheol" (Isa 38:10). Either way, it refers to the threshold of death, but more particularly to the place where human souls reside during the intermediate state between death and the resurrection.

When Jesus said of his church, "the gates of Hades will not prevail against it," it seems he meant that even though death would claim his disciples, they would rise in the resurrection. But he also may have referred to the martyrdom of his people. In the end times tribulation it will be pervasive, worldwide, and imposed by the Antichrist, yet it will not destroy the church. In CE 197, church father Tertullian wrote of this concept that was later paraphrased, "the blood of martyrs is the seed of the church."[11]

Should we think of Peter opening doors or gates of the kingdom of heaven? Gates seem to be a counterpart to Jesus' words "the gates of Hades." The book of Revelation says the city of New Jerusalem will have "twelve gates" inscribed with the names of the twelve tribes of Israel (Rev 21:12–15, 21.) Yet it also says, "There in heaven a door stood open" (4:1). And it relates that the heavenly Jesus said, "I have the keys of Death and of Hades" (Rev 1:18).

JESUS—"I WILL GIVE YOU THE KEYS OF THE KINGDOM OF HEAVEN"

After Peter made his classic confession about Jesus' identity, we learned that Mark and Luke do not record Jesus' saying in Matt 16:17–19. It is about Jesus building his church, giving Peter the keys of the kingdom, and Peter binding and loosing. Consequently, historical critics generally have

---

10. The OT says fourteen times that at the death of humans their souls go "down" to Sheol. Jesus, apparently speaking of his soul, predicted that between the time of his death and his resurrection that he would be "in the heart of the earth" (Matt 12:40), referring to Sheol.

11. Tertullian wrote in his book, *The Apology* in *ANF*, chapter 50, "the blood of Christians is seed."

deemed this portion of Jesus' saying as historically inauthentic, that is, a fictional addition by Matthew, largely because the other NT gospels do not attest to it. Yet the Roman Catholic Church has treated these words of Jesus with utmost importance, citing them as the foremost biblical support for its papacy dogma that we will examine in chapter 11.

Space prevents us from exploring the critics' other reasons for rejecting Matt 16:17–19, or parts of it.[12] Synoptic differences are based mostly on diversity in oral traditions about Jesus. That is, the various church communities wherein these oral traditions were developed did not always remember Jesus' sayings exactly the same. But such differences are minor and rarely substantial. And perhaps the synoptic authors themselves should be considered.

As stated above, few NT texts have stirred more discussion and controversy than Matt 16:17–19. Scholars generally have regarded the entire pericope of Matt 16:13–20 as central to Matthew's entire presentation of Jesus and his public ministry prior to Passion Week. Although the other synoptists do not include Jesus' words here to Peter, for Matthew they obviously were important. Interestingly, they caused the popular lore, which has no foundation in the Bible, that Peter is the gatekeeper of heaven. Joachim Jeremias informs, "A common view in the ancient world was that heaven is closed off by doors" or gates.[13]

WHAT IS "THE KEY OF THE HOUSE OF DAVID?"

During antiquity, sometimes a king would employ a trustworthy steward with a key for opening the door or gate to the king's royal household, or perhaps his palace where he conducted the business of ruling his kingdom. There is an OT passage about this regarding the kingdom of Israel. The Prophet Isaiah represents God in saying, "On that day I will call my servant Eliakim son of Hilkiah, and will clothe him with your robe and bind your sash on him. I will commit your authority to his hand, and he shall be a father to the inhabitants of Jerusalem and to the house of Judah. I will place on his shoulder the key of the house of David; he shall open, and no one shall shut; he shall shut, and no one shall open" (Isa 22:20–22).

There is a difference between this Isaiah text and what Jesus said to Peter. The Davidic king's steward was typically given a single key, whereas

---

12. For a brief refutation of this critical assessment, see Carson, *Matthew*, 366.
13. Jeremias, "*kleis*," 3:744.

Jesus told Peter he would give him multiple "keys." Thus, the king's steward was "the keeper of the key," but Peter would be "the keeper of the keys." One key works for one lock, but multiple keys work for multiple locks. Thus, Peter will use his keys to open multiple locked doors or gates.

There is another difference between this Isa 22:20–22 and what Jesus told Peter. The Davidic king's steward would continually open and shut a single gate; but in "the holy city, the new Jerusalem," which in the future will be "coming down out of heaven from God" (Rev 21:2), its twelve "gates will never be shut by day—and there will be no night there" (v. 25).

John Nolland seems right in saying of Matt 16:19, "Despite the fact that Is. 22:22 clearly intrigued Jews and early Christians, it is unlikely that 'the key of the house of David' lies behind Peter's keys. The ties are too tenuous, especially when a link between the clauses about the binding and loosing and the clauses about opening and closing of Is. 22:22 proves untenable." So, Nolland dismisses links to these Isaiah and Revelation texts and concludes, "Peter's possession of the keys primarily involves him in pointing to Jesus as the Christ and the Son of God."[14]

WHAT WERE PETER'S "KEYS OF THE KINGDOM OF HEAVEN?"

What did Jesus mean by "the keys of the kingdom of heaven" that he promised to give Peter? Obviously, he meant it metaphorically. Many NT scholars, both Catholic and non-Catholic, have claimed that the keys were a symbol of supreme authority which Jesus granted Peter regarding the church. The Roman Catholic Church interprets Peter's keys as symbols of its papal authority. That is, Peter is "the vicar of Christ," and he and his successors, called "apostolic succession," govern the whole Church through the ages.

Early Protestant leaders interpreted Peter's kingdom keys as the preaching of the word, that is, the good news about Jesus and his kingdom. Bruner quotes Zwingli as saying succinctly, "The keys are nothing else than this: the preaching of the pure, unfalsified Word of the gospel. Whoever believes this will be free of his sins and be saved. Whoever does not believe this will be damned (Mark 16:16)."[15] Luther and other Protestant leaders

---

14. Nolland, *The Gospel of Matthew*, 677.
15. Bruner, *Matthew: A Commentary*, 2:134.

The Apostle Peter's Keys of the Kingdom of Heaven

thought Peter's keys referred to his preaching plus judgment, and both do seem to be part of it.

The Presbyterians' Westminster Confession of 1647 declares in its later form (25.6.130), "The Lord Jesus Christ is the only head of the Church, and the claim of any man to be the vicar of Christ and the head of the Church is unscriptural, without warrant in fact, and is a usurpation dishonoring to the Lord Jesus Christ." But the Roman Catholic Church's explanation of its identification of Peter as "the vicar of Christ" is that he is the chief representative of Jesus, not the head of the Church. Yet we will see in chapter 11 that Vatican I differs.

All agree that Peter's kingdom keys represent a symbol of authority. But authority to do what? Jeremias says of Jesus' words "I will give" in Matt 16:19, "This means that the handing over of the keys is not just future. It is regarded as taking place now."[16] Then, why did he state it as futuristic? Jesus surely meant that this role he was going to give Peter would be significant in building the church. We will see in the Acts of the Apostles that it will begin to happen soon, on the day of Pentecost, mostly by Peter proclaiming his confession that Jesus is "the Christ."[17] But we also will learn that there is more to Peter's kingdom keys than him preaching the gospel.

Sometime after Jesus promised Peter his kingdom keys, Jesus said something that sheds light on the nature of the keys. Luke informs that he said, "Woe to lawyers! For you have taken away the key of knowledge; you did not enter yourselves, and you hindered those who were entering" (Luke 11:52; lawyers=scribes). He apparently meant entering a house of knowledge.[18] Matthew says Jesus spoke similarly, perhaps saying on a different occasion, "But woe to you, scribes and Pharisees, hypocrites! For you lock people out of the kingdom of heaven. For you do not go in yourselves, and when others are going in, you stop them" (Matt 23:13).

So, Jesus seems to have envisioned a same or similar role for Peter as he did of those scribes and Pharisees. That is, *Peter would use the keys to open doors to the kingdom of God by preaching the good news about Jesus and loosening God's power by means of his Spirit.* W. D. Davies and Dale Allison better explain Matt 16:19 concerning Peter's preaching and his binding and loosing, that "both had to do with Peter's evangelistic mission. . . . Peter was to open that door by his missionary activity. The apostle had the keys of the

---

16. Jeremias, "*kleis*," 3:750.
17. Acts 2:36; 3:18, 20; 4:10; 10:36.
18. Fitzmyer, *The Gospel According to Luke X-XXIV*, 946, 951.

kingdom in so far as he proclaimed the good news.... The one eschatological message effects salvation for some, condemnation for others."[19]

In contrast, those scribes and Pharisees locked people out of the kingdom of God by taking away the true knowledge of God. That is similar to what Jesus said in his parable of the sower. He taught that the sower's "seeds fell on the path, and the birds came and ate them up" (Matt 13:4). Then he explained about Satan, saying "the evil one comes and snatches away what is sown in the heart" (v. 19).

So, *Peter's kingdom keys refer to him opening doors, or gates, to the kingdom of heaven and loosening God's power.* When Peter opens the doors, do they stay open or not? They seem to stay open so that all people will have opportunity to believe in Jesus, thereby enter the kingdom, and receive God's Holy Spirit. Accordingly, *Peter's use of kingdom keys must be temporary, thus not permanent.* When he has opened all kingdom doors for all people groups to enter, his task of using the keys will be finished. We will examine this concept further in chapter 11.

Jesus often taught about entering the kingdom of heaven. He said in his Sermon on the Mount, "Enter through the narrow gate; for the gate is wide and the road is easy that leads to destruction, and there are many who take it. For the gate is narrow and the road is hard that leads to life, and there are few who find it" (Matt 7:13–14). Later, Jesus likewise said of the kingdom, "Strive to enter through the narrow door; for many, I tell you, will try to enter and will not be able" (Luke 13:24). The rest of this parable, especially vv. 25–27, seems to mean the door will remain open until the end of the age, when it will be shut (cf. Matt 25.1–13). And the heavenly Jesus said of himself, "These are the words of the holy one, the true one, who has the key of David, who opens and no one will shut, who shuts and no one opens" (Rev 3:7).

Arno C. Gaebelein says of Matt 16:18–19, "Can it be thought that the door once opened simply *remained* open, and needed no more opening? On the contrary, I believe it can conclusively be shown that the administration of the kingdom, which these keys stand for, is not yet over, is not at all come to an end in one initial authoritative act."[20] But Gaebelein does not show how this is so. Instead, in comparison to Jesus, (1) Gaebelein says "the door," but Jesus said "keys," indicating multiple doors; (2) Gaebelein says the keys continue in use even now by others, which supports Catholicism's

---

19. Davies and Allison, *Matthew*, 2:641.
20. Gaebelein, *Matthew*, 352. Emphasis his.

apostolic succession, but Jesus only promised to give the keys to Peter; (3) Gaebelein implies that a single door is continually opened and shut whereas Jesus doesn't say this in Matthew's text.

Frederick Dale Bruner insightfully connects Peter's keys with the book of Acts and says, "What were these 'keys' in Acts? Preaching the gospel."[21] Indeed, but Peter is not the only person who preached the gospel as reported in Acts. So, there must be more to Peter's kingdom keys that distinguished his role with them from the other apostles.

WHAT IS THE BINDING AND LOOSING?

Soon after Jesus promised Peter his kingdom keys and authority to bind and loose, he told all his traveling disciples, Peter included, the same thing about binding and loosing. It has often been called "church discipline." Jesus said, "If another member of the church sins against you, go and point out the fault when the two of you are alone. If the member listens to you, you have regained that one. But if you are not listened to, take one or two others along with you, so that every word may be confirmed by the evidence of two or three witnesses. If the member refuses to listen to them, tell it to the church; and if the offender refuses to listen even to the church, let such a one be to you as a Gentile and a tax collector" (Matt 18:15–17). Then he added, "Truly I tell you, whatever you bind on earth will be bound in heaven, and whatever you loose on earth will be loosed in heaven" (v. 18).

It is significant that, just as Matthew is the only synoptist who says Jesus promised to give Peter the keys of the kingdom with authority to bind and loose, only Matthew records the instruction in Matt 18:15–18 that Jesus gave to all his apostles about church discipline.

Many Christians and scholars have thought Jesus meant the same thing both times he spoke of the binding and loosing. That is, the same authority he promised Peter he now gave to the other apostles. But the context of each saying differs, which suggests that Jesus did not mean the same thing each time. The fact that Matthew is the only synoptist who records both sayings makes this even more evident. And if Jesus meant the same think both times, it would have been redundant for Peter that second time.

Consequently, Jesus must have had a different meaning for Peter than he later did for all of the disciples, with Peter included. Indeed, the binding and loosing authority that Jesus gave only to Peter involves him opening

---

21. Bruner, *Matthew: A Commentary*, 132.

doors for people to enter the church or kingdom; but the binding and loosing authority that Jesus gave to all of the disciples, including Peter, involves disciplining those who are already members of the church.

Context is important. The first time Jesus spoke of binding and loosing he said it only to Peter and in the context of Jesus' question about his own identity. Peter replied that Jesus is the Messiah, the Son of God. That is the gospel message Jesus will send with his disciples to evangelize the world. Jesus then replied to Peter, "I will build my church." The church is increased in size mostly by evangelism. That is largely how Peter will use the keys, by being the first to preach the gospel and thereby loose God's power. So, Jesus first spoke to Peter about binding and loosing in the context of Peter's imminent, evangelistic mission to grow the church.

The second time Jesus spoke of binding and loosing he said it to all of his disciples in the context of church discipline, not church growth. He meant he was giving all of them authority to bind and loose within the church regarding discipline of its members. They were to follow Jesus' steps laid out in Matt 18:15–17. If the sinning man refuses to repent, they are to metaphorically bind him by treating him as a nonbeliever. Such an act is often referred to as "excommunication" from the church. If he repents, the disciples are to loose him by forgiving him and accepting him again as a genuine brother, freeing him from guilt and condemnation.

Furthermore, it seems that Jesus intended that the authority he gave all of the disciples to bind and loose be passed down to successive church leaders. This is true succession. Joachim Jeremias informs about this concerning Matt 18:18 by saying of antiquity, "The power of binding was interpreted by the Palestinian and Syrian churches as the power to exclude from the congregation,"[22] thus excommunication.

The wording about binding and loosing in Matt 16:19b and 18:18 is nearly identical. Consequently, some NT scholars have interpreted Peter's kingdom keys in Matt 16:19 as the three-step process of church discipline in Matt 18:15–17. That is, the first key is that the offended brother privately reprimands the erring brother (v. 15); the second key is a repetition of this step by adding two or three witnesses to hear the rebuke (v. 16); the third key is to declare the offense of impenitence before the church (v. 17). If the erring brother makes no amends after these three steps are taken, the church is to excommunicate him.

---

22. Jeremias, "*kleis*," 3:752.

The Apostle Peter's Keys of the Kingdom of Heaven

But this interpretation of Peter's kingdom keys is inadequate since it has nothing to do solely with Peter, as Jesus indicates in Matt 16:19b. The pronouns and verbs in the Greek text of Matt 16:19b are singular, but in Matt 18:18 they are plural, as would be expected. For in Matt 16:19b, Jesus spoke only to Peter; but in Matt 18:18, he spoke to his "disciples" (v. 1).

Nevertheless, the binding and loosing seem to convey the same overall concept in both of Jesus' sayings in Matt 16:19b and 18:18. That is, the binding refers to judgment and the loosing refers to blessing. Many past scholars, especially Protestants, insisted that due to the tense of these two Greek verbs they should be translated as if heaven decides and the church implements those decisions. But isn't that a twisting of these two sayings? Grant Osborne thinks so. He explains concerning this grammatical difficulty in Matt 16:19b:

> The first issue is the force of the future perfect passive periphrastic "will have been bound" (*estai dedemenon*); should the two expressions in each clause retain their perfect force ("will have been bound/loosed") or be translated as futures ("will be bound/loosed")? It has been common to stress a past aspect of the perfect to say that the decisions on earth "have already been made" in heaven, so that the church moves as guided by divine inspiration.
>
> While this makes good sense, the more recent [scholarly] appraisal of the perfect tense shows that it often does not have past time sense but rather is stative in force, thus emphasizing the present and future aspect ("will be bound/loosed"). So some [scholars] make God's decision subsequent, thus ratifying Peter's/the church's decision.[23]

Craig L. Blomberg further explains concerning Matt 16:19b, "in Hellenistic Greek this construction was often roughly equivalent to a simple future passive (as in the main text of the NIV), in which case Jesus teaches that God had delegated his authority to the church." Blomberg prefers a "mediating solution, supported by recent linguistic research, . . . that God promises that all who enter the kingdom do so in accordance with God's sovereign will, without specifying one way or the other whose action caused whose response."[24]

Protestants obviously have had good reasons for interpreting that God first does the binding and loosing, and the church then recognizes it. Many

---

23. Osborne, *Matthew*, 628–29. Osborne does not accept the latter treatment.
24. Blomberg, *Matthew*, 255.

powerful men in the church have decided things quite contrary to God's will. But the context of these two sayings of Jesus in Matt 16:19b and 18:18 suggest he assumed his disciples, such as Peter, would be living according to God's will and thus have God's wisdom in making such decisions.

It generally has been understood that Peter's loosing and binding depicted in Matt 16:19 refers to him opening and closing kingdom doors, respectively. But are these not different concepts? If Peter closes a kingdom door, so that someone cannot enter through that doorway, why then does he need to bind that person?

Rather, it seems that Peter will open a kingdom door and leave it open so that all may have the opportunity to enter. Then, under certain circumstances, Peter may decide to *bind a person so that he or she cannot enter through the open doorway*. We will consider this concept in later chapters when we examine Luke's reports in his book of Acts about Peter's binding and loosing activities. Leon Morris makes a distinction in Matt 16:19, saying, "we must be guarded in our understanding of this passage, . . . on the whole it seems that the right to 'bind' and 'loose' refers primarily to the regulation of conduct, while the keys point to admission and exclusion."[25] Indeed, we will learn in Acts that Peter binds people due to their unrighteous conduct.

Distinguishing Peter's role of spiritually binding and loosing people from his role of opening kingdom doors may coincide better with the ancient, Jewish tradition of rabbis "tying" or "untying" people by declaring what was forbidden or permitted in Torah. And Jesus may have given the order of binding and loosing to correspond with this late rabbinic tradition despite the fact that, according to Acts, Peter loosed before he bound.

Some scholars understand "heaven" in certain synoptic texts—such as the binding and loosing "in heaven" in Matt 16:19 and 18:18—as a euphemism for God. But that may be too narrow. A few biblical texts indicate that, although God is the supreme ruler of the highest heaven, to some degree he shares some of his heavenly authority with select angels.

The primary biblical text that depicts God sharing his authority with some angels is Dan 7:9–10. It presents a yet future scene in heaven in which "thrones were set in place, and an Ancient One took his throne;" then "the court sat in judgment" (cf. v. 26). This is a court scene, and the Ancient One is God. The "thrones" that are set in place seem to be those of the angelic

---

25. Morris, *Matthew*, 426–27.

members of God's royal council in heaven.[26] They likely are the enthroned, twenty-four elders mentioned in the book of Revelation.[27] So, "heaven" endorsing Peter's binding and loosing may refer to God *and* his royal council. These "elders" are judges who rule heavenly life on behalf of God and lead in its worship of him.

DOES THE NEW TESTAMENT TELL ABOUT PETER USING HIS KINGDOM KEYS?

In 1953, German historical-critical NT scholar, Gunther Bornkamm, began to have a profound impact on German scholarship concerning Jesus' promise to give Peter his keys of the kingdom. Bornkamm affirmed its historicity yet asserted, "There is no indication that historically Peter ever had the role which is ascribed to him in Matt. 16.17–19."[28]

In this book's preface, I relate that the hypothesis of this book arose one day in 2012 when I asked myself the question, "Does the NT say anything about Peter using his kingdom keys?" I said, "If it does, it must be in the book of Acts." I then read Acts again and concluded, "Yes, it does." So, I think Bornkamm is wrong about that.

A few non-Pentecostal scholars, and these quite recently, have recognized this truth about Peter using his kingdom keys as recorded in the book of Acts. They have identified it exclusively as Peter preaching the gospel. But does that role also include Peter's relationship to the early development of baptism with the Holy Spirit? To this question we now turn.

---

26. See God's royal council in Ps 82:1; 89:5–7; cf. 135:5; 136:2; 138:1; 1 Kgs 22:19–22; Job 1:6–12; 2:1–6.

27. Bauckham, *The Theology of the Book of Revelation*, 34. See Rev 4:4, 10; 5:6, 8, 11, 14; 19:4. See my book *Warrior from Heaven*, 45–46.

28. Bornkamm, "The Authority to 'Bind' and 'Loose' in the Church in Matthew's Gospel," 93.

CHAPTER 5

Spirit Baptism on the Day of Pentecost (Acts 2)

The remainder of this book focuses primarily on The Acts of the Apostles mostly for two reasons. It contains the only information in the NT about Peter using his kingdom keys. And Gordon Fee says of the Pentecostals' belief in post-conversion Spirit baptism with tongues, "the sole biblical support for these teachings consists of passages from the book of Acts."[1]

Thus, Pentecostals have been known for having a "canon within a canon." They have viewed Luke-Acts with a more inspired prominence in the Bible than its other documents. There have been other groups in Jewish-Christian tradition that have done this. Most notable are the Jewish Sadducees who ruled the religious life in Jerusalem during the time of Jesus. They treated the Pentateuch—the first five books of the Bible—as fully inspired by God, yet they assigned a secondary degree of divine inspiration to the remaining books of the Tanaach, that is, the Jewish Bible. And the Roman Catholic Bible contains the Apocrypha, which the Church deems less inspired than the rest of the Bible. But such a procedure adopted by Pentecostals has shortcomings. The main one is that certain portions of Acts cannot be properly understood apart from another NT book that Luke didn't write, namely, the Gospel of Matthew.

---

1. Fee, *Gospel and Spirit*, 84.

Spirit Baptism on the Day of Pentecost (Acts 2)

LUKE THE PHYSICIAN, HISTORIAN, AUTHOR, AND PREACHER

Most modern, NT scholars have believed that the Gospel of Luke and the book of Acts were written in the CE 80s. Yet these two books do not divulge their author. Such scholars treat them as complimentary volumes written by the same author. It is mostly because their writing style, Greek grammar, and vocabulary are similar. Greek scholars claim the author was skilled at Koine Greek, the language in which the whole NT was written. Most modern scholars and all church fathers have believed the author is mentioned in the NT as "Luke."

The Apostle Paul writes about "Luke, the beloved physician" (Col 4:14). He may have been Paul's personal physician. And a man named "Luke" was one of Paul's "fellow workers" on his second and third missionary journeys (2 Tim 4:11; Phlm 24). Also, the author of Acts includes himself in several "we" passages, indicating he was a member of Paul's missionary team.[2] Ben Witherington views much of Acts as the author's eyewitness accounts.[3]

Luke was a Gentile name. Paul has two lists of his missionary associates. He includes "Luke" in his Gentile list (Col 4:12–14). In Acts, the author seems to include himself with other preachers (Acts 16:10–17).

The Gospel of Luke and the book of Acts are addressed to the same man—Theophilus (Luke 1:3; Acts 1:1). This name is the Latin form of the Greek name Theophilos, which means "friend of God." This fellow may have been a Roman official since Luke addresses him as "most excellent Theophilus" (Luke 1:3). And he may have financed both literary projects.

The author of Luke-Acts was an accomplished historian and author (Luke 1:3; Acts 1:1). Should he be regarded as a theologian writing these two books? That is how scholars, including Pentecostals, increasingly have viewed him.[4]

The author of Luke-Acts certainly had theological designs in selecting his written sources (Luke 1:1–4). But I think it is more accurate to view him predominantly as a historian than as a theologian in writing Luke-Acts. That is how he traditionally has been perceived, with his sole purpose having been to write the gospel as a historical narrative of Jesus' life and passion, and the other volume about the historical development

---

2. Acts 16:10–17; 20:5–21:18; 27:1–28:16.
3. Witherington, *The Acts of the Apostles*, 280–81.
4. A Pentecostal exception is Stronstad, *The Charismatic Theology of St. Luke*, 7.

of the Jesus Movement.[5] He states in the introduction of his gospel that his purpose is to present "an orderly account of the events" of Jesus' life that were seen by "eyewitnesses" (vv. 1–2). And he begins Acts by saying, "In my first book, Theophilus, I wrote about all that Jesus did and taught" (Acts 1:1). Throughout Acts, I think it is doubtful the author interjects his theology very much; rather, he writes another orderly account, that is, a history of events he claims were accomplished by the Holy Spirit. So, the life-experiences he records *reflect* his theology more than that he *interjects* his theology into them.

One of the features in Acts that verifies it is intended as a historical document is that it is all narrative with many speeches, the latter being summaries (cf. Acts 2:40). So, Acts is a historically reliable document that tells about a particular, religious-social movement. Yet the author embraces a rhetorical (persuasive) purpose and a theological viewpoint. Acts conforms to standards of conventional history writing of its time, in a mostly Hellenistic world.[6]

As stated above, more is said about the Holy Spirit in Luke-Acts than in the rest of the NT. For example, in the Gospel of Matthew, Jesus says the Father will "give good things," yet the Gospel of Luke has "give the Holy Spirit" (Matt 7:11; Luke 11:13). Many students of Acts rightly claim it is not about the twelve apostles but mostly about Peter and Paul. Thus, it has been suggested that a more appropriate title is "The Acts of the Holy Spirit."[7]

Luke-Acts uniquely presents a global vision of all of humanity. Thus, the Gospel of Luke has a worldview that is more prevalent than in the other synoptics, and it fits the book of Acts very well. Acts relates the evangelistic, world mission that the fledgling church carries out, starting with Peter and then Paul. The message of these apostles was the same: Jesus is Israel's Messiah who died for our sins, arose from the dead, ascended to heaven, sat down with God the Father on his throne, and he awaits his return to earth

---

5. Contra eds. Dennis E. Smith and Joseph B. Tyson, *Acts and Christian Beginnings: The Acts Seminar Report* (Salem, OR: Poleridge, 2013). This book has twelve contributing authors who were members of the Acts Seminar. It was an eleven-year, collaborative, research project of the Westar Institute that produced the Jesus Seminar. These scholars concluded Acts is fiction written in CE 110–120. Their stated purpose was "to produce a red-letter edition of Acts modeled on the Jesus Seminar." Acts' silence on Jerusalem's destruction in CE 70 is fatal to this thesis.

6. See Witherington, *The Acts of the Apostles*, 24–51; Peterson, *The Acts of the Apostles*, 8–32.

7. Textual critics claim that people other than the original authors later added titles to NT books and letters.

to resurrect dead saints, conduct the judgment, and establish his worldwide kingdom.[8]

Herein, we will assume the man Paul calls "Luke" is the author of Luke-Acts.

THE COMING OF GOD'S KINGDOM

Among the synoptic gospels, only Luke tells about Jesus' disciples expecting the kingdom of God to appear immediately. Luke says they expressed this belief twice. Concerning the first time, Luke says Jesus "proceeded to tell a parable, because he was near Jerusalem, and because they supposed that the kingdom of God was to appear immediately. He said therefore, 'A nobleman went to a far country to receive for himself a kingdom and then return'" (Luke 19:11–12 ESV). He finished the parable with the exhortation that the nobleman's servants must serve him faithfully during his absence and that at his return they would be well rewarded (vv. 13–27). Jesus characterizes himself as that nobleman who goes to the far-away heaven to receive a kingdom. In doing so, he alludes to the Son of Man in Dan 7:13–14 who is escorted before the enthroned God of heaven and given a great kingdom.

The second time the disciples thought the kingdom would appear was just before Jesus ascended to heaven. They said, "Lord, is this the time when you will restore the kingdom to Israel?" (Acts 1:6) This question indicates they had not understood his earlier parable, in Luke 19:12–27. Jesus replied, "'It is not for you to know the times or periods that the Father has set by his own authority. But you will receive power when the Holy Spirit has come upon you, and you will be my witnesses in Jerusalem, in all of Judea and Samaria, and to the ends of the earth'" (Acts 1:7–8). This answer, which foretells their Spirit baptism again as in v. 5 ("you will be baptized with the Holy Spirit"), is part of a prologue of Acts. Since Acts 1:5 and v. 8 are central to understanding Acts, we will consider these two verses repeatedly throughout this book.

Luke says next about Jesus, "When he had said this, as they were watching, he was lifted up, and a cloud took him out of their sight. While he was going and they were gazing up toward heaven, suddenly two men in white robes stood by them. They said, 'Men of Galilee, why do you stand

---

8. Peter: Acts 2:22–49; 3:19–21; 4:10–12; 5:29–32; 10:38–43. Paul: Acts 9:20–22; 13:28–39; 16:31; 17:30–31; 20:21; 26:20–23; 28:23, 31.

SOLVING THE SAMARITAN RIDDLE

looking up toward heaven? This Jesus, who has been taken up from you into heaven, will come in the same way as you saw him go into heaven'" (Acts 1:9–11). Apparently, these "two men" were angels.

Putting these episodes together, Jesus taught his disciples, and those who would believe their message, that between his first and second comings they were to be his faithful witnesses in the world, proclaiming the good news about him and his kingdom, and they would do it by means of the power of the Holy Spirit. Then, sometime in the future, Jesus literally would return to earth with his glorious kingdom.

Luke next says of the disciples, "Then they returned to Jerusalem from the mount called Olivet, which is near Jerusalem, . . . When they had entered the city, they went to the room upstairs where they were staying" (Acts 1:12–13). It probably was the so-called Upper Room where they ate the Passover with Jesus the night (before?) he was betrayed.[9] Luke then names all eleven of the apostles and says, "these were constantly devoting themselves to prayer" with others, which included women and even Jesus' mother (v. 14).

Then Luke informs, "In those days Peter stood up among the believers (together the crowd numbered about one hundred twenty persons) and said, 'Friends, the scripture had to be fulfilled, which the Holy Spirit through David foretold concerning Judas'" (Acts 1:15). Peter quoted from two psalms and said Judas' apostleship must be replaced (vv. 20–25). So, "they cast lots for them, and the lot fell on Matthias" (v. 26).

SPIRIT BAPTISM ON THE DAY OF PENTECOST

When Peter said Judas' vacant office needed to be filled, it was the first of many instances in which Peter was the leader among his fellow apostles in undertaking the grand mission Jesus had given them. The next time Peter so led was only a few days later. We read about it in Acts 2:1–41 as follows:

> 1When the day of Pentecost had come, they were all together in one place. 2And suddenly from heaven there came a sound like the rush of a violent wind, and it filled the entire house where they were sitting. 3Divided tongues, as of fire, appeared among them, and a tongue rested on each of them. 4All of them were filled with

---

9. On whether Jesus and his disciples ate the meal on Passover or before, see *The Gospels Interwoven*, 340–43.

Spirit Baptism on the Day of Pentecost (Acts 2)

the Holy Spirit and began to speak in other languages, as the Spirit gave them ability.

5Now there were devout Jews from every nation under heaven living in Jerusalem. 6And at this sound the crowd gathered and was bewildered, because each one heard them speaking in the native language of each. 7Amazed and astonished, they asked, "Are not all these who are speaking Galileans? 8And how is it that we hear, each of us, in our own native language? 9Parthians, Medes, Elamites, and residents of Mesopotamia, Judea and Cappadocia, Pontus and Asia, 10Phrygia and Pamphylia, Egypt and the parts of Libya belonging to Cyrene, and visitors from Rome, both Jews and proselytes, 11Cretans and Arabs—in our own languages we hear them speaking about God's deeds of power." 12All were amazed and perplexed, saying to one another, "What does this mean?" 13But others sneered and said, "They are filled with new wine."

14But Peter, standing with the eleven, raised his voice and addressed them, "Men of Judea and all who live in Jerusalem, let this be known to you, and listen to what I say. 15Indeed, these are not drunk, as you suppose, for it is only nine o'clock in the morning. 16No, this is what was spoken through the prophet Joel: 17'In the last days it will be, God declares, that I will pour out my Spirit upon all flesh, and your sons and your daughters shall prophesy, and your young men shall see visions, and your old men shall dream dreams. 18Even upon my slaves, both men and women, in those days I will pour out my Spirit; and they shall prophesy. 19And I will show portents in the heaven above and signs on the earth below, blood, and fire, and smoky mist. 20The sun shall be turned to darkness and the moon to blood, before the coming of the Lord's great and glorious day. 21Then everyone who calls on the name of the Lord shall be saved.'

22You that are Israelites, listen to what I have to say: Jesus of Nazareth, a man attested to you by God with deeds of power, wonders, and signs that God did through him among you, as you yourselves know—23this man, handed over to you according to the definite plan and foreknowledge of God, you crucified and killed by the hands of those outside the law. 24But God raised him up, having freed him from death, because it was impossible for him to be held in its power.

. . .

32This Jesus God raised up, and of that all of us are witnesses. 33Being therefore exalted at the right hand of God, and having received from the Father the promise of the Holy Spirit, he has poured out this that you both see and hear. 34For David did not ascend into the heavens, but he himself says, 'The Lord said to my Lord, "Sit at my right hand, 35until I make your enemies your footstool."' 36Therefore let the entire house of Israel know with certainty that God has made him both Lord and Messiah, this Jesus whom you crucified."

37Now when they heard this, they were cut to the heart and said to Peter and to the other apostles, "Brothers, what should we do?" 38Peter said to them, "Repent, and be baptized every one of you in the name of Jesus Christ so that your sins may be forgiven; and you will receive the gift of the Holy Spirit. 39For the promise is for you, for your children, and for all who are far away, everyone whom the Lord our God calls to him." 40And he testified with many other arguments and exhorted them, saying, "Save yourselves from this corrupt generation." 41So those who welcomed his message were baptized, and that day about three thousand persons were added.

Luke doesn't say in Acts 2 that the 120 disciples were baptized with the Holy Spirit at this first Pentecost festival following the Christ event. But Luke does say they were "filled with the Holy Spirit." Later, we will learn that the prerequisite of being filled with the Spirit is now to be baptized with the Spirit. During OT times, select individuals such as prophets, priests, or Israel's king were filled with the Spirit and often spoke the word of God. But now, *all* of Jesus' disciples are filled with the Spirit and can speak the word of God.

WHY SPIRIT BAPTISM WITH TONGUES AT PENTECOST?

So, the 120 disciples were baptized with the Holy Spirit on the day of Pentecost in fulfillment of some prophecies that had been uttered by the Prophet Joel, John the Baptist, and Jesus. John had said to his disciples about Jesus, "He will baptize you with the Holy Spirit and fire" (Matt 3:11; cf. Luke 3:16; John 1:33). Again, Jesus had said to his disciples, "you will be baptized with the Holy Spirit not many days from now" (Acts 1:5).

Luke says "tongues, as of fire," appeared among these 120 disciples, "and a tongue rested on each of them" (Acts 2:3). The word in the Greek text that is here translated "tongues" is *glossai*. Then Luke says they "were filled with the Holy Spirit and began to speak in other languages" (v. 4). "Other languages" is the rendering for *heterais glossais* in the Greek text. A prominent Greek lexicon says this expression "may mean either *speak with*

Spirit Baptism on the Day of Pentecost (Acts 2)

different (even *other* than their own) *tongues* or *speak in foreign languages*."[10] The Greek word *glossolalia* means "speaking in tongues." They obviously spoke actual, human languages since the Diaspora Jews heard them and so testified.

Luke quotes these Diaspora listeners as saying, "in our own languages we hear them speaking about God's deeds of power" (Acts 2:11). Frederick Dale Bruner says of this text, "nothing more aptly expressed the will of God for the world mission of the church than proclaiming the great deeds of God in the world's languages. This is what gives the Pentecost story its beauty and meaning."[11] Many have claimed it was a reversal of Genesis 11, which tells about people building the tower of Babel and God then confounding their language.

Why did the 120 disciples speak in foreign languages? Jesus caused this supernatural activity as evidence that the Holy Spirit was being universally poured upon them and to verify the truth of Peter's message. The miracle was their speech, not the hearing of the audience as a few scholars have insisted.[12]

Also, the 3,000 Jews were saved because of hearing Peter's message and believing it. Thus, they were *not* saved due to hearing the 120 disciples speak in tongues. In fact, Luke doesn't say they preached the gospel.

To summarize Acts 2, the Spirit came upon the 120 disciples and they spoke in foreign languages unknown to them. Peter said it was what the Prophet Joel had predicted, and he quoted an extensive portion of Joel's prophecy (Joel 2:28–32; cf. Isa 44:3–4; 39:29). Peter then rebuked his listeners for their part in calling for, or approving of, Jesus' death while attending the previous feasts. (Torah required men in Israel to attend Passover and the Feast of Pentecost every year.) Three thousand of Peter's listeners were convicted and asked him what they should do. Peter replied, "Repent, and be baptized . . . and you will receive the gift of the Holy Spirit" (Acts 2:38).[13]

---

10. BAGD, 315. Emphasis not mine.

11. Bruner, *A Theology of the Holy Spirit*, 163.

12. Contra Lloyd-Jones (*Great Doctrine of the Bible*, 2:273), who says of Acts 2:4–13, "The people who were listening were enabled to hear in their own language though their own language was not being spoken." Yet Acts 4:4 says they "began to speak in other languages."

13. Luke here quotes Peter saying "the Holy Spirt" (Gr. *tou agiou pneumatos*). Elsewhere in Acts, Luke sometimes does not include the article, thus "Holy Spirit" is anarthrous, such as in Jesus' quotation in Acts 1:5. This difference does not appear to be significant.

SOLVING THE SAMARITAN RIDDLE

What Peter proclaimed in Acts 2:38 has been very important in the history of Christian theology. Although he didn't mention the word "believe" in this sentence, it is inferred from what he previously said of Jesus—"God has made him both Lord and Messiah" (v. 36). Dunn does well in endorsing the common view of Acts 2:38 that "repentance and faith" are "the opposites of the same coin."[14]

Did Peter mean in Acts 2:38 that people must repent-believe *and* be water baptized to be saved? This question has been much debated. It centers on the Greek preposition *eis*, which can mean "for" the forgiveness of sins, "on account of," or the like. Translating it "for" indicates baptism is the prerequisite of forgiveness, signifying baptismal regeneration. I think John Polhill rightly states, "The connection of baptism with the forgiveness of sins in v. 38 has often been a matter of controversy. . . . There is ample evidence in the New Testament, however, that *eis* can also mean *on the ground of, on the basis of*, which would indicate the opposite relationship—that forgiveness of sins in Luke-Acts is with repentance and not with baptism."[15]

PETER PREACHES TO JEWS AT PENTECOST

Most scholars regard Acts 2:38 as a paradigm for all peoples thereafter. But we should realize that Peter was speaking to Jews. He said if they repented, and (presumably) believed in Jesus, they would then receive the Spirit (Acts 2:36–38). Peter may have meant repentance generically, thus acknowledging their sins generally. But he especially meant a specific sin: their acquiescence in the condemnation and execution of Jesus (vv. 23, 36).

In recent decades—largely due to guilt from historic, Christian anti-Semitism and the WWII Holocaust—many Christians have refused to accuse Jesus' generation of guilt for his death, as if it was only the fault of the Sanhedrin and Roman Governor Pilate. A prime example is Vatican II. But Peter afterwards repeated this allegation in public speeches to Jews (Acts 3:14–15; 4:10; 5:30; cf. 7:52; 10:39). He said they were guilty for the following reasons: (1) their representative "elders of the people," who were members of the council, condemned Jesus (Matt 27:21; Luke 22:66; cf. Num 11:17b); (2) the crowd shouted for Pilate to release Barabbas and crucify Jesus against Pilate's judgment that Jesus was innocent (Matt 27:20–24; Mark 15:11); (3) and the crowd defiantly shouted to Pilate, "His blood be

---

14. Dunn, *Baptism in the Holy Spirit*, 91.
15. Polhill, *Acts*, 117.

Spirit Baptism on the Day of Pentecost (Acts 2)

on us and on our children" (Matt 27:25). Also, Peter said in his second sermon that the promised restoration of Israel, which includes Jesus' return, will not occur until a substantial Jewish remnant repents of this sin against Jesus and God who sent him (Acts 3:19–21). Yet we have seen that Israel's penitence as a prerequisite of the coming kingdom was the message of John the Baptist and Jesus (Matt 3:2; 4:17; Mark 1:15).

Peter said of the Spirit in his Pentecost message, "For the promise is for you, for your children, and for all who are far away, everyone whom the Lord our God calls to him" (Acts 2:39). Who are far away? Although God and Luke, though after the event, may have had Samaritans and Gentiles in mind, Peter himself could not have. That is why Craig Keener says Acts 2:38–39 is "on the Lukan level, not that of Peter in the narrative world."[16]

As we will learn in Acts 10, Peter was a typical Jew in observing Judaism's religious customs about not associating with Samaritans or Gentiles even though there was no Torah law against it. But God was going to teach Peter a new lesson by overturning this Jewish tradition—that Jews must remain separate from Gentiles.

So, when Peter first preached at Pentecost, he thought Samaritans and Gentiles did not partake in the Jews' covenantal blessings (cf. Acts 3:25; Gal 3:14). Therefore, in Acts 2:38–39 he seems to mean only Diaspora Jews by saying, "All who are far away."[17] It is unlikely that he meant it for Gentile proselytes to Judaism since he began his message, "Men of Judea and all who live in Jerusalem, . . . Fellow Israelites" (Acts 2:14, 29). And he added, "Let the entire house of Israel know . . . " (v. 36).

The importance of this realization—that Peter preached Acts 2:38–39 solely to Jews and that he intended the words "far away" only for Diaspora Jews—will become evident when we consider the Samaritans in Acts 8. In that text, Luke says they received the Spirit days after their conversion. Then we will see that it is an error to regard Acts 2:38–39 as a paradigm for all people, thus despite their ethnicity, during this early period of church history.

Many scholars cite Isa 57:19 as evidence that Joel and Peter applied the expression "far away" to Gentiles. It reads, "Peace, peace, to the far and the near, says the LORD; and I will heal them." But Isaiah 57 refers only to Israel. For instance, "possess the land and inherit my holy mountain" refers to the

---

16. Keener, *Acts: An Exegetical Commentary: Volume 1*, 987.

17. E.g., Witherington, *The Acts of the Apostles*, 155–56; Peterson, *The Acts of the Apostles*, 156, 156n93.

land of Israel and Mount Zion (v. 13; cf. 65:9; Matt 5:5); "my people's way" in Isa 57:14 refers to "the way to Zion" that Diaspora Jews will take during the future ingathering (cf. Isa 35:8; Jer 50:4–5); and the expression, "I hid and was angry," in Isa 57:17 echoes God's abandonment of Israel spoken sometimes by the prophets.[18] So, "far away" in Acts 2:39 can only refer to Diaspora Jews.

Some may ask, "What about Jesus' great commission declarations?" Indeed, the risen Jesus told his disciples, "Go therefore and make disciples of all nations" (Matt 28:19; cf. Mark 16:15; Luke 24:47). And he said likewise in the Acts prologue, "You will be my witnesses . . . to the ends of the earth" (Acts 1:8). Yet some things Jesus told his disciples, such as predictions that he would be killed and rise from the dead, perplexed them so that they didn't understand or believe it.[19] We will learn in Acts 10 that, even after Jesus taught this great commission, God had to teach Peter that he could now associate with, and thus evangelize, Gentiles.

WHY DID SPIRIT BAPTISM BEGIN AT PENTECOST?

To repeat, Luke does not say the 3,000 Jewish converts at Pentecost were then baptized with the Holy Spirit. But Peter seems to have indicated in Acts 2:38 that they would be by saying, "you will receive the gift of the Holy Spirit." And Peter had applied Joel's quotation of God, "I will pour out my Spirit upon all flesh," to that very moment. Apparently, "all flesh" refers to all of God's people just as Moses had wishfully declared (Num 11:29).[20] Also in Acts 2:38, Peter does not say physical evidence would accompany Spirit baptism, such as the 120 disciples speaking in foreign languages unknown to them.

The Spirit coming at Pentecost fulfilled those two promises Jesus had made to his disciples days earlier. We have already considered them: (1) "you will be baptized with the Holy Spirit not many days from now" (Acts 1:5), and (2) "you will receive power when the Holy Spirit has come upon you, and you will be my witnesses in Jerusalem" (v. 8). Jesus also told them regarding Jerusalem, "Stay here in the city until you have been clothed with

---

18. E.g., Deut 31:17–18; 32:20–21, 30; Ps 104:29; Isa 1:15; 8:17; 30:20; 45:15; 54:8; 57:17; 59:2; 64:7; Ezek 39:23–24, 29; Hos 5:6, 15.

19. Matt 16:21–22/Mark 8:31–32/Luke 9:22; Matt 17:22–23/Mark 8:31–32/Luke 9:44–45; Matt 20:18–19/Mark 10:33–34/Luke 18:31–34.

20. Cf. Dunn, *Jesus and the Spirit*, 170.

Spirit Baptism on the Day of Pentecost (Acts 2)

power from on high" (Luke 24:49). So, all they had to do was stay in Jerusalem to be baptized with the Holy Spirit. Luke doesn't say that during that ten-day interval between Jesus' heavenly ascension and the day of Pentecost that they needed to ask God for Spirit baptism. It was going to happen because it was in God's plan.

One of God's purposes for Spirit baptism on the day of Pentecost was that it was to be the birthday of the church due to the symbolism of that feast. "Pentecost" is the translation of the Greek word *pentekoste*, which means "fiftieth." The Feast of Pentecost is also called the Feast of Weeks because seven weeks transpire between Passover and Pentecost (though there is dispute as to when these fifty days begin). The main feature of Pentecost is the offering of two loaves of wheat bread in celebration of the wheat harvest (Lev 23:17). The meaning of these two loaves has not been well understood, thus it contains mystery. Christians generally believe one loaf symbolizes Israel and the other loaf the church. After Pentecost, the heavenly Jesus taught his disciples that Jews, Samaritans, and Gentiles were being joined together into one body, the church, by means of the Holy Spirit (1 Cor 12:13).

But why did the 120 disciples speak in tongues at Pentecost? Peter said of it, "This is what was spoken through the prophet Joel" (Acts 2:16; cf. Joel 2:28–32)? But Joel's prophecy that Peter quoted doesn't say anything about *glossolalia*. The answer seems to be that actual languages were spoken as irrefutable, physical evidence of people receiving the Spirit, which verifies the truth of the speakers' messages. Joel's prophecy says the Spirit poured out would cause people to prophesy, see visions, and have dreams, all being signs of wonder. People speaking in foreign languages unknown to them are a comparable sign. Peter must have meant that *glossolalia* was evidence of the prophetic Spirit being poured out as Joel had predicted.

PETER'S FIRST USE OF KINGDOM KEYS

There is another promise Jesus made prior to these two promises about Spirit baptism as empowerment for witness, and it also began to be fulfilled on that blessed day of Pentecost. As stated in chapter 4, Jesus promised to give Peter "the keys of the kingdom of heaven" (Matt 16:19). *On that day of Pentecost, for the first time Peter used his keys Jesus gave him to open a door of the kingdom to Jews* by preaching the good news about Jesus. Then Jesus presumably Spirit baptized those 3,000 Jews who believed Peter's message.

Peter thereby opened the first door of the kingdom to Jews, and 3,000 apparently were Spirit baptized then.

Merrill F. Unger affirms this regarding the gospel by saying, "To Peter Jesus had given 'the keys of the kingdom of heaven' (Matt 16:19). This meant that to him would be delegated the authority to open the door of gospel opportunity at the beginning of this age. This he did to Israel on the day of Pentecost (Acts 2:38–42). That is why he was the God-chosen preacher for that day."[21] Yes, but we will see that there is more to Peter's keys than gospel preaching.

WAS THERE SEPARABILITY AND SUBSEQUENCE AT PENTECOST?

Pentecostals claim that on the day of Pentecost the 120 disciples had already been genuine believers in Jesus as the Messiah and that they had been making him Lord of their lives. They were regenerated, thus saved throughout the time they followed Jesus during his itinerant ministry. In those few days leading up to that day of Pentecost in Acts 2, they had been waiting in Jerusalem as Jesus had commanded them.

Pentecostals also claim that those 120 disciples previously had an association with the Holy Spirit. For we have seen that the risen Jesus appeared to these 120 disciples, or most of them (Thomas being absent), on the first Easter evening and said, "'Peace be with you. As the Father has sent me, so I send you.' When he had said this, he breathed on them and said to them, 'Receive the Holy Spirit'" (John 20:21–22).

Thus, some Pentecostals assert that when the Holy Spirit came upon the 120 disciples on the day of Pentecost, for some of them it was their third experience with the Holy Spirit due to their previous regeneration as well as that experience with Jesus in John 20:22. So, these Pentecostals contend that the 120 disciples were baptized with the Spirit at Pentecost *subsequent* to their previous conversion experiences when they initially believed in Jesus and began following him. This is what Pentecostal scholars call "the doctrine of subsequence."

Craig Keener says of the book of Acts, "one could argue for some subsequence even in most cases of the first mention of people receiving the Spirit; in 2:4, 8:16–17, 9:1–7, and (by at least a few minutes) 19:6, receiving

---

21. Unger, *The Baptism and Gifts of the Holy Spirit*, 74.

Spirit Baptism on the Day of Pentecost (Acts 2)

the Spirit followed faith, being absolutely simultaneous with it only in 10:44."[22]

So, Pentecostals are known most for their doctrine of "separability and subsequence." Separability means conversion and Spirit baptism are separate events, and subsequence means Spirit baptism follows conversion. In chapter 2, we learned that Article 7 in Fundamental Truths of the Assembly of God (AOG) church declares, "All believers are entitled to and should ardently expect and earnestly seek the promise of the Father, the baptism in the Holy Spirit and fire.... This experience is distinct from and subsequent to the experience of the new birth."

Most Pentecostals further insist that all recipients of Spirit baptism must then speak in tongues as evidence verifying that it happened. They call this "initial physical evidence" or "evidential tongues." In chapter 2, we learned that the AOG's Article 8 of Fundamental Truths states, "The baptism of believers in the Holy Spirit is witnessed by the initial physical sign of speaking with other tongues."

Consequently, Pentecostals contend that what happened to the 120 disciples at Pentecost is a paradigm that is normative for all Christians thereafter in order for them to be baptized with the Holy Spirit. Many Pentecostals therefore claim that Spirit baptism is "a second work of grace" or "the second blessing."

This Pentecostal doctrine of subsequence with tongues has another form of separability—*it separates Pentecostals from their Christian brethren*! Ever since their origin in 1906, Pentecostals have been marginalized, especially by the Christian academic community. But this situation began to change with its acceptance in biblical scholarship and the emergence of the Charismatic movement in mainstream church denominations.

Are Pentecostals right about subsequence? More specifically, are they right in saying the 120 disciples were regenerated prior to Pentecost, so that they were baptized with the Holy Spirit subsequent to their conversion? This distinctive pneumatology of Pentecostals is that the Spirit regenerates at conversion but baptizes later.

---

22. Keener, *Acts: An Exegetical Commentary: Volume 2*, 1524.

SOLVING THE SAMARITAN RIDDLE

WERE JESUS' DISCIPLES REGENERATED PRIOR TO PENTECOST?

Most non-Pentecostal Christians agree with Pentecostals, that the 120 disciples at Pentecost had become believers in Jesus as the Messiah, and thus were converted, when they started following him years earlier. But we have seen that Dunn says they were unregenerate prior to Pentecost.[23] Nevertheless, he adopts the common view, as I do, by saying, "Pentecost is the beginning of the Church." And then he explains, "A Christian is by definition a member of the Church."[24]

In Dunn's *Baptism* book, he uses the word "Christian" often in denying a previous regeneration of any of Jesus' disciples. Is this practice common among Bible readers and/or scholars? Joseph A. Fitzmyer says of "all who believed" in Acts 2:44, "'the believers,' is a Lucan way of saying 'Christians.'"[25] And Ben Witherington says of the Gentile converts in Acts 10, "This story delineates how Luke views the issue of conversion—receiving the gift of the Holy Spirit is essential to being a Christian, as is belief in Jesus as the Christ."[26]

I think the word "Christian" muddies the water here. This word was not created until a few years after the church began. Luke informs, "It was in Antioch that the disciples were first called Christians" (Acts 11:26). Antioch was in Syria, thus a Gentile land. (It now exists in far southern Turkey.) Even well after that happened, the Jewish disciples in Jerusalem and Judea were still called "Nazarenes," and their sect was called "the Way" (Acts 9:2; 19:9; 24:5, 14, 22). Luke uses the word "Christian" only one more time, in Acts 26:28.

So, to be precise, in Dunn's *Baptism* book he often uses the word "Christian" anachronistically as he argues against subsequence in Acts. He asserts, "There were no Christians (properly speaking) prior to Pentecost." He says of the 120 disciples, "As the disciples began their Christian lives at Pentecost with the outpouring of Christ's Spirit and God's love in

---

23. For a refutation of Dunn's view on this, see Turner, *Power from on High*, 318–47. He is a former Pentecostal who sides mostly with Dunn.

24. Dunn, *Baptism in the Holy Spirit*, 51.

25. Fitzmyer, *The Acts of the Apostles*, 271.

26. Witherington, *The Acts of the Apostles*, 361. Yet Ben (p. 286) views the Samaritans in Acts 8 as converted under Philip's preaching and later Spirit baptized through Peter and John.

Spirit Baptism on the Day of Pentecost (Acts 2)

their hearts, so did each one begin his Christian life in these early days of Christianity."[27]

I don't think it is important what label is attached to the 120 disciples in Acts 1-2, whether "Christians," "believers," or some other. Rather, it should first be asked, "During Jesus' public ministry, did these 120 Jewish disciples believe in Jesus as the Messiah of Israel and make him their Lord?"

Pentecostal scholar James B. Shelton takes it a step further by rightly explaining that the 120 disciples were saved prior to Pentecost because they had already done as Paul later writes, "If you confess with your lips that Jesus is Lord and believe in your heart that God raised him from the dead, you will be saved" (Rom 10:9).[28] Except for doubting Thomas, many of these 120 disciples were doing that ever since encountering Jesus that first Easter evening, several weeks before Pentecost. But as I stated in chapter 3, I think Jesus' genuine disciples were saved-regenerated before that. It was when they began following him, thus believing in his messiahship and making him their Lord.

Also in chapter 3, we learned that Jesus spoke at the Festival of Booths about living water metaphorically flowing from the believer's heart (John 7:37-39). The Fourth Evangelist explains about Jesus, "Now he said this about the Spirit, which believers in him were to receive, for as yet there was no Spirit, because Jesus was not yet glorified" (v. 39). So, Jesus said that these "believers in him" would receive the Spirit after he was glorified. Later, we will consider when this glorification of Jesus occurred.

Much NT gospel evidence can be marshaled to support this assertion, that Jesus' true disciples were born again and therefore saved prior to Pentecost. Foremost is Jesus' foot-washing ceremony at the Last Supper. Jesus washed his disciples' feet and said, "One who has bathed does not need to wash, except for the feet, but is entirely clean. And you are clean, though not all of you," this latter referring to Judas (John 13:10; cf. 15:3).[29]

What did Jesus mean by "clean?" He meant God had forgiven Jesus' genuine disciples of their sins so that they were redeemed, justified, saved, and regenerated.

---

27. Dunn, *Baptism in the Holy Spirit*, 139.

28. Shelton, *Mighty in Word and Deed*, 159.

29. Another leading Evangelical scholar who disagreed with Dunn about when the 120 disciples were converted, and cites John 13:10 as evidence, is Packer, *Keep in Step with the Spirit*, 87.

Jesus then added, "'You call me Teacher and Lord—and you are right, for that is what I am'" (John 13:13). So, Jesus said the eleven rightly called him Lord, meaning Master. Despite Matt 7:21, the Apostle Paul later writes, "no one can say 'Jesus is Lord' except by the Holy Spirit" (1 Cor 12:3).

Similar to calling Jesus "Lord," Jesus said people belong to God who sincerely call him "Father." He taught his disciples to address God in prayer as "Father" (Matt 6:9; Luke 11:2). And he said, "Whoever does the will of my Father in heaven is my brother and sister and mother" (Matt 12:50). He also said, "Not everyone who says to me, 'Lord, Lord,' will enter the kingdom of heaven, but only the one who does the will of my Father in heaven" (Matt 7:21). He didn't mean they live perfectly, never sinning, but that their lives reflect their love for him (cf. John 14:23). For he said, "They who have my commandments and keep them are those who love me" (v. 21).

So, prior to Passion Week, those disciples who genuinely called Jesus "Lord" and God their "Father" were "clean," that is, forgiven of their sins and born again. They belonged to God and Jesus. The timing of future events in God's salvation history—Jesus' imminent death, resurrection, ascension, and gift of the Spirit at Pentecost—did not deny the disciples a prior relationship with God and Jesus, or eternal destiny with them.

DOES DUNN DO RIGHT WITH THE 120 DISCIPLES AT PENTECOST?

So, Dunn thinks that prior to Pentecost the 120 disciples did not really believe in Jesus. Dunn asserts, "So far as Peter was concerned their belief in him and commitment to him as Lord and Christ did not begin until Pentecost. . . . It was only at Pentecost that the one hundred and twenty became Christians."[30]

Some other Evangelical scholars who have written books on this subject agree with this Dunn assertion. For example, Merrill Unger asserts that Pentecostals are wrong about the 120 disciples being "regenerated before Pentecost, and what happened on that day is explained as a second experience, the baptism with the Holy Spirit."[31]

Jimmy Dunn continues with this same argument by saying,

---

30. Dunn, *Baptism in the Holy Spirit*, 52–53.
31. Unger, *The Baptism and Gifts of the Holy Spirit*, 25

Spirit Baptism on the Day of Pentecost (Acts 2)

> The act of faith which resulted in the gift of the Spirit to the one hundred and twenty did not take place till Pentecost. However highly they esteemed their Master while with him on earth, however deep their insights into his character and person (Luke 5.5; 9.20), and however greatly they reverenced him when gone from them (Acts 1.21), so far as Peter was concerned their belief in him and commitment to him as Lord and Christ did not begin until Pentecost. It was only at that moment of believing committal that they received the Spirit, only at Pentecost that their faith reached the level of Christian committal, only then that they became Christians in the NT sense of that word.
>
> ... Only at Pentecost did they enter into that relationship with the Father which was made possible through the death, resurrection and exaltation of the Son, and which was effected through the ascension gift of the Spirit. Whatever their old covenant experience of the Spirit, it was only at Pentecost that they entered into what Paul might have called the *abba*-relationship with the Father. ... it was only at Pentecost that the one hundred and twenty became Christians.[32]

On the contrary, we saw above that Jesus taught his disciples to address God in prayer by saying, "Our Father" (Matt 6:9; cf. Luke 11:2). If this confession is sincere, it indicates they had a relationship with him.

With all due respect for Jimmy Dunn, I think Clark Pinnock is right in saying of him and others, "Some of our best people, like Dale Bruner and James Dunn, have tried to impose their reading of Paul upon Luke's writings and have distorted it."[33] Nearly all Pentecostal scholars and many Evangelical scholars agree. Dunn and likeminded scholars obviously have taken their position in an effort to reconcile Luke and Paul.

Pentecostals sometimes cite the following comment by Dr. Martin Lloyd-Jones (1899–1981), who was the chaplain of London's Westminster Chapel for thirty years:

> What is the baptism of the Holy Spirit? Now there are some, as we have seen, who say that there is really no difficulty about this at all. They say it is simply a reference to regeneration and nothing else. It is what happens to people when they are regenerated and incorporated into Christ, as Paul teaches in 1 Corinthians 12:13: 'By one Spirit are we all baptized into one body.' You cannot be a Christian

---

32. Dunn, *Baptism in the Holy Spirit*, 52–53.

33. Clark Pinnock in his Foreword to Stronstad's *The Charismatic Theology of St. Luke*, vii.

without being a member of that body and you are baptised into that body by the Holy Spirit. Therefore, they say, this baptism of the Holy Spirit is simply regeneration.

But for myself, I simply cannot accept that explanation, and this is where we come directly to grips with the difficulty. I cannot accept that because if I were to believe that, I should have to believe that the disciples and the apostles were not regenerate until the Day of Pentecost—a supposition which seems to me to be quite untenable. In the same way, of course, you would have to say that not a single Old Testament saint had eternal life or was a child of God.[34]

TRANSITION FROM THE OLD COVENANT TO THE NEW COVENANT

Some of the Dunn Debate concerns the transition from the old covenant God made with Israel to the new covenant he promised Israel of which the church partakes. This transition is the in-breaking of the new age. Most scholars claim the pivotal point is the critical day of Pentecost, though a few say it is John's baptism of Jesus. Merrill Unger says of this transitional period:

> Old Testament saints were regenerated by faith, . . . [and so were] the disciples of Jesus before Pentecost (Luke 10.20). This does not mean, however, that what happened to Jesus' disciples at Pentecost was something in addition to salvation, a sort of second work of grace. They received the common salvation of the new era, purchased by Christ. . . . All of this means . . . that both the content and character of pre-cross salvation were not the same as the content and character of post-cross salvation mediated for the first time to fallen humanity at Pentecost. This does not mean that God has more than one way of salvation or more than one kind of salvation.[35]

I think Unger is unconvincing in explaining this transition about salvation and that it is because he is a classic Dispensationalist. They often were accused of teaching two separate salvations—one for Israel and another for the church. Unger tries here to distance himself from that. But

---

34. Lloyd-Jones, *Great Doctrines of the Bible*, 2:236–37.
35. Unger, *The Baptism and Gifts of the Holy Spirit*, 64.

Spirit Baptism on the Day of Pentecost (Acts 2)

his above statement also allows him to say, "The Gentile Cornelius, who doubtless was regenerated before Peter came to Caesarea (Acts 10:2–4), apparently did not receive the common salvation" until Peter ministered to him.[36] So, Unger arguably still posits two salvations. But his assessment, I think, indicates it is difficult to explain salvation for this transitional period.

SOME ELEMENTS IN ACTS 2–5 THAT DON'T FIT SUBSEQUENCE

Pentecostals insist that after people believe in Jesus and thereby are converted, they need to seek in prayer the baptism in the Holy Spirit. Recall that Article 7 of the AOG's Fundamental Truths states, "All believers . . . should . . . earnestly seek . . . the baptism in the Holy Spirit. . . . This experience is distinct from and subsequent to the experience of the new birth." Pentecostals usually cite the 120 disciples at Pentecost for support. But there is no evidence in Acts 2 that they prayed asking God or Jesus to Spirit baptize them. Nor had Jesus told them to do so. He told them to stay in Jerusalem so they *would* receive the Spirit. It had nothing to do with them seeking it; rather, God had already decided it, and I think his decision had to do with the meaning of Pentecost. That is, the two loaves of bread symbolizing Israel and the church meant Jews and Gentiles would be made one.

Pentecostals cite the 120 disciples experiencing subsequence with evidential tongues at Pentecost as a paradigm for all people thereafter. But Luke says there was "a violent wind, . . . divided tongues, as of fire, appeared among them, and a tongue rested on each of them" (Acts 2:2–3). How can Pentecostals require *glossolalia* yet omit these as necessary Spirit manifestations? And Pentecostals don't claim to speak human languages unknown to them as Luke says these 120 disciples did.

Also, we have seen that Peter proclaimed at Pentecost, "Repent . . . and you will receive the gift of the Holy Spirit" (Acts 2:38). That seems to be what happened to the 3,000 Jews—when they repented they received the Spirit. Now, Luke doesn't say they did. But days later the high priest "arrested the apostles" (5:18), and Peter gave a defense by saying, "we are witnesses to these things, and so is the Holy Spirit whom God has given to those who obey him" (v. 32). Peter meant at Pentecost those 3,000 Jews, who obeyed what he said about "repentance" and faith in Jesus as "Savior" (v. 31), were baptized with the Holy Spirit. So, Peter's statement in Acts

---

36. Ibid., 66.

5:31–32 serves as an explanation of his declaration in Acts 2:38 and thus militates against classic Pentecostals insisting that Spirit baptism occurs after conversion.

It is ironic that Pentecostals fix their distinctive belief about subsequence on the 120 disciples being Spirit baptized at Pentecost, yet many of them ignore that the 3,000 Jews who believed Peter's message did not provide any evidence of subsequence. Rather, they apparently repented and believed, and according to Peter's message they must have then received the Spirit just as the Gentiles later did in Acts 10. Many Pentecostals choose certain texts in Acts to support subsequence while ignoring other texts in Acts that are contrary to it.

Also, the AOG's Article 7 cites Acts 10:44–46 for support. Yet this text says the Cornelius household was converted and Spirit baptized while Peter was preaching. So, not only does this text not support the AOG's Article 7, which says all in the early church normally experienced subsequence, it opposes it.

Some folks ask, "Why this difference between the 120 disciples and 3,000 Jewish converts in Acts 2?" They mean the 120 disciples already were believers and the 3,000 Jews became believers that day, yet both were then Spirit baptized. There had to be a time when Spirit baptism began. For the 120 disciples, it necessarily must have been an event subsequent to their conversion. But for the 3,000 Jews, their Spirit baptism was not an event subsequent to their conversion. Pentecostals need to reconcile this fact with their doctrine of subsequence, and they have not convincingly done so. Christians generally agree that Spirit baptism on the 120 disciples at Pentecost was a unique, unrepeatable act that inaugurated the church age.

ONE BAPTISM, MANY FILLINGS

Interestingly, Luke does not say the 120 disciples were "baptized" with the Holy Spirit on that blessed day of Pentecost. But we know they were because of Jesus' previous promise, "But you will be baptized with the Holy Spirit not many days from now" (Acts 1:5). Plus, Peter said as much in Acts 11:15. But Luke does say, "All of them were filled with the Holy Spirit" (2:4). This theme of being "filled with the (Holy) Spirit" appears five times in Acts (Acts 4:8, 31; 9:17; 13:9; cf. 13:52).

Pentecostal Howard Ervin claims, "Baptized in the Spirit, filled with the Spirit, these are one and the same experience. It follows therefore, that

Spirit Baptism on the Day of Pentecost (Acts 2)

if there is one baptism in the Holy Spirit, there is one filling with the Spirit. The cliché, 'one baptism, but many fillings,' cannot be true." Ervin provides much exposition in explaining the NT use of the Greek verb *pimplemi*, translated "fill" or "filled," in relation to the Spirit. He insists, "Baptism in and fullness of the Spirit are synonymous terms."[37] Pentecostal scholar Roger Stronstad refutes Ervin on this.[38]

Indeed, Spirit baptism is a one-time gift. After that, believers are admonished to submit continually to God to be filled with his Spirit. The Apostle Paul exhorts people to "be filled with the Spirit" in order to produce "the fruit of the Spirit" (Eph 5:18; Gal 5:22).

The Bible uses words to describe the Spirit's work in a person's life other than "filled" or "filling." Pentecostals often refer to it with the word "anointing." Spirit filling or anointing can be viewed alike. Anointing means "poured out" (Acts 10:45; Titus 3:6).

PETER LOOSES PEOPLE FROM PHYSICAL INFIRMITIES

Recall that Jesus told Peter, "I will give you the keys of the kingdom of heaven, and whatever you bind on earth will be bound in heaven, and whatever you loose on earth will be loosed in heaven" (Matt 16:19). Peter first exercised this role when he proclaimed the gospel and loosed the power of the Spirit at Pentecost.

Soon afterwards, Peter loosed the power of the Holy Spirit upon a single person. Luke informs that he and John were walking up to the temple in Jerusalem for the three o'clock hour of prayer (Acts 3:1). They encountered a man begging for alms who had been born a paralytic. Peter declared to him, "I have no silver or gold, but what I have I give you; in the name of Jesus Christ of Nazareth, stand up and walk" (v. 6). He did, jumping and praising God. A large crowd gathered and Peter preached. Then we read, "Many of those who heard the word believed; and they numbered about five thousand" (4:4).

Luke also tells of other instances in his book of Acts in which Peter loosed people from physical maladies. For instance, he says at Jerusalem people "even carried out the sick into the streets, and laid them on cots and mats, in order that Peter's shadow might fall on some of them as he came by" (Acts 5:15). And later, at Lydda, Peter "found a man named Aeneas,

---

37. Ervin, *Spirit-Baptism*, 44–45, 67.
38. Stronstad, *The Charismatic Theology of St. Luke*, 54.

who had been bedridden for eight years, for he was paralyzed. Peter said to him, 'Aeneas, Jesus Christ heals you; get up and make your bed!' And immediately he got up. And all the residents of Lydda and Sharon saw him and turned to the Lord" (Acts 9:33–35). Next, at Joppa, Peter prayed for a female disciple named Tabitha who had died, and she came back to life (vv. 36–42).

PETER BINDS ANANIAS AND SAPPHIRA

Luke reports that at Jerusalem, soon after the day of Pentecost, "The whole group of those who believed were of one heart and soul, and no one claimed private ownership of any possessions, but everything they owned was held in common. . . . There was not a needy person among them, for as many as owned lands or houses sold them and brought the proceeds of what was sold. They laid it at the apostles' feet, and it was distributed to each as any had need" (Acts 4:32, 34–35).

Luke next reports the first time Peter exercised his exclusive role of binding as follows:

> 1But a man named Ananias, with the consent of his wife Sapphira, sold a piece of property; 2with his wife's knowledge, he kept back some of the proceeds, and brought only a part and laid it at the apostles' feet. 3"Ananias," Peter asked, "why has Satan filled your heart to lie to the Holy Spirit and to keep back part of the proceeds of the land? 4While it remained unsold, did it not remain your own? And after it was sold, were not the proceeds at your disposal? How is it that you have contrived this deed in your heart? You did not lie to us but to God!" 5Now when Ananias heard these words, he fell down and died. And great fear seized all who heard of it. 6The young men came and wrapped up his body, then carried him out and buried him.
>
> 7After an interval of about three hours his wife came in, not knowing what had happened. 8Peter said to her, "Tell me whether you and your husband sold the land for such and such a price." And she said, "Yes, that was the price." 9Then Peter said to her, "How is it that you have agreed together to put the Spirit of the Lord to the test? Look, the feet of those who have buried your husband are at the door, and they will carry you out." 10Immediately she fell down at his feet and died. When the young men came in they found her dead, so they carried her out and buried her beside

Spirit Baptism on the Day of Pentecost (Acts 2)

her husband. 11And great fear seized the whole church and all who heard of these things. (Acts 5:1–11)

Although Luke doesn't say, it seems Ananias and Sapphira sold their property and told the apostles they were contributing the full amount of the sale to the church. As Peter exposed their lie, divine judgment fell upon them as they collapsed to the ground, dead. This first binding occurred in Jerusalem.

Was this binding an exercise of Peter's temporary role in using "the keys of the kingdom of heaven" (Matt16:19)? When Jesus promised Peter those keys, he seems to have meant Peter's use of them would include binding as well as loosing. Jesus told him, "Whatever you bind on earth will be bound in heaven" (v. 19). When this lying incident occurred, in Acts 5, Peter had been building Jesus' church by loosing people from their sins and physical infirmities. Jesus also had told Peter, "I will build my church, and the gates of Hades will not prevail against it" (v. 18). At that time did this binding by Peter prevent the gates of Hades from prevailing against the church?

Some may think God was too harsh on Ananias and Sapphira. But unexposed lying in church can be like a cancer that grows and spreads. Paul later addressed a similar, immoral situation in the church at Corinth by saying, "Do you not know that a little yeast leavens the whole batch of dough? Clean out the old yeast so that you may be a new batch" (1 Cor 5:6–7).

Peter's binding of Ananias and Sapphira had a dual purpose. It brought judgment on that couple and produced godly fear in the infant church at Jerusalem. After Luke says, "great fear seized the whole church and all who heard of these things" (Acts 5:11), he adds, "Now many signs and wonders were done among the people through the apostles" (v. 12). And he later says of the church, "Living in the fear of the Lord and in the comfort of the Holy Spirit, it increased in numbers" (9:31). This increase in numbers was about to spread beyond Jerusalem and Judea.

CHAPTER 6

Spirit Baptism on the Samaritans (Acts 8)

JESUS MINISTERED ONLY TO THE HOUSE OF ISRAEL

After Jesus began his public ministry, he chose twelve apostles (Matt 10:1–4). Apostle means "one sent out." Matthew informs, "These twelve Jesus sent out with the following instructions: 'Go nowhere among the Gentiles, and enter no town of the Samaritans, but go rather to the lost sheep of the house of Israel. As you go, proclaim the good news, "The kingdom of heaven has come near." Cure the sick, raise the dead, cleanse the lepers, cast out demons'" (vv. 5–8). So, Jesus forbade his disciples to go to Gentiles or Samaritans with this good news.

Thus, throughout Jesus' itinerant ministry he rarely traveled outside Israel. His intention was to minister only to Jews in their homeland. But one time he ventured briefly into the Gentile region of Tyre and Sidon (Matt 15:21). It may have been to temporarily escape trouble due to his having offended some Pharisees (v. 12). He then said, "I was sent only to the lost sheep of the house of Israel" (v. 24).

Why did Jesus say and do that? God's plan was to offer the kingdom to Jews first. Then during Passion Week, Jesus taught two parables about it in Matt 21:33—22:14. They vividly portray God offering the kingdom to Jews, them rejecting it, and then offering it to Gentiles.

Spirit Baptism on the Samaritans (Acts 8)

So, John the Baptist, Jesus, his apostles, and seventy others went only to Israel proclaiming the message, "Repent, for the kingdom of heaven has come near" (Matt 3:2; 4:17; cf. Luke 10:9, 11). While some Jews repented and believed, most did not. But after Jews condemned Jesus and got him crucified, God raised him from the dead.

Then God's plan advanced to a new phase. It was to evangelize the world with this good news about the risen Jesus. Just before Jesus' heavenly ascension, he told his disciples how it would happen. He said, "You will be baptized with the Holy Spirit not many days from now" in order to "be my witnesses in Jerusalem, in all Judea and Samaria, and to the ends of the earth" (Acts 1:5, 8). Then Jesus ascended to heaven (Act 1:9).

Ten days later the Holy Spirit came upon the 120 disciples in Jerusalem on the day of Pentecost (2:1–4). They "began to speak in other languages" (v. 4). Three thousand Jews were saved and thousands more soon afterwards (v. 41; 4:4; 5:14).

THE "GOOD NEWS" SPREADS BEYOND JUDEA INTO SAMARIA

After Stephen was martyred (Acts 6:5—7:60), the gospel was preached next in Samaria. Luke tells of some Samaritans hearing and then seemingly believing the gospel, yet receiving the Holy Spirit days later. *Pentecostals cite this text, Acts 8:1-25, as the strongest biblical support for their doctrine of separability and subsequence.* It reads as follows:

> 1That day a severe persecution began against the church in Jerusalem, and all except the apostles were scattered throughout the countryside of Judea and Samaria. 2Devout men buried Stephen and made loud lamentation over him. 3But Saul was ravaging the church by entering house after house; dragging off both men and women, he committed them to prison.
>
> 4Now those who were scattered went from place to place, proclaiming the word. 5Philip went down to the city of Samaria and proclaimed the Messiah to them. 6The crowds with one accord listened eagerly to what was said by Philip, hearing and seeing the signs that he did, 7for unclean spirits, crying with loud shrieks, came out of many who were possessed; and many others who were paralyzed or lame were cured. 8So there was great joy in that city.
>
> 9Now a certain man named Simon had previously practiced magic in the city and amazed the people of Samaria, saying that he

was someone great. 10All of them, from the least to the greatest, listened to him eagerly, saying, 'This man is the power of God that is called Great.' 11And they listened eagerly to him because for a long time he had amazed them with his magic. 12But when they believed Philip, who was proclaiming the good news about the kingdom of God and the name of Jesus Christ, they were baptized, both men and women. 13Even Simon himself believed. After being baptized, he stayed constantly with Philip and was amazed when he saw the signs and great miracles that took place.

14Now when the apostles at Jerusalem heard that Samaria had accepted the word of God, they sent Peter and John to them. 15The two went down and prayed for them that they might receive the Holy Spirit 16(for as yet the Spirit had not come upon any of them; they had only been baptized in the name of the Lord Jesus). 17Then Peter and John laid their hands on them, and they received the Holy Spirit. 18Now when Simon saw that the Spirit was given through the laying on of the apostles' hands, he offered them money, 19saying, 'Give me also this power so that anyone on whom I lay my hands may receive the Holy Spirit.' 20But Peter said to him, 'May your silver perish with you, because you thought you could obtain God's gift with money! 21You have no part or share in this, for your heart is not right before God. 22Repent therefore of this wickedness of yours, and pray to the Lord that, if possible, the intent of your heart may be forgiven you. 23For I see that you are in the gall of bitterness and the chains of wickedness.' 24Simon answered, 'Pray for me to the Lord, that nothing of what you have said may happen to me.'

25Now after Peter and John had testified and spoken the word of the Lord, they returned to Jerusalem, proclaiming the good news to many villages of the Samaritans.

DOES DUNN DO RIGHT WITH THE SAMARITANS IN ACTS 8?

Jimmy Dunn disputes the Pentecostals' interpretation of Acts 8:4–25. His treatment of it in his *Baptism* book is entitled "The Riddle of Samaria," from which the title of this book is derived. He writes, "Acts 8, long the chief stronghold of Pentecostal (baptism in the Spirit) and Catholic (Confirmation) alike, centers on two facts: the Samaritans believed and were baptized; they did not receive the Spirit until some time later. The problem is that in the context of the rest of the NT these facts appear to be mutually exclusive

Spirit Baptism on the Samaritans (Acts 8)

and wholly irreconcilable."[1] He means that Paul's NT teaching on Spirit baptism conflicts with the interpretation that the Samaritans in Acts 8 believed and were Spirit baptized days later. We will consider Paul's teaching on this in chapter 10.

So, how does Dunn handle this seeming contradiction? He says the Samaritans "went through the form but did not experience the reality."[2] Anthony Hoekema agrees by saying, "The Samaritans were not true believers when Philip baptized them, and therefore did not receive the Spirit for salvation until the apostles laid hands on them . . . to bring the Samaritans from a merely nominal acceptance of Christian truth to genuine faith. . . . There was no interval of time between the Samaritans' coming to true faith and their receiving the Spirit."[3]

Dunn continues this interpretation by saying, "For Luke the . . . gift of the Spirit is the *beginning* of a man's Christian experience and life."[4] Jimmy writes years later, "Luke shared the regular view among the major NT writers that it is the gift of the Spirit which constitutes a Christian."[5] Dunn writes decades later, "It is reception of the Spirit which constitutes a person as a member of Christ."[6]

I think all of that is right after Acts 19, but not before. Jimmy says of Acts 8, "The two senior apostles came down hot-foot from Jerusalem to remedy a situation which had gone seriously wrong somewhere."[7] His humorous word "hot-foot" is reminiscent of brothers James and John being hotheads about an incident when Samaritans did not accept Jesus in their villages (Luke 9:51–53). Luke reports, "When his disciples James and John saw it, they said, 'Lord, do you want us to command fire to come down from heaven and consume them?'" (v. 54). Such behavior may be why Jesus earlier nicknamed them "Sons of Thunder" (Mark 3:17).

Dunn again alleges that before Peter and John came to the Samaritans, their "response and commitment was defective."[8] He insists that Luke "does

---

1. Dunn, *Baptism in the Holy Spirit*, 55.
2. Ibid., 66.
3. Hoekema, *Holy Spirit Baptism*, 36–37.
4. Dunn, *Baptism in the Holy Spirit*, 58. Emphasis his.
5. Dunn, *The Christ and the Spirit*, 220, similarly 13. Dunn cites Rom 8:9 and 1 Cor 12:13 for support, to be examined in chapter 10.
6. Dunn, *The Acts of the Apostles*, 255.
7. Dunn, *Baptism in the Holy Spirit*, 58.
8. Ibid., 63.

not mean that Philip's preaching was defective, only that his particular emphasis (perhaps due to a desire to speak in terms familiar to his audience) could well have given the Samaritans a false impression and resulted in a response which was sincere and enthusiastic, but wrongly directed."[9]

Nine years after *Baptism* Dunn wrote, "Luke understood the Samaritans' faith to be defective to some degree." He added, "Luke suggests that their faith was defective. How could that be? The answer may be simply that they were a people of a rather volatile sentiment who misrepresented Philip's preaching."[10] Later, Dunn said the Samaritans' experience was "insufficient," and Philip was "ineffective . . . in dealing with the Samaritans."[11]

So, throughout Dunn's career he has denied that these Samaritans believed when Philip preached to them. And Jimmy has never suggested any "terms" that Philip could have used that might have caused the Samaritans to have the right "impression." Many scholars, including Gordon Fee,[12] claim that the words Philip *did* use in Acts 8:5–14 are Lukan for good gospel preaching. D. A. Carson says of this text, "It has been ably pointed out, in some detail, that the language of belief and baptism, applicable to the Samaritans *before* the Holy Spirit descends on them, is regular Lukan terminology for becoming a Christian. . . . In my judgment the attempt to make Luke say the Samaritans were not believers until they received the Holy Spirit is not true to Luke's purposes."[13]

What words did Philip use? Luke says he "proclaimed the Messiah to them" (Acts 8:5). Since Samaritans were half-Jew and half-Gentile, they believed in the concept of a future Jewish Messiah (cf. John 4:19–26). Luke adds, "They believed Philip, who was proclaiming the good news about the kingdom of God and the name of Jesus Christ" (Acts 8:12). What better words could be used? Luke later says similarly of Paul that he was "proclaiming the kingdom of God and teaching about the Lord Jesus Christ" (28:31).

Dunn, in his commentary on Acts, seems to have retreated somewhat from his suggestion in *Baptism* that Philip could have used better terms in preaching to the Samaritans. Dunn says of Acts 8:12, "Luke uses two

---

9. Ibid., 64.
10. Dunn, *The Christ and the Spirit*, 220–21.
11. Dunn, *The Acts of the Apostles*, 111, 124.
12. E.g., Fee, *Gospel and Spirit*, 97; Fee, "Baptism in the Holy Spirit: The Issue of Separability and Subsequence," 90.
13. Carson, *Showing the Spirit*, 144.

Spirit Baptism on the Samaritans (Acts 8)

phrases to indicate that Philip's preaching was wholly in accord with the gospel as preached elsewhere in Acts." Jimmy is right in saying of Luke's phrase, "they believed Philip," that "it is an unusual formulation."[14] But does Luke mean only that the Samaritans thought well of Philip without believing his message? Most scholars think not.

Luke also says the apostles at Jerusalem were told that the Samaritans "accepted the word of God" (Acts 8:14; cf. 4:4; 11:1). Joseph Fitzmyer explains, "'Acceptance of the Word' would mean that those Samaritans have become Christians (see 11:1; 17:11; Luke 8:13; cf. 1 Thess 1:6; 2:13; Jas 1:21)."[15]

David Peterson asks of Acts 8:12–17, "Are we to conclude that there was something deficient in the faith of the Samaritans?" He cites Dunn and Max Turner and tries to refute their position by saying, "Luke seems to be at pains to stress the orthodoxy of Philip's preaching, the close attention paid by the Samaritans to what they heard, and the genuineness of their response.... With the words *not yet* (*oudepo*), Luke indicates that the Samaritan incident provides 'a clear break with the "norm" we might expect from Acts 2:38–39,'" quoting Turner in the last clause.[16]

The word in the Greek text translated "believed" in Acts 8:12 is *pisteuo*, the common NT word meaning "to believe." Peterson explains, "The meaning is rather that they were convinced by the truth of Philip's message." Regarding Greek grammar in Acts, Peterson says of Dunn's *Baptism* book that on p. 65, Dunn "claims that *pisteuein* with the dative here indicates intellectual assent rather than commitment of heart. However, the same construction in 16:34; 18:8 is used for genuine belief."[17]

But is there any evidence in Acts 8:5–14 that the Samaritans' "response" was "defective" due to a "false impression" as Jimmy claims? Philip surely could not have been the problem. In the Jerusalem church he was selected among the seven deacons as being "full of the Spirit and wisdom," and the apostles ordained him (6:3–6). And Philip's evangelization of the eunuch shows he could articulate the gospel quite well (8:26–40).

Three decades after Dunn's *Baptism* book was published he acknowledged "my much criticized exegesis of Acts 8:12." And he said of his treatment of Acts 8:4–24, "I readily admit that this was not the strongest part

---

14. Dunn, *The Acts of the Apostles*, 110.
15. Fitzmyer, *The Acts of the Apostles*, 405.
16. Peterson, *The Acts of the Apostles*, 286.
17. Ibid., 284, cf. 284n38. See also Dunn, *Baptism in the Holy Spirit*, 66n41.

of my discussion of Acts, and that if my interpretation of Luke's intention is correct, Luke could have made his meaning a good deal clearer. But I was driven to search for an alternative explanation by the unsatisfactory nature of the other interpretations offered for what all are agreed is a rather difficult passage which raises several puzzling questions." Surely all can appreciate this candid admission. Jimmy then adds, "The explanation is not as compelling as I would wish, but where Luke has left us only a few clues as to his meaning in this very compressed passage, we have to be content with those he did provide.... Can any alternative explanation claim as much?"[18]

Forty years after the publication of Dunn's *Baptism* he concedes, "My suggestion that perhaps Luke intended his readership to infer that the Samaritan's faith was somehow faulty was justifiably criticized."[19] Yet he still had the same conviction about Acts 8:4–24, saying, "There is *no* thought in Acts that the Samaritans were 'regenerate'... as a result of Philip's ministry.... The evangelism was incomplete.... Something had gone wrong." He then says in a footnote, "In *Baptism* ch. 5 I try to offer an explanation as to why the Spirit had not come in Acts 8. My attempt may not be very successful, and need not be given much weight." Yet he still insists, "The absence of the Spirit meant that something had gone wrong."[20]

WAS THE SAMARITAN EPISODE AN ANOMALY?

In 1985, Gordon Fee said of Acts 8:1–25, "Thus in the case of Samaria, the Pentecostals do seem to have a biblical precedent, both for subsequence and, almost certainly, for tongues as evidence. But is this single precedent the intended divine pattern, or is it, as most New Testament scholars think, a unique event in the early history?"[21] Fee cautions, "The Pentecostal must be wary of reforming the biblical data to fit his or her own experience."[22]

While most NT scholars think the Samaritans in Acts 8:4–24 believed Philip's message, many of them deem this incident an anomaly, thus not a paradigm, by comparing it to Peter's statement in Acts 2:38–39. For instance, John Stott says this Samaritan incident was "something unusual,

---

18. Dunn, *The Christ and the Spirit*, 240n53, 216, 221.

19. Dunn, *Baptism in the Holy Spirit*, 2nd ed., xii.

20. Dunn, "Baptism in the Holy Spirit: Yet Once More—Again," 34. See also Dunn, *Baptism in the Holy Spirit*, 2nd ed., xiii–xiv.

21. Fee, "Baptism in the Holy Spirit: The Issue of Separability and Subsequence," 91.

22. Ibid., 96.

Spirit Baptism on the Samaritans (Acts 8)

something irregular." He also says of these Samaritans, "Many have believed and been baptized. There can be little, if any, doubt that they were genuine Christian believers; no hint is given that their response had been defective. The only exception is Simon Magus. . . . There does not appear to have been anything faulty either in the Word of God which they heard or in the reception which they gave it."[23] Stott concludes, "The reason why the Spirit was not given seems to lie in the historical situation. And since this historical situation was unique and cannot be repeated . . . I cannot myself see how the abnormality in the Samaritan reception of the Spirit could be taken as a precedent for today."[24]

So, like many Evangelical scholars, Stott regards this Samaritan episode in Acts 8 as an anomaly, that is, something that deviates from the standard, the normal, or the expected. Those who take this position think Peter's proclamation in Acts 2:38 is the standard paradigm for all people, and the Samaritans' experience in Acts 8 is not.

If Luke and Peter meant Acts 2:38 as a paradigm for all people, why didn't Luke make this clear in Acts 8? He surely would have been aware of the supposed discrepancy between Acts 2:38 and 8:5–14. Such silence impugns his competence as a theologian and a historian, especially if the Samaritans' response was defective. Dunn says it was and that Luke "intended his readers to know this."[25] But that is not evident in the text.

In contrast, Pentecostals cite the Samaritans' subsequence in Acts 8 as a paradigm for all people. Stott and others deny this without offering a rationale other than deeming it an abnormality, which is arbitrary. Evangelicals are quick to assert that God only has to say something one time in the Bible for it to be true. What about a one-time, Spirit-induced episode in which these Samaritans believed in Jesus yet were Spirit baptized days later?

So, if the Samaritans had a post-conversion Spirit baptism, was it an anomaly that contrasts with Peter's message in Acts 2:38? Not if Spirit baptism could occur only by Peter using his kingdom keys in both instances.

---

23. Stott, *Baptism & Fullness*, 31–32, 34.

24. Ibid., 34.

25. Dunn, *Baptism in the Holy Spirit*, 63. See pp. 63–68 for his reasons. I think Menzies (*Empowered for Witness*, 207–10) makes a compelling refutation of them.

SOLVING THE SAMARITAN RIDDLE

HISTORICAL PRECEDENCE OR DIDACTIC TEACHING?

Gordon Fee says of the Pentecostals' belief in post-conversion Spirit baptism with tongues, "Those who disagree with Pentecostals on these points usually argue in two closely related veins. First, they argue that one must distinguish between *didactic* and *historical* portions of Scripture, and that for the formulation of Christian doctrine and experience one must go primarily to the didactic portions, and only secondarily to the historical. Secondly, what is *descriptive history* of the primitive church must not be translated into *normative experience* for the ongoing church."[26] Fee agrees with both points, and it makes him a renegade to many of his Pentecostal brethren.

In contrast, Pentecostal scholars Stronstad, Shelton, and Menzies embrace the Pentecostal distinctive and cite the Samaritan episode in Acts 8 as a paradigm for all people.[27] As indicated above, some Evangelicals contend that in forming a pneumatology, Paul's didactic teaching should supersede experiences narrated in Acts.[28] Yet both sides believe deeds done in the power of the Holy Spirit cannot conflict with the Bible's didactic teaching.

WHY DID THE APOSTLES SEND PETER AND JOHN TO THE SAMARITANS?

Luke says when the apostles at Jerusalem heard that the Samaritans had "believed," then "they sent Peter and John to them" (Acts 8:14). Why? Various answers have been proposed. Foremost is that the apostles needed to verify that these Samaritans truly received salvation and thus approve of their acceptance into the community.

The Roman Catholic Church says the Samaritans received the Spirit in both Samaritan episodes, with the second as a confirmation of the first. Some church fathers did say this. John Chrysostom, called "goldenmouthed" for his preaching skill, said Philip bestowed on the Samaritans "the Spirit, namely, of remission of sins: but the Spirit of miracles they had not received."[29] At times, the Roman Church has insisted this episode

---

26. Fee, *Gospel and Spirit*, 85. Emphasis his.

27. E.g., Stronstad, *The Charismatic Theology of St. Luke*; Shelton, *Mighty in Word and Deed*; Menzies, *Empowered for Witness*.

28. E.g., Stott, *Baptism & Fullness*, 15–17; Hoekema, *Holy Spirit Baptism*, 23–24.

29. John Chrysostom, *The Acts of the Apostles* in NPNF[1], 18.4.

Spirit Baptism on the Samaritans (Acts 8)

shows that the Spirit can be received only by the laying on of hands of Jesus' original apostles and their successors, thus affirming what it calls "apostolic succession." But Luke and Paul never say this, and it is negated in Acts 9:17, 10:44–46, and 19:6.

Dunn relates that Protestant leader John Calvin said these Samaritans secretly received the Spirit when they believed Philip's message, but they only manifested the Spirit outwardly with Peter and John.[30]

G. R. Beasley-Murray similarly claims the Samaritans were Spirit baptized when Philip ministered to them, but they received spiritual gifts when Peter and John laid hands on them.[31]

All of these interpretations of Acts 8:4–25 seem incompatible with what appears to be Luke's answer to the question about why Peter and John were sent. He says, "The two went down and prayed for them that they might receive the Holy Spirit" (Acts 8:15). So, the Samaritans had not received the Spirit in any sense, neither secretly nor otherwise, and so the apostles sent Peter and John to impart the Spirit to them.

Philip probably sent word to the apostles telling them that the Samaritans believed but did not receive the Spirit. He had been at Pentecost and, being among the 120 disciples, had received the Spirit there. Philip also heard Peter proclaim that if those Jews repented (and believed), they would then receive the Spirit as well (Acts 2:38). So, Philip and the apostles at Jerusalem likely were perplexed as to why they themselves, the other 120 disciples, and (presumably) the 3,000 Jews had received the Spirit that blessed day, yet these Samaritans had not.

When Peter and John arrived at Samaria they must have accepted the Samaritans' profession of faith and water baptism as authentic or they would not have prayed for them to receive the Spirit; instead, they would have preached the gospel to them. Ben Witherington is right on the mark by saying of Acts 8, "*Vv. 15–17* indicates that Peter and John did not attempt to start over from scratch with the Samaritans, which would have suggested that the work of Philip was invalid or defective. They are not said to preach or to baptize or to perform miracles for the audience Philip had previously approached."[32]

Craig Keener makes another important point by explaining this Samaritan incident in Acts 8, "Apostolic baptism always presupposes faith in

---

30. Dunn, *Baptism in the Holy Spirit*, 55, 55n1.
31. Beasley-Murray, *Baptism in the New Testament*, 118–20.
32. Witherington, *The Acts of the Apostles*, 286. Emphasis his.

Christ (22:16), and the apostles accepted Philip's baptism of the believing Samaritans as legitimate. We know that the apostles accepted the Samaritans' baptism because, in contrast to Acts 19:5 (a defective baptism by John alone), they do not rebaptize the Samaritans."[33] Keener then cites the rebaptism in Acts 19:1–7, and we will examine it in chapter 9.

Luke adds a parenthetical explanation by stating, "For as yet the Spirit had not come upon any of them; they had only been baptized" (Acts 8:16). This, too, suggests that Luke, but especially those ministering—Philip, Peter, and John—were convinced that these Samaritans were true believers. And Luke's addition, "baptized in the name of the Lord Jesus," further suggests this. Otherwise, it would have been inappropriate for Luke to inform that they had not received the Spirit since the NT says a person must first believe in Jesus to receive the Spirit.

Furthermore, the apostles at Jerusalem likely sent Peter due to his preeminent leadership among them. But they also may have thought the difference between the episodes at Jerusalem and Samaria was that Peter was the preacher at Jerusalem, but not at Samaria. If so, why did they also send John? King Solomon wrote, "Two are better than one" (Eccle 4:9). Plus, Peter and John were close friends and already had been successful in ministry as a duo-team (Acts 3–4:22). Yet Luke Timothy Johnson says, "John . . . remains silently in Peter's shadow."[34] And Dunn says similarly, "In the Peter and John narratives (3.1—4.22; 8.14–24) John almost fades from view, although as active as Peter (4.13; 8.18); all attention is on Peter."[35]

Here is the most important question in the Dunn Debate. How could Philip have been a skilled, Spirit-filled evangelist (Acts 8:29–35), who healed paralytics and cast out demons, yet he could not impart the Holy Spirit to these Samaritans who had "believed?" Dunn states, "The most contentious of all the Luke-Acts passages on this topic: Acts 8:14–24. . . . In this very brief and spare narrative, Luke elected to tell his readers the barest details. Beyond that, everyone, on all sides of the debate, has to indulge in speculation and guesswork, not least in any attempt to work out why the coming of the Spirit to the Samaritans was so delayed."[36] Jimmy adds, "The question which has posed the greatest puzzles for successive generations

---

33. Keener, *Crucial Questions about the Holy Spirit*, 58.
34. Johnson, *The Acts of the Apostles*, 148.
35. Dunn, *Baptism in the Holy Spirit*, 60.
36. Dunn, *The Christ and the Spirit*, 228.

Spirit Baptism on the Samaritans (Acts 8)

of commentators is the relation between faith, baptism, and the gift of the Spirit in Acts 8."[37]

So, many scholars claim the apostles at Jerusalem sent Peter and John to investigate whether or not the Samaritans had truly believed Philip's message. But many also suggest it was to prevent the centuries-old, Jewish-Samaritan schism from infiltrating the new, fledgling church. That faction had surfaced in Jesus' encounter with the Samaritan woman at Jacob's well (John 4:9, 20–22; cf. Luke 10:29–37). And the text about it says, "Jews do not share things in common with Samaritans" (John 4:8). So, it is thought that the Jerusalem apostles wanted the Samaritans to know the truth that Jesus had proclaimed to her, "Salvation is from the Jews" (v. 22), thus not from the Samaritans.

Here is how D. A. Carson explains this Samaritan lack of the Holy Spirit in Acts 8 and the avoidance of schism:

> It appears, then, that in Acts 8 the gift of the Holy Spirit is withheld to draw the connection between the Samaritans and the Jerusalem church through the apostles, Peter and John. Judging from what we know of relations between Jews and Samaritans, if this connecting link had not been forged, the Samaritans may well have wished to preserve an autonomy that would have divided the church from its inception, and which became principially [sp.] impossible once their reception of the Holy Spirit was so publicly dependent on the Jerusalem apostles. For their part, the Christian Jews may well have been less than eager to accept the Samaritans as full Christian brothers and sisters unless such a link had been forged.[38]

Maybe, but are these the only reasons the apostles sent Peter and John to the Samaritans? John Stott states, "No other explanation of the Samaritan story (*a*) brings it into harmony with the apostles' general teaching, from which it deviates, and (*b*) at the same time sets it in its historical context."[39]

Although the main reason Peter and John were sent was probably to impart the Spirit, these two concepts—imparting the Spirit and avoiding a schism—could be connected. Since the Jewish believers at Pentecost were Spirit baptized and these Samaritan believers were not, that difference could have provided Jewish believers with further leverage in claiming a spiritual superiority over Samaritan believers.

---

37. Ibid., 216.

38. Carson, *Showing the Spirit*, 145.

39. Stott, *Baptism & Fullness*, 33.

SOLVING THE SAMARITAN RIDDLE

WHAT IS GOD'S CHRONOLOGICAL ORDER FOR FAITH, FORGIVENESS, AND SPIRIT BAPTISM?

Dunn asserts in the following statements that God forgives and saves people by giving them his Spirit:

- "God's giving of the Holy Spirit is equivalent to his cleansing of their hearts; these two are one."[40]
- "The baptism in the Spirit is God's act of acceptance, of forgiveness, cleansing and salvation."[41]
- Acts "15:8–9: the gift of the Spirit was God's way of 'cleansing their hearts by faith.'"[42]
- "It is God's giving of the Spirit which makes a man a Christian, and ... nothing else."[43]

I think the NT evidence reveals that God saves people *because* they believe, and that is why he gives them his Holy Spirit. Hermann Gunkel explains likewise more fully, "The reception of the Spirit is thus God's witness to the existence of faith (Acts 15:8ff.; 11:17). Faith, then, is not derived from the Spirit but is held to be the prerequisite for receiving the Spirit. Even the first disciples—this is the view of Acts—had long been believers, even in Jesus' lifetime."[44] However, after Peter finished his role in using his kingdom keys in Acts 10, except for Acts 19, people were and still are always converted and Spirit baptized simultaneously, as Dunn says.

David Petts states similarly, "We must with Dunn (and Acts 2:38) add the gift of the Spirit. But that is not to make the gift of the Spirit salvation itself. It is distinct from salvation as it is distinct from water-baptism. Yet it is intimately connected to both, and, in a sense, without it salvation, in the full NT use of the term, is incomplete."[45]

Peter affirms this distinction at Pentecost. He declares, "Repent, and be baptized every one of you in the name of Jesus Christ . . . and you will receive the gift of the Holy Spirit" (Acts 2:38). So, repentance and faith are

---

40. Dunn, *Baptism in the Holy Spirit*, 81–82.
41. Ibid., 82.
42. Dunn, "Yet Once More—Again," 35.
43. Dunn, *Baptism in the Holy Spirit*, 68.
44. Gunkel, *The Influence of the Holy Spirit*, 17.
45. Petts, "The Baptism in the Holy Spirit in Relation to Christian Initiation," 87.

Spirit Baptism on the Samaritans (Acts 8)

God's prerequisites for giving people salvation. If they will repent and believe in Jesus, God will then save them and give them his Spirit.

So, God does not save people by giving them his Spirit. He *does* accomplish the new birth *by means* of his Spirit (John 3:3–5), as we saw in chapter 3. But being born again by the Spirit is *not* the same as being baptized with the Spirit as Dunn seems to say. This is not a moot point in this debate since this aspect of Dunn's viewpoint disallows a time interval between conversion and Spirit baptism as I think Luke narrates in Acts 8 and 19.

THE SAMARITANS HAVE A POST-CONVERSION SPIRIT BAPTISM

So, Philip preached to these Samaritans and they truly believed. But it was a few days later, when Peter and John came and laid hands on them, that they received the Spirit. So, *Pentecostals rightly insist that these Samaritans were baptized with the Spirit subsequent to their initial faith in Jesus. But are they right in citing this narrative as a paradigm for all believers?*

I don't think so. Peter's instruction at Pentecost—"Repent . . . and you will receive the gift of the Holy Spirit" (Acts 2:38)—was the core of his message. If he was right, those 3,000 Jews who repented and believed that day then received the Spirit. No subsequence there. Why this difference between the Jews and the Samaritans?

The difference was Peter's presence. He was there at Pentecost preaching the gospel. He used his keys to open a door of the kingdom for Jews and for them to enter and simultaneously receive the Spirit. *But Peter was not there at Samaria when Philip preached the gospel to those Samaritans and they believed. They did not receive the Spirit until Peter came there and used his keys to open a door of the kingdom for Samaritans.*

That is why Peter proclaimed that those Jews simultaneously would receive the Spirit when they repented and believed. But it appears Philip did not promise this to the Samaritans. Yet he had received the Spirit at Pentecost and heard Peter make that promise. If so many scholars are right, that Peter's proclamation in Acts 2:38 is a paradigm for all people, why didn't Philip promise the same—"You will receive the gift of the Holy Spirit?" The answer is that *the Spirit could only be initially given through Peter's presence, which was him using his keys.*

There is another difference between these two episodes. Luke says, "Simon saw that the Spirit was given through the laying on of the apostles'

SOLVING THE SAMARITAN RIDDLE

hands" (Acts 8:18). At Pentecost, Peter could not have laid his hands on the 3,000 Jewish converts for them to presumably receive the Spirit. And we will learn from Acts 10 that, while Peter was preaching to Gentiles, they believed and received the Spirit simultaneously, thus without Peter laying hands on them either. Why this difference with the Samaritans? It may have been due to Peter's presence more than laying hands on them. But it could have been due to Samaritans always arguing with Jews about religion and the proper place to worship (cf. John 4:20). Perhaps Jesus wanted these Samaritans to know with certainty what he told the Samaritan woman at Jacob's well, "You worship what you do not know; we worship what we know, for salvation is from the Jews" (v. 22), and now so is Spirit baptism.

As we learned in chapter 2, most Pentecostals contend that all Christians who don't speak in tongues have not been baptized with the Holy Spirit and that they need to seek this experience through prayer. They tell people to pray fervently, pleading to God for it to occur. Classical Pentecostals insist that if it does, these seekers will speak in tongues as evidence. But Frederick Dale Bruner observes, "There is no record in Acts of men praying that they might receive the Holy Spirit."[46] While true, Peter and John did pray for these Samaritans that they would.

So, when these Samaritans believed the gospel and later received the Spirit, it was the first fulfillment of Jesus telling his disciples, "You will be my witnesses in . . . Samaria" (Acts 1:8).

Were Peter's words in Acts 2:38—about conversion and Spirit baptism occurring simultaneously—a paradigm for all subsequent believers, thus rendering the Samaritans' post-conversion Spirit baptism abnormal? Well, God had planned both situations, and they involved Peter using his kingdom keys.

DO PETER'S KINGDOM KEYS EXPLAIN EARLY SPIRIT BAPTISM?

Dunn apparently is like nearly all NT scholars who have written on the relationship of conversion and Spirit baptism in Acts—they have not considered Peter's kingdom keys as a solution to this Samaritan riddle.

In my research for this book, I did not discover any writer who proposes that Peter's role in using kingdom keys explains early Spirit baptism in Acts and thus solves the Samaritan riddle in Acts 8. But near the end of

---

46. Bruner, *A Theology of the Holy Spirit*, 171.

Spirit Baptism on the Samaritans (Acts 8)

my research and writing of this book, I discovered one scholar who does so or comes very close. He is Michael J. Wilkins, an authority on the Gospel of Matthew. In one of his commentaries on Matthew, he makes the following comment on Matt 16:17–19, which Grant R. Osborne endorses in his own commentary on Matthew:

> Peter, the representative disciple who gives the first personal declaration of the Messiah's identity, is the one in the book of Acts who opens the door of the kingdom to the Jews on Pentecost (Acts 2), to the Samaritans (Acts 8), and finally to the Gentiles (Acts 10).... Peter leads the fledgling church to accept all peoples as recipients of God's kingdom blessings. His presence on three critical occasions (Acts 2, 8, 10) signified that God had bestowed his Spirit on all peoples—Jews, Samaritans, and Gentiles. As the utilizer of the keys of the kingdom of heaven, Peter signifies that God has opened the door of salvation-historical blessing for all peoples.... all that is directed to Peter is temporarily limited to his lifetime. It is therefore right for us to give due regard to this blessed apostle as one used in a special way in opening the doors of the kingdom of God and in the establishment of the church. But nowhere does Jesus indicate that Peter will play a perpetual role through successors.[47]

Notice that Wilkins says Spirit baptism occurred in all three instances in Acts 2, 8, and 10 due to Peter's presence, which was him using his kingdom keys. Wilkins just doesn't say this interpretation solves the Samaritan riddle, referring to subsequence in Acts 8 and its lack in Acts 2 and 10. But we should not expect a commentary on the Gospel of Matthew to provide a solution to an apparent problem in another book of the Bible.

Again, those who say Peter and John were sent to the Samaritans to prevent schism in the church may be right. But I doubt it is the only reason, or the main reason, the apostles sent them. Surely they knew the Samaritans had not received the Spirit, and that was the primary reason Peter and John went there. Whether any of the apostles at Jerusalem knew it or not, under God's guidance *they sent Peter to use his kingdom keys and thereby become the conduit, the channel, whereby Jesus would pour out the Holy Spirit upon these Samaritans.*

Some may allege that this viewpoint makes Peter look like the Spirit baptizer instead of Jesus. Cessationists often have made this allegation

---

47. Wilkins, *Matthew*, 566, 579–80. But see Matt 14:33. Osborne (*Matthew*, 628) has this quote of Wilkins.

against faith healers such as Oral Roberts. But Oral always wisely replied that Jesus healed through him. That is surely how healings occurred that are recorded in Acts. Sometimes the apostles laid hands on people and they were healed; other times, it happened without the laying on of hands.[48] Yet the Apostle Paul tells of imparting spiritual gifts through the laying on of hands (1 Tim 4:14; 2 Tim 1:6; cf. Rom 1:11).

It was the same with people who were Spirit baptized in Peter's presence. Peter and John laid their hands on the Samaritans and they received the Spirit. Yet we will learn in chapter 8 that Cornelius and his household, mentioned in Acts 10, received the Spirit in Peter's presence without him laying hands on them. Thus, the crucial requirement for Spirit baptism in the early days of the Jesus Movement seems to have been Peter's presence rather than the implementation of some other practice, such as one or more apostles laying hands on people.

DID THE SAMARITANS SPEAK IN TONGUES WHEN THEY WERE SPIRIT BAPTIZED?

It is ironic that classical Pentecostals cite Acts 8:4–25 as the strongest biblical support for their doctrine of subsequence, which includes evidential tongues, yet Luke doesn't say the Samaritans spoke in tongues. Pentecostal Howard Ervin cites Acts 2, 10, and 19, which say tongues accompanied Spirit baptism; yet he avoids discussing the apparent absence of tongues regarding the Samaritans' Spirit baptism in Acts 8.[49]

Since Luke doesn't say those Samaritans spoke in tongues when they received the Holy Spirit, this silence suggests that they didn't, and that Luke did not regard tongues-speaking as necessary evidence of Spirit baptism. And the same silence occurs regarding the multiple thousands of Jewish converts that Luke mentions three times (Acts 2:41; 4:4; 5:14). This realization should cause classical Pentecostals to pause and ponder, thus questioning the validity of their distinctive doctrine of subsequence with evidential tongues.

Also, for many Pentecostals it is difficult for them to discuss Spirit baptism with non-Pentecostal Christians without making tongues a *major* part of the conversation, and for some of them *the* conversation. Menzies

---

48. With hands: Acts 5:12 NASB, ESV; 9:12, 17–18; 14:3 NASB, ESV; 28:8; cf. 3:1–8; 5:15. Without hands: Acts 9:40; 19:11.

49. Ervin, *Spirit-Baptism*, 83.

Spirit Baptism on the Samaritans (Acts 8)

explains that many Pentecostals fail to distinguish *glossolalia* from Spirit baptism. He says, "This failure has led many of them to erroneously equate the Pentecostal gift with tongues."[50] I have noticed this.

Non-Pentecostal scholar Frederick Dale Bruner convincingly says of this situation:

> If it were Luke's or the early church's conviction that no one should suppose he had received the Holy Spirit until he had spoken in tongues . . . why does Luke so consistently fail to mention this *sine qua non*? Why does he not mention it at all places and, *of* all place, here, where for a period there was knowledge that the Holy Spirit had not yet been received? Here, certainly, on the one occasion in the New Testament where momentarily Christian baptism appears to be without the spiritual gift, the doctrine of tongues as the Spirit's only initial evidence should have been taught with prominence. Our only conclusion can be that Luke had no such doctrine.[51]

Although Luke does not say these Samaritans spoke in tongues, he does relate, "Now when Simon saw that the Spirit was given through the laying on of the apostles' hands, he offered them money, saying, 'Give me also this power so that anyone on whom I lay my hands may receive the Holy Spirit'" (Acts 8:18–19). So, Luke implies that outward signs accompanied the Samaritans' reception of the Spirit since that must have been how Simon knew they had been Spirit baptized. But it seems that if it had included tongues, Luke would have said so. Dunn says of Acts, "Luke certainly believes that the glossolalia was *a* manifestation of the Spirit's coming. . . . But it is equally certain that he has no intention of presenting glossolalia as *the* manifestation of the Spirit—otherwise he would have mentioned glossolalia in Acts 8 and made the point with greater force elsewhere."[52]

PETER SPIRITUALLY BINDS SIMON THE MAGICIAN

After Peter performed his initiatory role of binding Ananias and Sapphira, in Acts 5:1–11, the next time Peter did this was with this Simon the magician. The following points indicate Peter's unique binding role: (1) he did both bindings, (2) there is no mention of other bindings in Acts 2–8, and

---

50. Menzies, *Empowered for Witness*, 244.
51. Bruner, *A Theology of the Holy Spirit*, 179.
52. Dunn, *Jesus and the Spirit*, 191. Emphasis his.

SOLVING THE SAMARITAN RIDDLE

(3) these two bindings occurred in Jerusalem and then Samaria in accordance with Jesus' promise in Acts 1:8 to be "my witnesses in Jerusalem" and "in all Judea and Samaria," whether by loosing or binding.

Luke says this Simon "practiced magic" (Acts 8:9), the correct rendering of *mageuo* in the Greek text. Some scholars think it also indicates sorcery. The Latin word for magic is *magus*. That is why Latin Church fathers called him "Simon Magus." From him the term "simony" developed. It means the despicable practice of buying or selling church endowments.

Magic was practiced widely in the ancient world. Like most people, magicians believed in the existence of spiritual powers or beings, and magicians thought these powers or beings could affect human affairs on earth. Thus, magicians tried to manipulate, or otherwise influence, these powers or beings either for good or for evil by the use of amulets, incantations, rituals, potions, speeches, and prayers. Magicians typically hired out to clients to prosper them or harm their enemies by vocally calling on such celestial powers.

The Bible affirms the existence of spiritual beings, calling them "angels" and "spirits." It says good angels belong to God, and evil angels, also called "demons," belong to Satan. If Simon Magus ever contacted such beings, which is likely, they would have been demons.

A few scholars have proposed that Simon Magus became a real believer. For instance, Max Turner says, "There is little reason to suspect that Luke doubted Simon Magus was a *bona fide* convert."[53] And F. F. Bruce states, "Simon had believed Philip's message and been baptized, but he still manifested the signs of his old unregenerate nature. . . . Simon was terror-stricken" at Peter's condemnation of him.[54]

Terror-stricken is a bit of a stretch. However, among the five major families of Greek NT manuscripts, the *Codex Bezae* group adds this logion in Acts 8:24: "who did not stop weeping copiously." Textual critics and most NT scholars dismiss it as an interpolation.[55] If so, Simon does not appear to have repented and believed.

So, Dunn surely does right about this Samaritan in saying, "It is unlikely that Simon thereupon repented and was converted."[56] And Ben With-

---

53. Turner, *Power from on High*, 366.

54. Bruce, *Commentary on the Book of Acts*, 183–84. Contra Turner (*Power from on High*, 366–67), who says Simon was a genuine believer.

55. Metzger, A *Textual Commentary*, 358–59.

56. Dunn, *Baptism in the Holy Spirit*, 66n41.

Spirit Baptism on the Samaritans (Acts 8)

erington graphically explains the same concerning Acts 8, "v. 23 is as telling a description of an unregenerate person as one could want—trapped in the chains of wickedness."[57]

But does Dunn do right in saying, "Simon's faith and baptism were precisely like those of the other Samaritans, . . . they all went through the form but did not experience the reality?"[58] Yet Luke says the Samaritans "believed" and were "baptized;" but he also says "Simon himself believed" and was "baptized" (Acts 8:12–13). Were the Samaritans and Simon believers, or were they all pseudo-believers?

As in Acts 8:12, "believed" in v. 13 translates *pisteuo* in the Greek text, meaning "to believe." In nearly all NT texts that say people "believed," it means real faith. Yet there are rare exceptions, and they usually regard lack of perseverance.

For instance, the Fourth Evangelist says that Jesus spoke and "many believed in him. Then Jesus said to the Jews who had believed in him, 'If you continue in my word, you are truly my disciples; and you will know the truth, and the truth will make you free'" (John 8:30–32). This concept of Jesus' genuine disciples persevering in faith is pervasive in the NT.[59] In fact, we English speakers get our word "discipline" from the word "disciple."

So, Philip must have baptized Simon because he thought he truly "believed" (Acts 8:13). Yet days later it became apparent that Simon was a pseudo-believer due to his offering Peter money to get the power of the Holy Spirit.[60] Simon Peter said to this Simon Magus, "May your silver perish with you." That recalls what Jesus once said, "You cannot serve God and money" (Matt 6:24/Mark 16:13 ESV).

So, Peter exercised his role of binding false believers—Priscilla and Aquila at Jerusalem and Simon at Samaria. They had been accepted into the faith community. Like Judas, their downfall was "the love of money," which Paul deems "the root of all evil" (1 Tim 6:10 KJV).

We learned in chapter 4 that Jesus gave Peter an exclusive, initiatory role when Jesus said only to Peter, "Whatever you bind on earth will be bound in heaven" (Matt 16:19). Peter did exactly that when he denounced

---

57. Witherington, *The Acts of the Apostles*, 288.

58. Dunn, *Baptism in the Holy Spirit*, 66.

59. E.g., Matt 7:21–23; 13:21; Luke 8:13; 1 Cor 6:9; Eph 5:5–6; Gal 5:19–21; Titus 1:16; Heb 6:4–6; 10:26–27; Jas 2:14, 20–26; 1 John 2:4; 3:6–10; 4:7–8; 5:4, 18.

60. Dunn (*Baptism in the Holy Spirit*, 65–67), Fee (*Gospel and Spirit*, 97), and many other scholars rightly conclude Simon was unconverted.

Simon (Acts 8:20–22), telling him to repent of being "in the gall of bitterness and the chains of wickedness" (v. 23).

Simon Magus was not working his magic with God by then telling Peter rather flippantly, "Pray for me" (Acts 8:24). Peter had just told this man to repent and do his own praying, "that, if possible, the intent of your heart may be forgiven you" by God (v. 22). How many times have people responded that nonchalantly to men of God who exposed their sins? This sorry Simon sought the adulation of men who said of him, "This man is the power of God that is called Great" (v. 10). He was like some "scribes and the Pharisees" of whom Jesus alleged, "They do all their deeds to be seen by others" (Matt 23:2, 5).

Nevertheless, Simon Peter left room for Simon Magus to repent. But Peter offered no such opportunity to Ananias and Sapphira, pronouncing immediate curtains on them. Richard Pervo observes this difference by saying, "Simon, whose crime may seem more abominable than that of Ananias and Sapphira, is, unlike them, offered a chance for repentance."[61]

Simon Magus briefly saw miraculous acts done by the Spirit through Philip and perhaps Peter and John. But Ananias and Sapphira had been members of the apostolic community and thus had been exposed much more to God's power and maybe involved in ministry. Plus, they lied to God, which seems a greater sin than Simon's. Jesus once said, "Everyone to whom much has been given, much will be required" (Luke 12:48). So, in both situations there was binding, but the former was more severe since more divine revelation had been given.

Luke ends this story abruptly, suggesting Simon did not repent. Dunn convincingly concludes, "Such a notable success for the gospel would surely have been recorded."[62] Indeed, this non-closure probably indicates Peter's denunciation of Simon Magus came true. Some second century church fathers wrote stories about this Simon, depicting him as a Gnostic or some other kind of heretic, but these may be fictional tales.[63]

---

61. Pervo, *Acts*, 214–15.

62. Dunn, *Baptism in the Holy Spirit*, 66n41.

63. E.g., Pseudo-Clementine, *Homilies* 3.29–58; Justin Martyr, *First Apology* in *ANF*, 1.26; Justin Martyr, *Acts of Peter* 5, 9, 17.

Spirit Baptism on the Samaritans (Acts 8)

WHY DIDN'T THE ETHIOPIAN EUNUCH RECEIVE THE HOLY SPIRIT?

After this Samaritan episode, Luke says "An angel of the Lord said to Philip, 'Get up and go toward the south to the road that goes down from Jerusalem to Gaza'" (Acts 8:26). As he did, Philip saw "an Ethiopian eunuch, a court official of the Candace, queen of the Ethiopians, in charge of her entire treasury. He had come to Jerusalem to worship and was returning home; seated in his chariot, he was reading the prophet Isaiah" (vv. 27–28). No doubt he was reading aloud as literate ancients often did. Philip came alongside the man and told him the suffering servant he was reading about in Isaiah 53 is Jesus of Nazareth (vv. 30–35). The eunuch believed him, and Philip water baptized him (vv. 36–39).

This Gentile, Ethiopian official would have been a black man and probably a God-fearing Gentile, like Cornelius in Acts 10, rather than a proselyte to Judaism since it forbade castration.

Luke does not say this man received the Spirit. He merely writes, "Philip baptized him. When they came up out of the water, the Spirit of the Lord snatched Philip away; the eunuch saw him no more, and went on his way rejoicing" (Acts 8:38–39). Was his rejoicing evidence that he had received the Spirit? It is doubtful. Although joy is evidence of the Holy Spirit (Acts 13:52; Rom 14:17; Gal 5:22), "there was great joy in that city" of Samaria due to seeing Philip heal people before anyone received the Spirit there (Acts 8:8).

Ironically, Pentecostal Howard Ervin thinks this Ethiopian eunuch received the Holy Spirit when he believed. One would expect Ervin to say this man had *not* received the Holy Spirit then, but later, to support Ervin's doctrine of subsequence. Instead, Ervin cites a variant of Acts 8:39 that appears in some NT Greek manuscripts, but not in the large majority of them. This variant reads in English, "The Holy Spirit fell on the eunuch, and an angel of the Lord caught up Philip," and it replaces "the Spirit of the Lord snatched Philip away."

Bruce Metzger says some scholars have thought this variant in Acts 8:39 is original. They have asserted that a later scribe excised it by thinking Acts 8:15–17 requires that the Spirit could be received only by the laying on of the hands of the apostles. Metzger says the vast majority of scholars have deemed this variant a scribal interpolation inserted (1) to conform to at least Acts 8:17, which says these Samaritans received the Spirit, and (2) to complete Philip's ministry to this man.[64]

Most likely this Ethiopian, being a Gentile, was *not* Spirit baptized at that time. For that to occur, Peter must open the last door of the kingdom, and it will be for Gentiles.

SUMMARY

To summarize Luke's account of these Samaritans, he likely meant they truly believed Philip's message and thereupon were converted to faith in Jesus. Accordingly, Philip's preaching was not defective, nor did the Samaritans misunderstand him or exercise only an intellectual assent. And due to the Samaritans' subsequent Spirit baptism, *Pentecostals have a very strong case here for their doctrine of subsequence.*

But is this Samaritan episode a paradigm for all people afterwards who are converted to faith in Jesus, as Pentecostals claim? I don't think so. Subsequence happened to these Samaritans because *Peter was not present* when they first heard and believed the gospel, *but days later he was present*, performing his task of opening a kingdom door for Samaritans to enter and thereby receive the Spirit. And Luke not saying these Samaritans spoke in tongues militates against classical Pentecostals claiming the necessity of tongues with Spirit baptism.

So, Peter has now opened two doors of the kingdom, one for Jews and one for Samaritans, to begin the fulfillment of Jesus' prediction that his disciples would be "my witnesses in Jerusalem, in all Judea and Samaria" (Acts 1:8). After that, Jews and Samaritans who believed the gospel *simultaneously* received the Spirit. But Peter must open one more door of the kingdom for the disciples to begin to be "witnesses ... to the ends of the earth."

Before we examine this final episode of Peter's use of kingdom keys, in Acts 10, Luke tells a fascinating story in Acts 9 about a zealous, religious Jew who was breathing vile hatred upon Jesus' fledgling church by getting some of his disciples cast into prison. This young man was even involved in causing the first Christian martyrdom. Yet Jesus turned this fellow around so that he became the greatest, Spirit-filled Christian missionary of all time by taking the gospel to the Gentiles. To his most dramatic conversion story we now turn.

---

64. Metzger, *A Textual Commentary*, 360–61.

CHAPTER 7

Spirit Baptism on the Apostle Paul (Acts 9)

THE APOSTLE PAUL'S CONVERSION

The Apostle Paul's conversion is one of the most thrilling stories in the Bible. "Saul" seems to have been his pre-Christian name and "Paul" his Christian name, but this is uncertain. He was a young, zealous Pharisee who grew up in Jerusalem under the instruction of prominent rabbis who included the well-known Gamaliel (Acts 5:34; 22:3). Saul thought it his divine calling to persecute followers of Jesus, whom he deemed a messianic imposter. David Peterson says of Saul, "Luke shows his readers that even the hardest heart can be softened by God and the most formidable opponent can become a servant of Christ and a vigorous agent of his gospel."[1]

Right before telling about Saul's conversion, Luke relates how Stephen became the first Jewish, Christian martyr. Members of the Sanhedrin (religious council) stoned him to death, and "the witnesses laid their coats at the feet of a young man named Saul" (Acts 7:58). Luke adds, "Saul approved of their killing him. . . . Saul was ravaging the church by entering house after house; dragging off both men and women, he committed them to prison" (Acts 8:1, 3). Then Luke writes in Acts 9:1–19:

---

1. Peterson, *The Acts of the Apostles*, 311.

1Meanwhile Saul, still breathing threats and murder against the disciples of the Lord, went to the high priest 2and asked him for letters to the synagogues at Damascus, so that if he found any who belonged to the Way, men or women, he might bring them bound to Jerusalem. 3Now as he was going along and approaching Damascus, suddenly a light from heaven flashed around him. 4He fell to the ground and heard a voice saying to him, "Saul, Saul, why do you persecute me?" 5He asked, "Who are you, Lord?" The reply came, "I am Jesus, whom you are persecuting. 6But get up and enter the city, and you will be told what you are to do." 7The men who were travelling with him stood speechless because they heard the voice but saw no one. 8Saul got up from the ground, and though his eyes were open, he could see nothing; so they led him by the hand and brought him into Damascus. 9For three days he was without sight, and neither ate nor drank.

10Now there was a disciple in Damascus named Ananias. The Lord said to him in a vision, "Ananias." He answered, "Here I am, Lord." 11The Lord said to him, "Get up and go to the street called Straight, and at the house of Judas look for a man of Tarsus named Saul. At this moment he is praying, 12and he has seen in a vision a man named Ananias come in and lay his hands on him so that he might regain his sight." 13But Ananias answered, "Lord, I have heard from many about this man, how much evil he has done to your saints in Jerusalem; 14and here he has authority from the chief priests to bind all who invoke your name." 15But the Lord said to him, "Go, for he is an instrument whom I have chosen to bring my name before Gentiles and kings and before the people of Israel; 16I myself will show him how much he must suffer for the sake of my name." 17So Ananias went and entered the house. He laid his hands on Saul and said, "Brother Saul, the Lord Jesus, who appeared to you on your way here, has sent me so that you may regain your sight and be filled with the Holy Spirit." 18And immediately something like scales fell from his eyes, and his sight was restored. Then he got up and was baptized, 19and after taking some food, he regained his strength.

For some people, to speak of Paul's conversion is misleading. They may understand the word "conversion" to mean the devotee of one religion changing to another religion. But we are not talking about Saul being converted from Judaism to Christianity. That idea is anachronistic. Rather, Saul converted to faith in Jesus as Israel's promised Messiah. In so doing, he believed he was being faithful to his religious heritage. So, Paul afterwards did not try to start another religion. At least in his early years as a Christian, like Jesus, Paul was trying to reform Judaism.

WAS PAUL CONVERTED ON THE DAMASCUS ROAD?

Most Christians have thought Saul was converted on the Damascus road. Recall that Pentecostal scholars cite Acts 2, 8, and 19 as their three main Bible texts to support their doctrine of subsequence. Some also cite Paul's conversion in Acts 9 (also in Acts 22 and 26) as further support. For example, Pentecostal scholar Howard Ervin says of Paul's conversion, "It was in the Damascus road encounter that the persecutor of the Christians became a disciple of Christ Jesus. He was saved, and three days later he was healed of blindness, filled with the Holy Spirit when Ananias laid his hands upon him in the name of Jesus. Here too the Pentecostal pattern is consistent: (1) conversion with its concomitant new birth, and (2) subsequently baptized in/filled with the Holy Spirit."[2]

Many Christians have thought that when Saul called Jesus "Lord" on the Damascus road (Acts 9:5; 22:8), it means he then believed in Jesus and was converted. Also, years later Paul wrote that "no one can say 'Jesus is Lord' except by the Holy Spirit" (1 Cor 12:3), which means being a Christian. But two points indicate that these two texts don't mean the same thing.

First, Saul did not know who spoke to him on the Damascus road since he asked, "Who are you, Lord?" (cf. Acts 22:8; 26:15). He did not mean to call Jesus "Lord" as if his master. It was the same with the Cornelius incident that we will examine later. When an angel appeared to him in a vision and said, "Cornelius," he asked, "What is it Lord?" (Acts 10:3–4).

In contrast, Howard Ervin argues, ineffectively I think, that Saul was influenced by hearing Christians call Jesus "Lord," especially the martyr Stephen saying "Lord Jesus" (Acts 7:59), so that Saul would not have addressed Jesus as "Lord" unless he truly believed in him.[3]

Second, calling someone "Lord" was a respectful greeting commonly used in the ancient world. Paul's word "Lord," in Acts 22:8, translates *kurie* in the Greek text. Being in the vocative case, it means an address to someone. Usually, the vocative was used without any religious connotation. It was similar to the address, "Sir," which also was used in antiquity. Again, Paul did not mean Jesus had become his Lord on the Damascus road.

---

2. Ervin, *Spirit-Baptism*, 76.
3. Ervin, *Conversion-Initiation*, 41–44.

Dunn makes both of these two points,[4] as do many other scholars. For instance, Craig Keener says that during antiquity, "kingship language," such as the word Lord, "was in no way 'uniquely Christian,'" and he cites several pagan, ancient sources for support.[5]

What of Ananias saying three days later, "Brother Saul" (Acts 9:17; 22:13)? Many Christians, especially Pentecostals,[6] have thought it indicates Ananias would not have called Saul a "brother" unless he thought Saul already was converted, maybe on the Damascus road.

However, it was customary for Jewish men to call each other "brothers" (e.g., Acts 22:5; 28:21). This word in the Greek NT is *adelphoi*, the plural of *adelphos*. In the Greek text of Acts, *adelphoi* appears fifty-one times, and most of these instances refer to different occasions. In ten of them, Peter, Stephen, and mostly Paul so address a crowd of non-Christian, Jewish men.[7] And the crowd at Pentecost addressed the 120 disciples as "brothers" (Acts 2:37; cf. 13:15). So, Luke in Acts often uses *adelphoi* to refer to non-Christian Jews.

At first glance, it is difficult to tell from Luke's account in Acts 9 if Paul was converted on the Damascus road or three days later. Luke records two later incidents when Paul was permitted to tell his Christian testimony to a crowd and royalty (Acts 22:1–21; 26:1–23).

Although many classical Pentecostals cite Paul's conversion and Spirit baptism to support their doctrine of subsequence, they cannot cite anything from Luke's three accounts of it to support their other distinctive doctrine—that Spirit baptism must be evidenced by *glossolalia*. Luke doesn't say Paul spoke in tongues during this most significant time in his life or even thereafter. In fact, Luke doesn't say Paul was baptized with, or received, the Holy Spirit. He only quotes Ananias telling Paul he would "be filled with the Holy Spirit" (Acts 9:17).

If Saul was filled with the Spirit and spoke in tongues when Ananias laid hands on him, Luke would have said so in Acts 9. Years later, Paul wrote to the church at Corinth, scolded it for magnifying tongues, and said, "I speak in tongues more than all of you" (1 Cor 14:18).

---

4. Dunn, *Baptism in the Holy Spirit*, 73.

5. Keener, *Acts: An Exegetical Commentary: Volume 2*, 1663–64.

6. Contra Ervin (*Conversion-Initiation*, 41–50), who asserts both "Lord" and "brother" indicate Paul was converted on the Damascus, and he says on p. 41 that this is the common position taken by Pentecostals.

7. Acts 2:29; 3:17; 7:2; 13:26, 38; 22:1; 23:1, 5–6; 28:17. Crowds called them "brothers" twice (Acts 2:37; 13:15).

Spirit Baptism on the Apostle Paul (Acts 9)

OR WAS PAUL CONVERTED THREE DAYS LATER?

Many contemporary, non-Pentecostal scholars disagree with the traditional view that Paul was converted on the Damascus road. They think Saul was *in a process of conversion* during those three days and that he believed in, and committed his life to, Jesus upon meeting Ananias. Dunn says, "Paul's conversion-commissioning was one experience which extended over three days; his conversion was completed through Ananias just as much as was his commissioning."[8]

Simon Kistemaker says of Acts 9, "In a sense, Paul's conversion was sudden when Jesus arrested him on the way to Damascus and addressed him personally. But if we look at the broader context (vv. 10–19), we see a gradual development of his conversion and calling. In his loneliness, no one proclaimed the gospel to him until Ananias, sent by Jesus, extended to him the welcome of the Christian community."[9]

Ben Witherington states similarly, "In Luke's telling of Saul's story the conversion experience was not instantaneous. He was blinded for the three days and did not regain sight, receive the Holy Spirit, or receive baptism washing away his sins until the third day after the Damascus road experience. Conversion even in the case of Saul is seen as an event which precipitates a process, but the process of conversion is not completed till Saul receives sight, Spirit, and baptism."[10]

Indeed, Paul seems to have been baptized and filled with the Spirit simultaneously as Ananias laid hands on him and "his sight was restored. Then he got up and was baptized" (Acts 9:18). And the fact that Paul continued his full fast until his healing and baptism further suggests a conversion process (v. 19). Jews and some pagans combined fasting with penitence.[11] Jews did both on their holiest day of the year—Yom Kippur. So, *Paul most likely broke his fast, was converted, and water baptized all on the third day after his initial encounter with Jesus.*

Now, Luke's three accounts of Paul's conversion do not have the same details. In Luke's second account, which is a testimony by Paul himself, Paul says after he regained his sight that Ananias said to him, "Get up, be baptized, and have your sins washed away, calling on his [Jesus'] name" (Acts

---

8. Dunn, *Baptism in the Holy Spirit*, 75.
9. Kistemaker, *Exposition of the Acts of the Apostles*, 335.
10. Witherington, *The Acts of the Apostles*, 313–14.
11. Keener, *Acts: An Exegetical Commentary: Volume 2*, 1643.

22:16). If my explanation in chapter 5 about the meaning of water baptism is correct, Ananias meant Paul needed to then be water baptized since God, at that time, forgave him of his sins (=sins washed away) rather than three days prior. If so, Paul's conversion occurred at relatively the same time he received the Holy Spirit. Thus, *Paul's conversion and simultaneous Spirit baptism do not support the Pentecostals' doctrine of subsequence; rather, these elements militate against it.*

Furthermore, it would seem that Paul's temporary blindness paralleled, if not symbolized, his spiritual blindness, so that he was spiritually healed when he was physically healed.

So, I think Dunn's arguments are significantly more compelling, saying Paul was finally converted on the third day. Dunn says Paul would have been in shock by "being confronted with the glory of one whom he thought of as a blasphemer and a law-breaker justly done to death."[12] Jimmy adds, "When we realize how this encounter with Jesus cut to the very roots of Paul's personality and world-view it becomes impossible to think that he was converted in an instant."[13] Indeed! Dunn, who years later became a leading authority on Paul, continues:

> Perhaps the simplest way to regard Paul's blindness, so far as symbolism goes, is to see it as indicative of the deep and crushing sorrow and conviction which must have weighed him down like a millstone during these three days. He had sought to devastate the Church of God (Gal. 1.13); he had been resisting the Holy Spirit and had approved the murder of God's Righteous One (Acts 7.51f.); he had all that time gone on persecuting the risen Lord. Do those who think Paul was converted in an instant believe that he could sweep aside the enormity of his manifold crime in an instant? The three days abstinence and inactivity are difficult to explain on such a hypothesis; but they make excellent sense when seen as the occasion of a deep heart-searching and repentance.
> We conclude then that Paul's conversion was one single experience lasting from the Damascus road to the ministry of Ananias. As John Wesley—no stranger to instantaneous conversion—says of the three days, "So long he seems to have been in the pangs of the new birth." . . . Paul's conversion was only completed when he called on Jesus as Lord, was filled with the Spirit, and had his sins washed away.[14]

---

12. Dunn, *Baptism in the Holy Spirit*, 75.
13. Ibid., 75–76.
14. Ibid., 77–78.

Spirit Baptism on the Apostle Paul (Acts 9)

We will learn in chapter 10 that Paul teaches that conversion and Spirit baptism happen simultaneously, and his conversion experience surely would not have differed from this.

ARE "THREE DAYS" AND "THIRD DAY" EQUIVALENT?

How much time elapsed between Saul's encounters with Jesus and then Ananias? Luke says of Saul, "For three days he was without sight, and neither ate nor drank" (Acts 9:9). Ananias came, met Saul, healed him, and baptized him. Then, "After taking some food, he regained his strength" (v. 19). For us English speakers, this time interval could mean as much as three full days and thus seventy-two hours.

A similar question arises concerning Jesus' resurrection. The NT says repeatedly that he arose from the dead on the third day (Luke 24:7, 46; Acts 10:40; 1 Cor 15:4). Matthew and Luke say Jesus told his disciples on three occasions that he would be killed and arise from the dead "on the third day" (Matt 16:21/Luke 9:22; Matt 17:23; Matt 20:19/Luke 18:33). Mark relates the same predictions yet quotes Jesus saying it would be "after three days" (Mark 8:31; 9:31; 10:34). Another time, Jesus predicted his death and resurrection by saying, "For just as Jonah was three days and three nights in the belly of the sea monster, so for three days and three nights the Son of Man will be in the heart of the earth" (Matt 12:40).

Christian tradition is unanimous: Jesus died on Friday and arose from the dead early on Sunday morning, thus on the third day. But these "three days" texts have caused some Christians to assert that Jesus did not die on Friday but on Thursday; and a few people have contended it was Wednesday to accommodate seventy-two hours. But Bible culture and languages concerning this subject indicate otherwise.

"Three days" and "three days and three nights" in the Bible are Semitic idioms meaning "third day."[15] It is because those ancients customarily counted a portion of a day as one day.

Scripture affirms this. "Three days" and "third day" are used interchangeably regarding a single incident. Matthew says after Jesus' death and entombment, "The Pharisees gathered before Pilate and said, 'Sir, we remember how that imposter said, while he was still alive, "After three days I will rise." Therefore order the tomb to be made secure until the third

---

15. Delling, "*hemera* (day)," 2:949–50. Though the NT was written in Greek, the native tongue of Jesus and his disciples was Aramaic.

day, lest his disciples go and steal him away and tell the people, "He has risen from the dead," and the last fraud will be worse than the first'" (Matt 27:62–64 ESV). So, they equated "three days" and "third day."

It is the same with Queen Esther. When her Jewish people were about to be annihilated, "Esther said in reply to Mordecai, 'Go, gather all the Jews to be found in Susa, and hold a fast on my behalf, and neither eat nor drink for three days, night or day. I and my maids will also fast as you do. After that I will go to the king,' . . . On the third day Esther put on her royal robes and stood in the inner court of the king's palace" (Esth 4:15–16; 5:1), and then she spoke to the enthroned king.[16] So, the author of Esther equates "three days" and "third day."

Accordingly, Luke means in Acts 9 that Saul received his sight and was baptized on the third day following his encounter with the heavenly Jesus on the road to Damascus.

IS PAUL'S CONVERSION A TYPE OF ISRAEL'S ENDTIMES CONVERSION?

Some scholars think Paul was converted on the third day after his encounter with Jesus as a type of Jesus' resurrection on the third day. Dunn says of Paul's conversion, "The three days probably recalled Jesus' three days in the tomb." Yes, but he says in a footnote, "The comparison is certainly present to Paul himself (Rom. 6.4; Col. 2.12)."[17] Maybe, but Paul doesn't say so.

I think Paul's conversion on the third day is a type of Israel's conversion in the end times. This supports the thesis of my book, *The Third Day Bible Code*.[18] It examines a third-day motif that occurred in many of the most important events in the history of Israel recorded in the Bible. They include, in chronological order, Abraham offering Isaac, Israelites meeting God at Mt. Sinai, Joshua preparing Israel to take the promised land, King Hezekiah being healed, Queen Esther saving the Jews, and the boy Jesus

---

16. A Persian law required that a person could suffer the death penalty for visiting the enthroned king without permission. See also 2 Chr 10:5, 12. For more information about three days and third day being synonymous, see my *The Third Day Bible Code*, 14–18.

17. Dunn, *Baptism in the Holy Spirit*, 77n12.

18. I did not include Paul's conversion in my book as an example of the third-day motif in Scripture.

Spirit Baptism on the Apostle Paul (Acts 9)

being lost. In the following Scriptures that narrate these historical events, third-day and three-days motifs are placed in italics:

- "On *the third day* Abraham looked up and saw the place far away" to sacrifice Isaac (Gen 22:4).
- Moses said to Israel: "Prepare for *the third day*" when "the LORD will come down on Mt. Sinai" (Exod 19:11).
- Joshua said to Israel: "Prepare your provisions; for *in three days* you are to cross over the Jordan (Josh 1:11).
- God said to Hezekiah: "I have heard your prayer, . . . I will heal you; on *the third day*" (2 Kgs 20:5).
- "On *the third day* Esther put on her royal robes and stood in the inner court of the king's palace" (Esth 5:1).
- "When he [Jesus] was twelve years old, . . . *After three days* they found him in the temple" (Luke 2:42, 46).

It is surprising how many important events there are in Israel's biblical history that have a third-day/three-days motif, yet there is hardly any mention in the Bible about a second day, fourth day, fifth day, or sixth day in Israel's history. This phenomenon can be seen readily by examining these days in a Bible concordance.

In my *Third Day* book, I show that these events with a third-day/three-days motif are types that forecast Israel's future. Some foreshadow Jesus' death and resurrection on the third day. The most prominent that does so is Abraham offering Isaac (Gen 22:4; cf. Heb 11:17–19).

Types are fascinating, obscure, and mysterious. They also are most peculiar to Judaism and Christianity. Typology is the study of types and antitypes. Our English word "type" derives from the Greek word *typos*, meaning a "mark," "impression," "image," or "pattern." A type is a person, object, historical event, or institution that represents, symbolizes, or prefigures something else, often of like nature, which usually happens in the future, called an "antitype." So, a type is a symbol, emblem, token, or sign. When Jesus spoke of "the sign of the prophet Jonah," signifying his death and resurrection (Matt 12:40; cf. 16:4), he meant Jonah in the big fish was a type.

SOLVING THE SAMARITAN RIDDLE

WILL PAUL'S THIRD-DAY CONVERSION PARALLEL THE TIMING OF ISRAEL'S CONVERSION?

Also in *Third Day*, I show that most of these third-day and three-days motifs in Israel's biblical history indicate the approximate timing of Israel's end times conversion to Jesus and his return to establish his kingdom. Several Hebrew prophets predict this end times conversion of Israel. As we might expect, it starts with Moses in the Torah.

Due to Israel's future sins, Moses predicted, "The LORD will scatter you among the peoples; . . . From there you will seek the LORD your God, and you will find him if you search after him with all your heart and soul. In your distress, when all these things have happened to you in time to come, you will return to the LORD your God and heed him" (Deut 4:27, 29–30). Moses afterwards predicts the Diaspora and its penitent remnant in the end times (30:1–5).

The Apostle Paul puts it this way, "Understand this mystery: a hardening has come upon part of Israel, until the full number of the Gentiles has come in. And so all Israel will be saved; as it is written, 'Out of Zion will come the Deliverer'" (Rom 11:25–26), that is, Jesus at his return. So, it appears that even Paul's literal blindness was a type of Israel's spiritual blindness (cf. Isa 6:8–10; Jer 5:21; John 9:39–41).

None of the OT prophets predict God's abandonment of Israel and its final penitence more than Moses and Hosea. Hosea says, "For the Israelites shall remain many days without king or prince, without sacrifice or pillar, without ephod or teraphim. Afterward the Israelites shall return and seek the LORD their God, and David their king; they shall come in awe to the LORD and to his goodness in the latter days" (Hos 3:4–5). Israelites will approach the risen King David, yet "David" here also refers to Messiah Jesus. Hosea says on behalf of God, "I will return again to my place until they acknowledge their guilt and seek my face. In their distress they will beg my favor" (Hos 5:15), this latter referring to the end time.

Peter echoed Hosea, here, by preaching to Israel, "Repent . . . so that times of refreshing may come from the presence of the Lord; and that he may send the Messiah appointed for you, that is, Jesus, who must remain in heaven until the time of universal restoration" (Acts 3:19–21).

Then Hosea says of God's end times deliverance of Israel, "Come, let us return to the LORD; for it is he who has torn, and he will heal us; he has struck down, and he will bind us up. After two days he will revive us; on the third day he will raise us up, that we may live before him" (Hos 6:1–2).

Spirit Baptism on the Apostle Paul (Acts 9)

This text raises questions. Who is speaking? It seems to be representatives, perhaps priests, of this penitent remnant. Other biblical prophets predict this end times remnant, and some even indicate its size.[19]

When will Israel's penitence happen? It will be at the end of the age, right before the world-to-come. Hosea 6:1–3 is similar to Joel 2:11–17. Israel's penitence precedes Joel's prophecy that Peter quoted at Pentecost.

There is a strong rabbinical tradition that Hos 6:2 refers to the resurrection of the dead.[20] That supports the view that this text refers to the end of days. A Jewish Targum translates Hos 6:2, "He will give us life in the days of consolation that will come; on the day of the resurrection of the dead he will raise us up and we shall live before him."[21] Rabbis were so inclined to this understanding of Hos 6:2 largely because the same two Hebrew verbs, *chayah* ("revive") and *qam* ("raise up"), appear together in their Bible only in Hos 6:2 and Isa 26:19. Rabbis also regarded this Isaiah text as one of the few in their Bible that depicts resurrection. It reads, "Your dead shall live, their corpses shall rise. O dwellers in the dust, awake and sing for joy! . . . The earth will give birth to those long dead."

What do "two days" and "third day" mean in Hos 6:2?[22] Martin Luther said Hosea "is speaking of Christ's resurrection. . . . Paul glories about this passage when he says Christ was to rise on the third day (cf. 1 Cor. 15:4)."[23] But Hosea's context is not about the Messiah but Ephraim and Judah, thus the nation of Israel. Yet because Jesus embodies Israel, it also could implicitly refer to his resurrection on the third day as well.

Should Hosea's "two days" and "third day" as referring to Israel be taken literally? Douglas Stuart well insists it "should not be taken literally (in two days or third day, all will be well) or to mean 'soon.' . . . Its intent is more likely that after 'a set time' Yahweh would again visit his people in mercy."[24]

---

19. E.g., Isa 49:5; 66:2, 7–9; Mic 5:3–5; Zech 12:10–14; Mal 4:5–6.

20. Delling, "hemera," 2:294; McArthur, "On the Third Day," 81–86. McArthur quotes these rabbinical sources on pp. 83–84: *p. Sanhedrin* 97a; *b. Rosh Hashanah* 31a; *p. Berakoth* 5.2; *p. Sanhedrin* 11.6; *Midrash Rabbah, Esther* 9.2 (on Esther 5:1); *Midrash Rabbah, Deuteronomy* 7.6 (on Deut 28:12); *Midrash Rabbah, Genesis* 56.1 (on Gen 22:4); *Pirke de Rabbi Eliezer* 51 (73b–74a); *Tanna de-be Eliyyahu*, p. 29.

21. Cathcart and Gordon, *Targum of the Minor Prophets*, 41.

22. For an exposition of Hos 5:12—6:1–3, see the chapter "Hosea and the Third Day Motif" in my book, *The Third Day Bible Code*, 110–22.

23. *Luther's Works*, 18:31.

24. Stuart, *Hosea-Jonah*, 108.

In my book *Third Day*, I interpret Hos 6:2 and these other biblical texts having a third-day motif by applying to them what Moses said to God, "For a thousand years in your sight are like yesterday when it is past, or like a watch in the night" (Ps 90:4). Peter quotes this text from the LXX by saying, "With the Lord one day is like a thousand years, and a thousand years are like one day" (2 Pet 3:8). By interpreting third-day motif texts in the Bible with this concept, I call it the Thousand-Year Day Principle.

So, I conclude in my book (p. 121), "By applying the Thousand-Year Day Principle to Hos 6:1–3, it appears from v. 2 that the resurrection of the dead will occur sometime during the early part of the third millennium following Jesus' death and resurrection, in AD 30." I further explain that the resurrection will occur when Jesus returns, and I claim that will happen approximately between the years 2070 and 2250.

In conclusion, if the Apostle Paul's conversion is a type of Israel's conversion during the end times, then Paul likely was converted on the third day following his encounter with Jesus as a further parallel to Israel's conversion on "the third day" as Hosea says. If so, this third-day motif is further evidence that Paul's conversion does not support the Pentecostals' doctrine of separability and subsequence.

CHAPTER 8

Spirit Baptism on the Cornelius Household (Acts 10)

GENTILES RECEIVE THE GOSPEL

After the Apostle Peter used his kingdom keys to open two doors of God's kingdom—first to Jews at Jerusalem and then Samaritans in the city of Samaria (Acts 2, 8)—he used a key to open a third door of the kingdom, this one to the Gentiles. When he did, Peter finished his exclusive role Jesus had given him to "loose on earth" what was "loosed in heaven" (Matt 16:19). That loosing was the power of God by means of the Holy Spirit that fell upon those Gentiles. In each of these three episodes, Peter initiated the full ministry for all of Jesus' disciples to be his "witnesses in Jerusalem, in all Judea and Samaria, and to the ends of the earth" (Acts 1:8), and it included the baptism with the Holy Spirit. So, this third experience occurring in a Gentile land began to fulfill Jesus' words in that text, "to the ends of the earth."

Luke records in Acts a lengthy account of what happened that third time. He begins, "In Caesarea there was a man named Cornelius, a centurion of the Italian Cohort, as it was called. He was a devout man who feared God with all his household; he gave alms generously to the people and prayed constantly to God" (Acts 10:1–2). So, Cornelius was a Gentile

SOLVING THE SAMARITAN RIDDLE

God-fearer, not a circumcised proselyte to Judaism.[1] To summarize Acts 10:3–33, God gave Cornelius a vision in which an angel told him to send men to Joppa to fetch Peter, whom he did not know. Joppa was present-day Tel Aviv, and it was located thirty miles south of Caesarea. As these men were approaching Joppa, Peter "fell into a trance" (v. 10). He had a vision in which he saw a large sheet with animals in it that Jews previously were forbidden to eat due to the Torah designating them as ritually "unclean" (e.g., Leviticus 11). Then we read, "Peter heard a voice saying, 'Get up, Peter; kill and eat'" (Acts 10:13). When Peter objected the voice said, "What God has made clean you must not call profane" (v. 15). Why this change from unclean to clean?

David Peterson says of this new development,

> What was implicit in the teaching of Jesus is now made explicit. The clean and unclean provisions of the law were temporary, designed to keep Israel a holy and distinct people until the time when Jews and Gentiles could receive the forgiveness of sins and sanctification on the same basis, through faith in Christ (Acts 20:32; 26:17–18; cf. 15:9). . . . Association with Gentiles was a cause of defilement in Jewish tradition (cf. *Jub.* 22:16; *Test. Jos.* 7:1), rather than being strictly defined as such by the law of Moses. It was 'unlawful' (*athemitos*) in the more general sense of being against their custom. This was especially so because Gentiles did not observe the biblical rules about food. Such defilement would have to be removed by following the provisions of the law for cleansing. Even Gentile possessions needed to be purified before they were used by Jews.[2]

Luke next relates that Cornelius' men then arrived to meet Peter, and he went with them to Caesarea (Acts 10:17–24). This city was located on the Mediterranean coast. The Romans built it into a magnificent looking city that was populated almost entirely by Gentiles. Its main feature was a man-made harbor that was an engineering marvel. (All the coastland from Mount Carmel southward to Egypt has no natural harbors.) Caesarea served as the capital of Judea. It was also the home of Judea's Roman governor (procurator), and it had a military garrison.

This Caesarea later came to be called Caesarea Maritima ("by the sea") to distinguish it from the inland Caesarea Philippi, located at the base of

---

1. Keener, *Acts: An Exegetical Commentary: Volume 2*, 1750–53.
2. Peterson, *The Acts of the Apostles*, 330, 333.

Spirit Baptism on the Cornelius Household (Acts 10)

Mount Hermon. That is where Peter confessed Jesus as the Christ, and Jesus then promised to give him the kingdom keys (Matt 16:13–19). It is interesting that the promise about keys was made at one Caesarea, and Peter finished using the keys at the other Caesarea.

Craig Keener also observes, "Some scholars suggest that Peter's location in Joppa may providentially recall Jonah's story." Keener then compares six parallels in Acts with portions in the book of Jonah.[3]

Luke next relates concerning Peter and the others, "Cornelius was expecting them and had called together his relatives and close friends" (Acts 10:24). Peter arrived and began speaking to Cornelius and his household, saying, "You yourselves know that it is unlawful for a Jew to associate with or to visit a Gentile; but God has shown me that I should not call anyone profane or unclean" (v. 28). Cornelius then related his vision and asked Peter to tell them "all that the Lord has commanded you to say" (v. 33).

Luke then records in Acts 10:34–48 what ensued next, and it reads as follows:

> 34Then Peter began to speak to them: "I truly understand that God shows no partiality, 35but in every nation anyone who fears him and does what is right is acceptable to him. 36You know the message he sent to the people of Israel, preaching peace by Jesus Christ—he is Lord of all. 37That message spread throughout Judea, beginning in Galilee after the baptism that John announced: 38how God anointed Jesus of Nazareth with the Holy Spirit and with power; how he went about doing good and healing all who were oppressed by the devil, for God was with him. 39We are witnesses to all that he did both in Judea and in Jerusalem. They put him to death by hanging him on a tree; 40but God raised him on the third day and allowed him to appear, 41not to all the people but to us who were chosen by God as witnesses, and who ate and drank with him after he rose from the dead. 42He commanded us to preach to the people and to testify that he is the one ordained by God as judge of the living and the dead. 43All the prophets testify about him that everyone who believes in him receives forgiveness of sins through his name."
>
> 44While Peter was still speaking, the Holy Spirit fell upon all who heard the word. 45The circumcised believers who had come with Peter were astounded that the gift of the Holy Spirit had been poured out even on the Gentiles, 46for they heard them speaking in tongues and extolling God. Then Peter said, 47"Can anyone

---

3. Keener, *Acts: An Exegetical Commentary: Volume 2*, 1730.

withhold the water for baptizing these people who have received the Holy Spirit just as we have?" 48So he ordered them to be baptized in the name of Jesus Christ. Then they invited him to stay for several days.

GENTILES ARE SPIRIT BAPTIZED AND SPEAK IN TONGUES

So, those of Cornelius' household were the first Gentiles to receive the Holy Spirit, and they immediately manifested evidence of it by speaking in tongues. Some scholars nowadays call it the Gentile Pentecost. Both of these phenomena amazed Peter and his entourage that this happened to Gentiles. Why?

Out of all the nations of the world, God had made a covenant exclusively with the nation of Israel. He also promised to give his Spirit to Israel so that it could fulfill the law code, that is, the Torah, which he attached to that covenant. Thus, Jews had understood that this promise of the Spirit was restricted to Jews in the form of a new, or renewed, covenant with God.[4] And they thought these Spirit manifestations, such as those predicted in Joel 2:28–32 and quoted by Peter at Pentecost, would be experienced only by Jews.[5]

But when these Gentiles, in Acts 10, were "speaking in tongues" (Gr. *lalounton glossais*), were they actual languages unknown to them? Recall that when Spirit baptism first occurred at Pentecost, in Acts 2, the 120 disciples spoke "other languages" unknown to them but native to Diaspora Jews who heard them (Acts 2:4–13). But here, in Acts 10:46, Luke does not indicate that these Gentiles spoke in human languages. Neither does he say in Acts 19:6 that the Ephesians who "spoke in tongues" spoke actual languages. Why? There was no need to do that.

At Pentecost there were witnesses, Diaspora Jews, who testified that the 120 disciples spoke their native languages. But in Acts 10 and 19 there were no such witnesses. This raises the question of the nature of tongues in these two texts and Paul's teaching in 1 Corinthians 12–14. Scholars debate

---

4. E.g., Isa 44:4; 59:21; Jer 31:31–33; 32:40; Ezek 36:26–27; 37:14, 26; 39:29.

5. All of Joel 2–3 is a prophecy about the nation of Israel in the end times even though some of it in Joel 2 can also refer to an earlier time. So, "all flesh," "your sons and your daughters," "your old men," and "your young men" in Joel 2:28 refer exclusively to Israeli Jews.

Spirit Baptism on the Cornelius Household (Acts 10)

whether or not "tongues" mentioned in these three texts refer to actual languages or if they are no more than gibberish, that is, ecstatic speech. Whatever the correct answer, it does not affect the theme of this book, which is about how Peter's keys relate to Spirit baptism.

PREACHING AND BAPTIZING

Luke does not say Peter water baptized any of the Cornelius household. Rather, "he ordered them to be baptized" (Acts 10:48). So, those who did the baptizing no doubt were the disciples who accompanied Peter. He may have foreseen that if he baptized them it could have caused a later problem.

The Fourth Evangelist relates that soon after Peter and some of the other disciples left John the Baptist and began following Jesus, "Jesus and his disciples went into the Judean countryside, and he spent some time there with them and baptized. John also was baptizing at Aenon near Salim because water was abundant there" (John 3:22–23). At first glance, this appears to say Jesus water baptized people. But it must mean Jesus' party baptized them due to what follows. For we soon read, "Now when Jesus learned that the Pharisees had heard, 'Jesus is making and baptizing more disciples than John'—although it was not Jesus himself but his disciples who baptized—he left Judea and started back to Galilee" (4:1–3). So, this parenthetical remark clarifies the matter: Jesus' disciples did the baptizing, not him. Why? Peter probably knew why and knew it then.

Paul reports a problem that developed years later. Some in the church at Corinth were saying, "I belong to Paul," or "I belong to Apollos," or "I belong to Cephas," that is, Peter (1 Cor 1:12). Paul asks, "Were you baptized in the name of Paul? I thank God that I baptized none of you except Crispus and Gaius, so that no one can say that you were baptized in my name.... For Christ did not send me to baptize but to proclaim the gospel" (vv. 13–15, 17). The same was true of Jesus and Peter. Yet John the Baptist did both—preaching and baptizing.

Preaching the word was most important. Baptizing could be compared to the problem of food distribution that arose at Jerusalem. Luke says of the apostles, "The twelve called together the whole community of the disciples and said, 'It is not right that we should neglect the word of God in order to wait on tables. Therefore, friends, select from among yourselves seven men of good standing, full of the Spirit and of wisdom, whom we may appoint to this task, while we, for our part, will devote ourselves to prayer and to serving the word" (Acts 6:2–4).

There is a difference between the message Peter preached to the Jews at Pentecost and what he proclaimed to Gentiles at the house of Cornelius. Peter exhorted the Jews at Pentecost to repent and be water baptized. But here, with these Gentiles, he said of Jesus, "Everyone who believes in him receives forgiveness of sins" (Acts 10:43), and he did not mention water baptism. Since these Gentiles believed while Peter was preaching, and they were water baptized afterwards, this suggests Peter did not intend to teach baptismal regeneration at Pentecost.

WAS CORNELIUS SPIRIT BAPTIZED AFTER CONVERSION?

Some Pentecostal scholars think Cornelius was regenerated before he met Peter and heard him preach. So, they cite Acts 10 to support their doctrine of subsequence. Roger Stronstad says of all mention of Spirit baptism in Acts, "In every example there is a clear interval between conversion and being filled and/or baptized with the Holy Spirit."[6] In Acts 10, he refers only to Cornelius. What of the others in the house?

We have seen that Cornelius was "a devout man who feared God with all his household," and "he gave alms generously to the people and prayed constantly to God" (Acts 10:2). An angel told Cornelius in a vision, "Your prayers and your alms have ascended as a memorial before God" (v. 4). Cornelius' men described him as "an upright and God-fearing man" (v. 22). And Peter implies that God viewed Cornelius as a Gentile "acceptable to him" (v. 35).

Ben Witherington asks of Acts 10:35, "What does 'acceptable' mean? It appears it refers to a person being in an acceptable state (repentance) to hear and receive the message of salvation and release from sins. Luke is not advocating that Cornelius, because of his piety, is already saved, apart from having faith in Christ."[7]

Indeed. As stated earlier, this is a transitional period of time in which God's plan is changing from the old covenant to the new covenant. And Luke indicates that Cornelius and the Ethiopian eunuch in Acts 8 stand on the fringe of Judaism. It was the same with John baptizing the penitent; they still needed to believe in Jesus. The revelation of God's salvation was

---

6. Stronstad, "Forty Years On," 10.

7. Witherington, *The Acts of the Apostles*, 356.

Spirit Baptism on the Cornelius Household (Acts 10)

progressing from belief in Jesus as Messiah during his ministry to belief in his atoning death for sins. Thus, Cornelius still must believe in Jesus to be saved. As Peter declared earlier, "There is salvation in no one else, for there is no other name under heaven given among mortals by which we must be saved" (Acts 4:12).

Furthermore, Luke has two decisive texts indicating Cornelius was not saved prior to meeting Peter. First, Luke says that soon after this Cornelius episode, "When Peter went up to Jerusalem, the circumcised believers criticized him, saying, 'Why did you go to uncircumcised men and eat with them?'" (Acts 11:2–3). Peter then related that Cornelius "told us how he had seen the angel standing in his house and saying, 'Send to Joppa and bring Simon, who is called Peter; he will give you a message by which you and your entire household will be saved'" (vv. 13–14).

Second, Luke implies that at this time in Jerusalem, Peter spoke to "the apostles and the believers" (Acts 11:1). Then Luke says regarding what Peter said to them, "When they heard this, they were silenced. And they praised God, saying, 'Then God has given even to the Gentiles the repentance that leads to life'" (v. 18).

Thus, Cornelius was not regenerated-saved prior to hearing Peter preach. Rather, Cornelius' conversion and Spirit baptism occurred simultaneously. And it was the same with the members of his household.

Interestingly, Paul wrote years after this Cornelius incident, "I had been entrusted with the gospel for the uncircumcised, just as Peter had been entrusted with the gospel for the circumcised" (Gal 2:7). Then, why wasn't Paul the first to proclaim the gospel to Gentiles who then simultaneously received the Spirit? God chose Peter to be the first to open kingdom doors to all three racial classes, thus also to the uncircumcised Gentiles.

Peter, in this defense speech to the apostles at Jerusalem, said of those Gentiles at Cornelius' house, "The Holy Spirit fell upon them just as it had upon us at the beginning" (Acts 11:15), referring to the 120 disciples at Pentecost. Dunn interprets Peter's phrase here, "at the beginning," to mean "the beginning of their *Christian* experience."[8]

Dunn then quotes Peter as saying in Acts 11:17, "God gave the same gift to them as he gave to us *when we believed* in the Lord Jesus Christ."[9] In this translation of the Greek text, the last clause means three things happened at Pentecost: (1) the 120 disciples initially believed Jesus was the

---

8. Dunn, *Baptism in the Holy Spirit*, 52. Emphasis his.
9. Ibid., 52. Emphasis his.

Messiah, (2) they made him Lord of their lives, and (3) they were baptized with the Spirit. According to this translation the 120 disciples, who included the twelve apostles, were not saved until that day of Pentecost.

Most English versions render Acts 11:17 as Dunn here quotes, "when we believed in the Lord Jesus Christ" (NIV, NRSV, ESV); but some do not. The KJV is noncommittal on the timing by rendering it, "who believed in the Lord Jesus Christ." But the NASB has "after believing," indicating a post-conversion Spirit baptism. So, this NASB translation means that the 120 disciples were already believers prior to Pentecost.

The critical word in Acts 11:17 in the Greek text is the aorist participle *pisteusasin*, which can be rendered "when we believed" or "having believed."[10] I think Peter likely meant "having believed" because he only intended to say that those Gentiles had received the Spirit just as he and the accompanying Jewish believers had. In fact, that is how he described those Gentiles in their presence—"who have received the Holy Spirit just as we have" (10:47; cf. 15:8).

THE FIRST CHURCH COUNCIL

After the apostles settled the issue about Peter associating with Gentiles, another related disagreement arose. It was hatched in Jerusalem and spread to Antioch. Luke relates, "Then certain individuals came down from Judea and were teaching the brothers, 'Unless you are circumcised according to the custom of Moses, you cannot be saved.' And after Paul and Barnabas had no small dissension and debate with them, Paul and Barnabas and some of the others were appointed to go up to Jerusalem to discuss this question with the apostles and elders" (Acts 15:1–2).

Church historians call this first meeting of early church leaders "the first church council." Luke says some "believers," who were still "Pharisees," said of these Gentile converts, "It is necessary for them to be circumcised and ordered to keep the law of Moses" (Acts 15:5).

Luke then relates, "Peter stood up and said to them, 'My brothers, you know that in the early days God made a choice among you, that I should be the one through whom the Gentiles would hear the message of the good news and become believers'" (Acts 15:7). *Did Peter have in mind his role of using kingdom keys?*

---

10. But see Dunn's argument about its aorist tense in *The Christ and the Spirit*, 238–39.

Spirit Baptism on the Cornelius Household (Acts 10)

After Peter said these Gentiles had become "believers," he said of God, "In cleansing their hearts by faith he has made no distinction between them and us," that is, between Gentile believers and Jewish believers (Acts 15:9).

Peter also had said, "And God, who knows the human heart, testified to them by giving them the Holy Spirit, just as he did to us'" (Acts 15:8). Peter meant that those Gentiles were saved by faith without being circumcised since the Spirit fell on them while Peter was preaching, and they spoke in tongues to authenticate it. So, these Gentile men were saved without being either circumcised or water baptized, though they were soon water baptized.

To repeat, *since these Gentiles at Cornelius' house believed and were Spirit baptized at the same time, Pentecostals are unable to reconcile this important episode with their doctrine of subsequence.* Dunn explains:

> With Acts 10 the Pentecostal is in difficulty from the start: there appears to be no grasp between the conversion of Cornelius and his Spirit-baptism. Pentecostals usually argue along one of three lines:
> a) Cornelius "was born again before Peter preached to him."
> b) Cornelius came to faith and was cleansed in heart (15.9) during Peter's sermon. The gift of the Spirit followed in close succession, but as a distinct act of grace.
> c) The two things happened simultaneously, and though indistinguishable in this case, they were even here distinct acts of God.[11]

What Dunn calls "grasp" Pentecostals call "subsequence." They mean a time interval between conversion and Spirit baptism. But it is not in this Gentile episode.

To sum, Pentecostals who argue (a) do err since Luke says the following about these Gentiles: (1) Peter recalled that the angel said to Cornelius concerning Peter, "he will give you a message by which you and your entire household will be saved" (Acts 11:14); (2) when Peter preached they "accepted the word of God" (v. 1); (3) the apostles at Jerusalem said, "Then God has given to the Gentiles the repentance that leads to life" (v. 18); (4) Peter recalled, "the Gentiles would hear the message of the good news and become believers" (15:7); (5) "cleansing their hearts by faith" (v. 9). To repeat, these Gentiles believed and were Spirit baptized at the same time.

---

11. Dunn, *Baptism in the Holy Spirit*, 79.

SOLVING THE SAMARITAN RIDDLE

IS SPIRIT BAPTISM EQUIVALENT OR ADDITIONAL TO CONVERSION?

Jimmy Dunn goes on to say of this Gentile incident, "The Spirit was not something additional to God's acceptance and forgiveness but constituted that acceptance and forgiveness." He continues, "God's giving of the Holy Spirit is equivalent to his cleansing of their hearts; these two are one . . . the baptism of the Spirit is God's act of acceptance and forgiveness, cleansing and salvation."[12] Frederick Dale Bruner states likewise, "God cleanses men's hearts through faith by giving them the Holy Spirit through the gospel."[13]

In chapter 3, I objected to Jimmy's assertion, "The one thing that makes a man a Christian is the gift of the Spirit." And I agreed with Menzies' rejoinder to Dunn, "Luke does not view the gift of the Spirit as a necessary element in conversion." I said the Spirit was active in OT days in accomplishing the new birth. If true, Menzies and his Pentecostal dialogue partners are right, that Spirit baptism is *in addition* to the Spirit's work of regeneration-conversion. This seems obvious from Jesus saying to his disciples, "You will receive power when the Holy Spirit has come upon you, and you will be witnesses in Jerusalem, in all Judea and Samaria, and to the ends of the earth" (Acts 1:8). Jesus means that Spirit baptism would empower them for ministry. In regeneration, the Spirit imparts spiritual life from God; but Spirit baptism in Acts is about imparting God's power for service, just as Pentecostals insist.

Thus, Pentecostal Howard Ervin well argues against Dunn on this issue. But in doing so, Ervin fails to overcome Dunn's main argument, that there is no subsequence, "no grasp," in Acts 10. Ervin quotes Dunn and practically ignores this important subject in his own chapter on Acts 10 in his book *Conversion-Initiation*.[14] It is obvious why he does so, and it represents poor scholarship. We shouldn't treat the Bible as a smorgasbord. Dunn clearly is right that there is no time interval, no subsequence, between conversion and Spirit baptism in Acts 10 since they occurred together.

Robert Menzies does likewise in his book entitled *Empowered for Witness*. In an extensive treatment of the Samaritan episode in Acts 8, he rightly shows that the Samaritans experienced subsequence. And he acknowledges

---

12. Ibid., 80–82.

13. Bruner, *A Theology of the Holy Spirit*, 201.

14. Ervin, *Conversion-Initiation*, 51–54. And Ervin does not address it in his *Spirit-Baptism* (pp. 68–69, 77–79), wherein he treats Acts 2, with its 3,000 converts, and Acts 10.

Spirit Baptism on the Cornelius Household (Acts 10)

that the Gentiles in Acts 10 underwent conversion and Spirit baptism simultaneously. Yet Menzies ignores trying to reconcile this simultaneity in Acts 10 with his Pentecostal doctrine of subsequence affirmed in Acts 8.[15]

CONCLUSION

In sum, what Peter says in Acts 11:14–15 and 15:7–8 shows that Cornelius and the other Gentiles in his house were not saved prior to hearing Peter preach. Thus, the Gentiles in Acts 10 being converted and Spirit baptized at the same time is strong evidence that militates against the Pentecostals' doctrine of subsequence.

It should now be concluded that Luke provides no uniformity concerning the relation of conversion, Spirit baptism, and water baptism in Acts of the Apostles. So, it is an error for Pentecostals to cite the subsequence of the 120 Jewish disciples in Acts 2 and the Samaritans in Acts 8 as the basis for a paradigm of subsequence for all believers thereafter since it clashes with the Gentiles' simultaneity in Acts 10. *Pentecostals generally have chosen certain texts in Acts, especially Acts 8, to support their doctrine of subsequence while ignoring Acts 10 that militates against it.*

Luke's purpose in telling these incidents in Acts during the early period of the Jesus movement was not to provide a paradigm for conversion and Spirit baptism, but to reveal that all peoples—Jews, Samaritans, and Gentiles—are equals with the same opportunity to believe the good news about Jesus, be saved, enter the kingdom, and be Spirit baptized.

It should also be concluded from Acts 10 that at that time Peter finished his Christ-given role of metaphorically using his keys to open kingdom doors for Jesus to baptize people with the Spirit through Peter as conduit. Years later, after Peter finished this unique mission, a strange situation occurred regarding water baptism and Spirit baptism to which we now turn.

---

15. Menzies, *Empowered for Witness*, 204–18.

CHAPTER 9

Spirit Baptism on the Ephesians (Acts 19)

KNOWING ONLY THE BAPTISM OF JOHN

During the mid-first century, Ephesus was the third largest city in the Roman Empire. It was located in far western Asia Minor, which is present western Turkey. By land from Israel, it was about 800 miles north and west around the Mediterranean Sea. It was a commercial center due to being on a trade route and having a harbor (at that time quite silted) three miles from the Aegean Sea. People in this far away land may not have known much about Christian Jews in Israel.

Over twenty years after the Christ event, an unusual situation occurred in Ephesus. Luke relates in Acts 19:1–7 that the Apostle Paul came there and met some men who had undergone John's water baptism, yet they had not been baptized with the Holy Spirit. Modern NT scholars dispute whether or not they were genuine Christians before meeting Paul. Right before Acts 19:1–7, Luke relates information in Acts 18:24–28 that may affect how one understands this unusual situation at Ephesus. Luke seems to have purposely combined these two historical narratives for this reason. Acts 18:24–19:7 reads as follows:

> 18:24Now there came to Ephesus a Jew named Apollos, a native of Alexandria. He was an eloquent man, well-versed in the

Spirit Baptism on the Ephesians (Acts 19)

scriptures. 25He had been instructed in the Way of the Lord; and he spoke with burning enthusiasm and taught accurately the things concerning Jesus, though he knew only the baptism of John. 26He began to speak boldly in the synagogue; but when Priscilla and Aquila heard him, they took him aside and explained the Way of God to him more accurately. 27And when he wished to cross over to Achaia, the believers encouraged him and wrote to the disciples to welcome him. On his arrival he greatly helped those who through grace had become believers, 28for he powerfully refuted the Jews in public, showing by the scriptures that the Messiah is Jesus.

19:1While Apollos was in Corinth, Paul passed through the interior regions and came to Ephesus, where he found some disciples. 2He said to them, "Did you receive the Holy Spirit when you became believers?" They replied, "No, we have not even heard that there is a Holy Spirit." 3Then he said, "Into what then were you baptized?" They answered, "Into John's baptism." 4Paul said, "John baptized with the baptism of repentance, telling the people to believe in the one who was to come after him, that is, in Jesus." 5On hearing this, they were baptized in the name of the Lord Jesus. 6When Paul had laid his hands on them, the Holy Spirit came upon them, and they spoke in tongues and prophesied— 7altogether there were about twelve of them.

So, Apollos and these Ephesian men had something in common: they had been water baptized according to John's baptism, but they did not know about Christian baptism. They probably never knew John personally, but they knew of his ministry and probably much of what he had taught. At Pentecost, Jesus' disciples obviously reformed John's baptism to make it also symbolize Jesus' death and resurrection.

WAS APOLLOS A CHRISTIAN BEFORE MEETING PRISCILLA AND AQUILA?

Due to this seeming connection between Apollos and these twelve Ephesian disciples, if Apollos was a Christian before meeting Priscilla and Aquila, these Ephesians probably were also Christians before meeting Paul.

These Ephesian men likely were Diaspora Jews who attended the synagogue at Ephesus. If so, they no doubt knew Apollos and may have been taught by him. Joseph Fitzmyer says Apollos "was a diaspora Jew, who bore the name of the Greek god Apollo, but had already become a follower of Jesus."[1]

Luke says Apollos was an eloquent Jew who was born and reared in Alexandria, Egypt. That was the premier intellectual center of the Roman Empire, and it had the world's best library. Apollos knew the Jewish Bible well. All of this suggests he was highly educated in Judaism.

Luke says before Apollos met Priscilla and Aquila that he was "instructed in the Way of the Lord" and "taught accurately the things concerning Jesus." The expressions, "the Way of the Lord" and "the Way of God," are used here interchangeably and are peculiar to the book of Acts. Luke repeatedly calls the fledgling Jesus movement "the Way,"[2] as if it was known by that title perhaps due to Jesus' saying, "I am the way, and the truth, and the life" (John 14:6).

Next, Luke says of Apollos, "When Priscilla and Aquila heard him, they took him aside and explained the Way of God to him more accurately." Luke doesn't say what they explained. Since Apollos "knew only the baptism of John," they must have taught him about Christian baptism and probably Spirit baptism.

Some scholars think there were other groups of disciples of John the Baptist, perhaps at Ephesus, who believed in Jesus without knowing of Christian baptism and Spirit baptism.[3]

After that, Luke says of Apollos, "He powerfully refuted the Jews in public, showing by the scriptures that the Messiah is Jesus." In fact, Apollos became one of the greatest preachers of the early church. We have seen that Paul later wrote to the church at Corinth about a division it had. Four groups claimed loyalty to a different church leader. Those leaders were Paul, Apollos, Peter, and Jesus (1 Cor 1:10–13). So, this church rated Apollos in top company!

---

1. Fitzmyer, *The Acts of the Apostles*, 638.

2. Acts 9:2; 18:25; 19:9, 23; 22:4; 24:14, 22.

3. Barrett, "Apollos and the Twelve Disciples," 37. Menzies (*Empowered for Witness*, 220n1) cites the following scholars and their works: F. F. Bruce, G. R. Beasley-Murray, J. H. E. Hull, and I. Howard Marshall.

Spirit Baptism on the Ephesians (Acts 19)

WHAT DID APOLLOS AND THE EPHESIANS KNOW ABOUT JOHN AND JESUS?

Apollos and these Ephesian men probably knew about John baptizing Jesus and some things John had said about Jesus. Here is what the NT says John the Baptist said about Jesus, arranged in chronological order:

- "one who is more powerful than I is coming; I am not worthy to untie the thong of his sandals. He will baptize you with the Holy Spirit and fire" (Luke 3:16 par.).

- "Then Jesus came from Galilee to John at the Jordan, to be baptized by him. . . . when Jesus had been baptized, just as he came up from the water, suddenly the heavens were opened to him and he saw the Spirit of God descending like a dove and alighting on him. And a voice from heaven said, 'This is my Son, the Beloved, with whom I am well pleased'" (Matt 3:13, 16–17 par.).

- "The next day he [John] saw Jesus coming toward him and declared, 'Here is the Lamb of God who takes away the sin of the world! This is he of whom I said, "After me comes a man who ranks ahead of me because he was before me." I myself did not know him; but I came baptizing with water for this reason, that he might be revealed to Israel.' And John testified, 'I saw the Spirit descending from heaven like a dove, and it remained on him. I myself did not know him, but the one who sent me to baptize with water said to me, "He on whom you see the Spirit descend and remain is the one who baptizes with the Holy Spirit." And I myself have seen and have testified that this is the Son of God'" (John 1:29–34).

- "The next day John again . . . watched Jesus walk by, he exclaimed, 'Look, here is the Lamb of God!'" (John 1:35–36).

- "I am not the Messiah, but I have been sent ahead of him. . . . He must increase, but I must decrease" (John 3:28, 30).

So, John the Baptist said the reason he baptized was to prepare Israel for the coming of Jesus "that he might be revealed to Israel." And John clearly said Jesus was greater than himself. Due to the development of oral tradition then, Apollos and these Ephesians likely knew much if not all of these things John said about Jesus. Thus, they probably knew that Jesus was going to baptize with the Holy Spirit. They just didn't know it had already happened.

Also, while Jesus was still with John at the Jordan River, some of John's disciples claimed Jesus was "the Messiah," "the Son of God," and "the King of Israel" (John 1:41, 49). So, they left John and began following Jesus as their teaching rabbi. They included Peter, Peter's brother Andrew, Philip, and Nathanael (vv. 40–42, 44–45).

"DID YOU RECEIVE THE HOLY SPIRIT WHEN YOU BECAME BELIEVERS?"[4]

When Paul met these Ephesian men he asked them, "Did you receive the Holy Spirit when you became believers?" (Acts 19:2a). Did Paul think they were believers or not?

Pentecostal scholars cite Acts 19:1–7 as the final biblical support in Acts for their doctrine of subsequence. They claim these Ephesian men were believers in Jesus prior to meeting Paul, so they already had been regenerated. All Christians agree that Paul administered Christian baptism to them and that they then received the Holy Spirit with signs accompanying, included speaking in tongues.

Dunn says of these Ephesians in Acts 19:1–7, "They are disciples, but do not yet belong to *the* disciples; that is, they are not yet Christians." He adds, "They were not Christians at all. The absence of the Spirit indicated that they had not even begun the Christian life."[5] By then, the word "Christian" was in use (11:26).

Dunn also says of Spirit baptism in Acts, "one of Luke's purposes in recording these unusual instances is to show that the one thing which makes a man a Christian is the gift of the Spirit. Men can have been for a long time in Jesus' company, can have made profession of faith and been baptized in the name of the Lord Jesus, can be wholly 'clean' and acceptable to God, can even be 'disciples,' and *yet not be Christians*, because they lack and until they receive the Holy Spirit."[6]

In a later publication, Jimmy expresses the same viewpoint by saying concerning Acts, "Paul's question to the Ephesian 'disciples' in 19:2 . . . 'Did you receive the Spirit when you believed?'—the implication being that if

---

4. The NRSV's, "When you became believers," is no different than other versions having "when you believed" (NASB, NIV, ESV).

5. Dunn, *Baptism in the Holy Spirit*, 85–86. Emphasis his.

6. Ibid., 93. Emphasis his.

they had believed, taken the step of commitment, they would have received the Spirit."[7]

Jimmy also says of Acts 9:1 that the lack of the article in the expression *tinas mathetas* ("some disciples") in the Greek text "probably" indicates they were not genuine disciples.[8] But he recanted of this assertion in a later publication.[9]

Some Evangelical scholars agree with Dunn's view of Acts 19:1–7. Merrill Unger goes a step farther by saying, "The Ephesian disciples were not saved (Ac 11:14) with the common salvation of the new age before Paul preached to them the gospel of grace and free salvation.... They were evidently regenerated," yet they were "not Christians looking back to an accomplished redemption."[10]

Ben Witherington says of these Ephesian men, "From Luke's point of view, having received the Holy Spirit was the *sine qua non* of being a Christian.... One must conclude that Luke believed they were not Christians, and there is no sound reason to think he is wrong."[11]

John B. Polhill likewise says of these Ephesians, "They failed to recognize Jesus as the one whom John had proclaimed, as the promised Messiah.... This group was totally unacquainted with the gospel.... They immediately responded to Paul's good news that Christ the Messiah had come."[12] Polhill admits that John identified Jesus as the Messiah, yet Polhill assumes that the Ephesians didn't know this.

Surprisingly, Pentecostal Howard Ervin adopts the same view of these Ephesians as do these Evangelical scholars just mentioned, that these Ephesians were not Christians until they heard Paul. Ervin states, "Hearing from Paul that Jesus was the long-awaited Messiah, they believed and" that was "their regeneration."[13] One would expect Ervin to have viewed this

---

7. Dunn, *The Christ and the Spirit*, 219.

8. Dunn, *Baptism in the Holy Spirit*, 84.

9. Dunn, "Baptism in the Spirit: A Response to Pentecostal Scholarship on Luke-Acts," 24n1.

10. Unger, *The Baptism and Gifts of the Holy Spirit*, 89–90.

11. Witherington, *The Acts of the Apostles*, 570. See also p. 565.

12. Polhill, *Acts*, 399.

13. Ervin, *Spirit-Baptism*, 80. It is the same in the complex chapter, "The Ephesian 'Disciples,'" in Ervin's *Conversion-Initiation*, pp. 55–67. In chapter 6, we saw that he does the same with Acts 8:39, in which he adopts the variant that nullifies subsequence.

situation as his Pentecostal brethren did, that these Ephesians were believers before they met Paul since that supports the Pentecostals' doctrine of subsequence.

Yet Pentecostal Gordon Fee agreed with Dunn and Ervin by saying of the Ephesians in Acts 9:1–7, "They were obviously not Christians because the one essential ingredient was missing," referring to the Holy Spirit.[14]

Actually, saying that these Ephesian men were not Christians until they met and heard Paul supports the thesis of this book. Nevertheless, it seems to me from Luke's account that Paul did not see it that way.

WAS THE EPHESIAN EPISODE AN ANOMALY?

Was this Ephesian episode an anomaly? That is, did these Ephesians experience a post-conversion Spirit baptism that was abnormal? If so, why did Paul later teach in his epistles that Spirit baptism occurs at conversion? Paul taught in his epistles what was normative, but he first taught it after Peter had finished opening kingdom doors in Acts 10. I am inclined to think this Ephesian episode was abnormal and that Paul perceived it as such.

There is another way to comprehend Paul's question in Acts 19:2 than how the scholars mentioned above have understood it. That is, as Paul was talking to these Ephesians, he may have thought they were Christians, but suspected they didn't have the Spirit or didn't know that Spirit baptism had begun at Pentecost, thus years earlier. I think it is more likely that this is the correct way to understand Paul's question. Why?

First, Luke apparently arranged these two incidents together in Acts 18:24—19:7 since Apollos and these Ephesians underwent John's baptism without knowing of Christian baptism.

Second, Apollos may have taught these Ephesians. If so, they also would have been "instructed in the Way of the Lord," referring to Jesus, and known "accurately the things concerning Jesus" (Acts 18:25).

Third, Luke says that at Ephesus Paul "found some disciples" (Acts 19:1). This word "disciples" (Gr. *mathetai*) appears twenty-five times in Acts, and in all of the other instances it refers to true believers. Plus, Luke doesn't say these Ephesians were actual disciples of John, only that they underwent John's baptism.

---

14. Fee, "Baptism in the Holy Spirit: The Issue of Separability and Subsequence," 94.

Spirit Baptism on the Ephesians (Acts 19)

Fourth, Paul ended his question in Acts 19:2 with the words, "when you became believers." I think it is more likely that this means Paul thought they were believers.

Fifth, if Paul suspected these Ephesians were nonbelievers, his first question to them is irrelevant. Instead, he should have preached the gospel to them rather than ask this question or at least have asked if they believed in Jesus as the Messiah.

In sum, I think the more compelling understanding of this incident in Acts 19:1–7 is that *Paul thought these Ephesian men were genuine believers, but he began to suspect from his conversation with them that they had not yet received the Holy Spirit.* Most NT scholars who have written commentaries on Acts adopt this interpretation. For example, F. F. Bruce says in his popular commentary on Acts, "Paul's question, 'Did ye receive the Holy Spirit when ye believed?' suggests strongly that he regarded them as true believers in Christ."[15]

"WE HAVE NOT EVEN HEARD THAT THERE IS A HOLY SPIRIT"

These Ephesians answered Paul, "No, we have not even heard that there is a Holy Spirit" (Acts 19:2). Dunn and others take this answer to mean these men did not know of the existence of the Holy Spirit, indicating they were not Christians.[16] In Dunn's commentary on Acts he says of this response, "Since they ... had not even heard of the Spirit. ... their complete ignorance of the Spirit puts a question mark against the status of their discipleship."[17] And David Peterson remarks on this text, "How could genuine Christians make such a response? ... Their answer showed that they were definitely not Christians."[18]

On the contrary, these Jewish men of Ephesus surely knew their Jewish Bible somewhat. It mentions "the Spirit of the LORD" twenty-four times, "the Spirit of God" thirteen times, and "the/my Spirit" many more times. However, it mentions "holy spirit" only three times (Ps 51:11; Isa 63:10–11). So, these men surely knew about the Holy Spirit of God.

---

15. Bruce, *Commentary on the Book of Acts*, 385.
16. Dunn, *Baptism in the Holy Spirit*, 83.
17. Dunn, *The Acts of the Apostles*, 255–56.
18. Peterson, *The Acts of the Apostles*, 530.

D. A. Carson explains that Acts 19:2b "*may* simply mean 'that there is a Holy Spirit to be received,' not *necessarily* that they had not even heard the words *Holy Spirit* before."[19]

Indeed. We have seen that the same idea is in the Gospel of John. The author says Jesus said, "Out of the believer's heart shall flow rivers of living water" (John 7:38). The author adds, "Now he said this about the Spirit, which believers in him were to receive; for as yet there was no Spirit" (v. 39). He does not mean there is no Spirit but that the Spirit had not been given.

So, this reply about the Spirit by these Ephesians likely reflects that *they did not know something important that had occurred regarding the Holy Spirit*. What could it have been? We have learned that John the Baptist said to his disciples concerning Jesus that he would "baptize you with the Holy Spirit and fire" (Matt 3:11/Luke 3:16). So, these Ephesian men did not know about Jesus first baptizing his disciples with the Holy Spirit at Pentecost. Joseph Fitzmyer adopts this viewpoint by explaining, "The Ephesian disciples are Gentiles in background, who are unaware of what Jerusalem Jewish Christians have experienced or known."[20]

F. F. Bruce also says of these Ephesians, "Even if they only had been baptized with John's baptism, they conceivably knew that John had spoken of a coming baptism with the Holy Spirit; they did not know, however, that this expected baptism was now an accomplished fact."[21] And they likely would have known John said Jesus was greater than himself and that he would baptize with the Spirit, which is greater than baptizing with water.

Luke Timothy Johnson also says of Acts 19:2b that it "can mean only that they did not know there was a Holy Spirit in connection with baptism. . . . As in the case of Apollos (18:25), these 'disciples' and 'believers' are portrayed as yet unfinished and in need of the messianic baptism in the Spirit."[22]

Jewish scholar Darrell Bock likewise connects the two incidents in Acts 18:24–19:7 and says of these Ephesian men, "They have come to faith in Jesus (*pisteusantes*), so their problem is like that of Apollos, knowing about Jesus but not the work of the Spirit."[23]

---

19. Carson, *Showing the Spirit*, 149. Emphasis his.

20. Fitzmyer, *The Acts of the Apostles*, 643. See Dunn, *Baptism in the Holy Spirit*, 85, where he elaborates on this.

21. Bruce, *Commentary on the Book of Acts*, 385–86.

22. Johnson, *The Acts of the Apostles*, 337.

23. Bock, *Acts*, 599.

Spirit Baptism on the Ephesians (Acts 19)

D. A. Carson says of Acts 19:1–7, "Paul presupposes by this line of questioning that reception of the Spirit at conversion is normal and expected."[24] Yes, but after Peter finished opening all kingdom doors.

WHY DID PAUL RE-BAPTIZE THE EPHESIANS?

What did Paul mean by asking these Ephesians, "Into what then were you baptized?" He inquired about the meaning of their water baptism since they did not yet have the Spirit.

Paul's question also indicates that he closely connected water baptism and Spirit baptism. Much has been written about how these two are related in the NT. Paul later wrote a creedal statement in his letter to the Ephesians, saying, "one Lord, one faith, one baptism, one God and Father of all" (Eph 4:5). But to enter that discussion would take us far afield from the main purpose of this book—to learn how Peter's kingdom keys relate to Spirit baptism.

When these Ephesian men answered Paul, "Into John's baptism," he re-baptized them. It is the only mention of re-baptism in the NT. Before he did so Paul explained, "John baptized with the baptism of repentance, telling the people to believe in the one who was to come after him, that is, in Jesus" (Acts 19:4). Some scholars think this signifies that Paul was telling these men something they didn't know. As stated above, I think it more likely that Paul was merely reiterating what these Ephesian men already knew.

John's baptism was preparatory for Christian baptism that symbolizes Jesus' death and resurrection. Due to this additional meaning for water baptism, Paul deemed it necessary to re-baptize them. He obviously thought they should thereby demonstrate their belief in Jesus as their risen Savior. Yet there is no indication in Acts 19:1–7 that Paul thought these Ephesian men needed to be re-baptized to be saved.

Then, what about Apollos? Luke doesn't say Priscilla and Aquila re-baptized him. Maybe they didn't think it was necessary.[25] Or maybe they weren't sure about it, and Paul was.

This silence about Apollos being baptized raises the same question about the 120 disciples at Pentecost, especially the twelve apostles. John surely would have baptized several of them. Yet Luke does not say anything

---

24. Carson, *Showing the Spirit*, 150.
25. Witherington, *The Acts of the Apostles*, 567.

about them being re-baptized in Jesus' name, either. All such silence shows that Luke himself did not think water baptism was necessary for salvation.

Luke says these Ephesian men were "baptized in the name of the Lord Jesus" (Acts 19:5). This probably means the baptizer uttered Jesus' name just prior to baptizing the person.

So, John's baptism did not symbolize Jesus' death and resurrection. No one but Jesus foreknew about his death and resurrection, not even John or Jesus' mother. Yet Jesus predicted it several times.[26] Sometimes, he did it obscurely; other times, he was very explicit about it.[27] Yet no one who heard it believed him.

Then, what about John calling Jesus "the Lamb of God who takes away the sin of the world" (John 1:29)? John could not have referred to Jesus' death fulfilling the sacrificial paschal lamb as Paul does in 1 Cor 5:7. Otherwise, the imprisoned Baptist would not have doubted when he sent a message to Jesus asking if he was the coming one whom John had preached about or not (Matt 11:2–3; Luke 7:19–20).

John was an apocalyptic preacher. So, he must have called Jesus "the Lamb of God," and probably "the Son of God" (Psalm 2; 110), in an apocalyptic sense. The book of Revelation identifies Jesus as "the Lamb" twenty-eight times. Sometimes, it refers to his sacrificial death; other times, it identifies him as one who vents wrath upon his enemies by conquering them in battle (Rev 6:16–17; 17:14; cf. 19:11–21). The latter must have been how John applied the ascription "Lamb of God" to Jesus (cf. Matt 3:11–12; Luke 3:16–17).

DID THESE EPHESIAN MEN EXPERIENCE A POST-CONVERSION SPIRIT BAPTISM?

So, Luke says of these Ephesian men that after Paul spoke about Jesus to them, "On hearing this, they were baptized in the name of the Lord Jesus. When Paul had laid his hands on them, the Holy Spirit came upon them, and they spoke in tongues and prophesied" (Acts 19:5–6). Did they have a post-conversion Spirit baptism? If so, that would support the Pentecostals' doctrine of subsequence unless viewed as an anomaly.

Pentecostal Gordon Fee agrees with Jimmy Dunn about the Ephesians in Acts 19:1–7. Fee says, "It is extremely unlikely, despite his use of *mathetai*

---

26. E.g., John 2:19–22; Matt 12:38–40; 16:4 par.; Matt 26:6–12 par.
27. E.g., Matt 16:21 par.; Matt 17:22–23 par.; Matt 20:17–19 par.

Spirit Baptism on the Ephesians (Acts 19)

to describe them, that Luke intended us to see the people in Acts 19 as Christians in any real sense,"[28] that is, before "Paul had laid his hands on them" and "the Holy Spirit came upon them" (v. 6).

In 1972, reformed systematic theologian Anthony Hoekema agreed with Dunn and Fee by saying of these Ephesians, "It is quite obvious that these disciples were not full-fledged Christian believers when Paul first met them."[29] If it is so obvious, why do most non-Pentecostal commentaries on Acts say these Ephesians were already Christians? And was it possible for a Christian to be anything other than a full-fledged Christian? Hoekema adds, "What happened at Ephesus, therefore, was not a 'baptism in the Spirit' subsequent to and distinct from conversion, but a receiving of the Spirit at the same time as conversion. The whole point of the narrative—as is that of the story of the conversion of the Samaritans—is that one cannot be truly converted apart from the reception of the Holy Spirit."[30] Hoekema says of all the texts about Spirit baptism in Acts, "Conversion and reception of the Spirit, these passages tell us, must not be separated but must always be kept together."[31]

J. I. Packer says likewise, "The Ephesian 'disciples' who had not received the Spirit (*see* 19:2–6), were, as it seems, not yet Christians when Paul met them."[32] Packer also cites the Samaritans in Acts 8:12–17, the Ephesians in Acts 19:1–7, and then asserts, "The expectation that the Spirit's full ministry to Christians would begin at conversion is clear throughout Acts."[33] Not at all! Packer says this since he believes, as do Dunn and some other Evangelicals, that the Samaritans and Ephesians were not converted until they received the Spirit.

As stated above, if Paul had suspected that these Ephesians were not saved, he first would have preached the gospel to them. The same can be said of Peter with the Samaritans in Acts 8. Of course, this is an argument based on silence, but it would be a glaring silence. It would have been far more important for Luke to tell about Paul explaining the gospel correctly, and them believing it, than merely saying he re-baptized them.

---

28. Fee, "Baptism in the Holy Spirit: The Issue of Separability and Subsequence," 90.
29. Hoekema, *Holy Spirit Baptism*, 41.
30. Ibid., 42.
31. Ibid., 43.
32. Packer, *Keep in Step with the Spirit*, 204.
33. Ibid., 89.

SOLVING THE SAMARITAN RIDDLE

D. A. Carson is convincing in his tentative summary of this situation as follows:

> They had apparently become followers of John the Baptist, had received his baptism (whether personally or conceivably from one of the John's converts), and had followed the Baptist's ministry long enough to know he had pointed beyond himself to Jesus, the one whose sandals he was not worthy to loosen. Apollos at least (and probably the Ephesians) had also learned enough about Jesus to be described as one who "taught about Jesus accurately" (18:25). This probably suggests knowledge not only of Jesus' public ministry and teaching, but also of his death and resurrection. But apparently they knew nothing of Pentecost and what it signified of eschatological formation. This ignorance could have developed because they (or the people who taught them) left Jerusalem (like tens of thousands of other diaspora Jews) shortly after the Passover feast—that is, they learned of Jesus' death and resurrection, but not of the coming of the Spirit.[34]

Why could Paul impart Spirit baptism to these Ephesians, yet Philip could not do so to the Samaritans? Some scholars, especially Catholics, answer that imparting Spirit baptism was reserved only for the twelve apostles, and that is why Peter and John were sent. But that does not fit Paul and these Ephesians, since he was not one of the twelve. The correct answer seems to be that Peter already had opened all three doors for the three divisions of humanity in the Bible. Henceforth, Spirit baptism was available to all people, including these Ephesians, without the need of Peter's presence. In this case, as in Acts 8:17, it occurred with the laying on of hands.

Keeping this interpretation in mind about Luke's book of Acts—that Peter's kingdom keys explain Spirit baptism in Acts 2, 8, and 10, with Acts 19 as an anomaly—we now turn to see if this interpretation corresponds with what Paul teaches about receiving the Holy Spirit.

---

34. Carson, *Showing the Spirit*, 148–49.

CHAPTER 10

Paul's Teaching on the Holy Spirit and Spiritual Gifts

COMPARING THE PNEUMATOLOGIES OF LUKE AND PAUL

So far, we have learned that Pentecostals have relied almost entirely on Luke-Acts for their doctrine of separability and subsequence. But they earlier ignored Paul's teaching about receiving the Spirit at conversion. So, Dunn wrote in 1970, "Pentecostalism is built foursquare on Acts. . . . Paul seems to be more of an embarrassment than an asset, so that time and again expositions of this doctrine conveniently ignore him."[1] Recently, Pentecostal scholars have not ignored Paul's teaching, but have had difficulty reconciling it with their doctrine.

Pentecostal scholar Martin William Mittelstadt is an authority on Pentecostal literature about Luke-Acts. He affirms this accusation by Dunn and explains, "In early Pentecostal communities the Book of Acts and the Gospels were the primary narratives in shaping of Pentecostal belief and practice. The Epistles played a secondary and supportive role. Therefore, it was important to know which biblical book or passage has the final word

---

1. Dunn, *Baptism in the Holy Spirit*, 103.

on any given topic when one 'interpreted scripture in light of scripture.'"[2] Mittelstadt also says, "Pentecostals focus little on . . . the ministry of Paul (Acts 13 and beyond). A glance at the literature reveals Pentecostal proclivity to Acts 1–10 . . . but very little on the second half of Acts. Paul, the missionary and prisoner receives little attention. I suppose the marked decline of the Spirit language in the second half of Acts may serve as a contributing factor."[3] Yes, but it may be more due to the absence of *glossolalia* therein.

As stated earlier, some Evangelicals criticize Pentecostals for basing their doctrine of subsequence solely on the narrative structure of Acts. Merrill F. Unger alleges, "The Pentecostal interpretation of the book of Acts . . . is strongly suspect for a number of reasons. In the first place it fails to take into account the nondoctrinal and purely historical and experiential nature of the book of Acts."[4] Yes, but this allegation undermines the integrity of the disciples' actions. Being led of the Spirit, they would have acted in accordance with truth.

Most Pentecostal scholars disagree with some Evangelical scholars about the purpose of Spirit baptism in the NT. Robert Menzies, and to a lesser extent Roger Stronstad and James Shelton, contend that Luke viewed Spirit baptism as empowerment for ministry, especially evangelism, so it is missional. But Dunn and Max Turner insist that Spirit baptism in Acts always accompanies regeneration-salvation-conversion, so it is also soteriological. This debate goes back to the definition of regeneration-salvation that we examined in chapter 3.

Both of these positions are based on certain biblical authors and their works. These two positions are called pneumatologies, and they get a bit complex. The Pentecostal position is founded on Luke's book of Acts, and the Evangelical position rests on certain epistles of Paul. If both are right, some scholars think Luke and Paul have contrasting pneumatologies. A few Pentecostals think they do and cite G. W. H. Lampe for support. He alleges concerning Acts, "Luke's apparently inconsistent account of the practice of baptism . . . at times appear to be self-contradictory, but it also seems to be at variance with the evidence of St. Paul on the subject. Consequently, commentators on Acts and dogmatic theologians alike have produced a remarkable variety of theories to account for these supposed inconsistencies, and drawn totally divergent inferences for baptismal theology. . . . Luke

---

2. Mittelstadt, *Reading Luke-Acts in the Pentecostal Tradition*, 43–44.

3. Ibid., 157–58.

4. Unger, *The Baptism and Gifts of the Holy Spirit*, 16.

Paul's Teaching on the Holy Spirit and Spiritual Gifts

has an insufficient appreciation of the Spirit as the inner principle of the ordinary believer's life in Christ."[5]

But isn't this difference in pneumatologies between Luke and Paul partly due to them having different purposes in their writings, resulting in different genres? Luke wrote two history books whereas Paul wrote letters to churches and missionary associates to address problems, teach truths, and strengthen faith.

As stated earlier, many scholars have accused Dunn of trying to reconcile Luke and Paul by using Paul's pneumatology in his epistles as a grid to interpret Luke's pneumatology in Acts. Dunn acknowledges "the charge being that I fell into the trap of reading Acts too much with Pauline spectacles."[6] They so accuse him for saying such things as, "The pneumatology of Luke is essentially one with the pneumatology of Paul."[7] Scholars call this supposed agreement in pneumatology "continuity." But we saw in chapter 6 that Dunn is unconvincing in his denial that the Samaritans in Acts 8 had a post-conversion Spirit baptism. If they did, some think that subsequence appears to conflict with Paul's teaching that conversion and Spirit baptism happen simultaneously. Pentecostal scholar Youngmo Cho thus concludes, "There is a considerable difference between Paul's pneumatology and that of Luke."[8]

Pentecostal Roger Stronstad insists on a unity with diversity in the NT writings of Luke and Paul on this matter.[9] But Pentecostal Robert Menzies forthrightly admits his belief in the "discontinuity" between the pneumatologies of Luke and Paul. He says his persuasion on this goes back to the influence that early form critics Hermann Gunkel and Eduard Schweizer had on him.[10] Menzies, in his book *Empowered for Witness*, has done a valuable service in making us (more?) aware of Luke's emphasis on the pro-

---

5. Lampe, *The Seal of the Spirit*, 64–65.

6. Dunn, *The Christ and the Spirit*, 242. On p. 223, he lists the main writers (and their books) who so accuse him, the first being W. Hollenweger, then "H. D. Hunter, H. Ervin, R. Stronstad, F. L. Arrington, J. B. Shelton, and R. P. Menzies."

7. Ibid., 242.

8. Cho, *Spirit and Kingdom in the Writings of Luke and Paul*, 161.

9. Stronstad, *Spirit, Scripture and Theology*, 169–92. Some claim irony in Dunn denying this since he is the champion of this subject due to his book, *Unity and Diversity in the New Testament*.

10. Menzies, *Empowered for Witness*, 18–26; Menzies, *The Development of Early Christian Pneumatology*; Gunkle, *The Influence of the Holy Spirit*; Schweizer, *The Holy Spirit*.

phetic ministry of the Spirit and the Spirit's empowerment of Christians for witness. Yet I think Menzies goes too far in contrasting these points with Paul's emphasis on the Spirit's soteriological ministry and spiritual formation. And from Menzies' position, I don't think he succeeds in reconciling Luke and Paul.[11]

For instance, Menzies asserts, "Luke not only fails to refer to the soteriological aspects of the Spirit's work so prominent in the epistles of Paul, his narrative presupposes a pneumatology which excludes this dimension. Rather than presenting the Spirit as the source of Christian existence, Luke consistently portrays the Spirit as the source of prophetic inspiration."[12] But saying Luke's missional pneumatology excludes soteriology sounds like it denies Paul's soteriological pneumatology. Menzies also states, "Luke's pneumatology is *different* from—although *complementary* to—that of Paul. . . . Luke's distinctive penumatology is ultimately reconcilable with that of Paul and that both perspectives can be seen as contributing to a process of harmonious development." Menzies repeats, "The pneumatology of Luke and Paul are different but compatible."[13]

Menzies also says these "differences . . . are particularly acute. . . . It indicates that the task of articulating a holistic biblical theology of the Spirit is more complex than is often assumed. More specifically, it calls into question attempts at theological synthesis which do not adequately account for the distinctive pneumatological perspectives of the primitive church (Mark, Matthew) and particularly Luke-Acts."[14] So, Menzies implicitly criticizes scholars who rely only, or nearly so, on Paul's pneumatology.

Of course, Menzies saying Luke and Paul have compatible pneumatologies as he understands them doesn't make it so. This is further evident by Menzies saying of the Samaritans' subsequence in Acts 8, "Paul would not—indeed, could not—have interpreted and narrated the event in this way."[15]

On the contrary, the Samaritan incident in Acts 8 occurred a few years before Paul was converted. Peter was still exercising his temporary role of using kingdom keys with those Samaritans, and he completed this role

---

11. E.g., Menzies and Menzies, *Spirit and Power*, 55–58.

12. Menzies, *Empowered for Witness*, 230, 240. He repeats the clause with "excludes" on pp. 237, 256, and 257.

13. Ibid., 238. Emphasis his.

14. Ibid., 257.

15. Ibid., 247.

Paul's Teaching on the Holy Spirit and Spiritual Gifts

soon afterwards with the Gentiles in Acts 10. To repeat, Peter had opened kingdom doors to all three people groups and thus finished this mission. After that, and the anomaly of the Ephesians in Acts 19, Spirit baptism has always occurred for all people at conversion, as Paul writes years later.

Thus, if Paul had reported the Samaritan incident rather than Luke, being a man of the Spirit Paul would have recorded what Luke did. Luke did not intend to write his own pneumatology in his book of Acts. Rather, he wrote history in Acts 1–8 that probably occurred prior to his own conversion and certainly prior to Paul's. So, Luke likely got his information in Acts 8 from oral reports of eyewitnesses, perhaps even Philip, and maybe from written sources.

Pentecostal scholar Roger Stronstad, in his 1984 book entitled *The Charismatic Theology of Paul*, applies redaction criticism to the NT and concludes that Luke provides subsequence and Paul does not. Then Stronstad tries to reconcile Luke and Paul on this. I think his conclusion is right, that Luke has subsequence and Paul does not, but I don't think Stronstad's explanation of this difference is convincing. Instead, the difference is due to Luke telling about an instance of Peter using kingdom keys when Saul/Paul wasn't even saved. So, the timing between the two covenants in this transitional period and Peter's use of the keys are important factors in trying to reconcile Luke and Paul on whether or not Spirit baptism is subsequent to conversion.

Forty years into the Dunn Debate, Roger Stronstad wrote, "The clash between Dunn's conversion-initiation paradigm of Spirit baptism and the Pentecostals' commissioning-empowerment paradigm remains unresolved. The two paradigms cannot both be discovered in Luke's data."[16] I agree. This is why *we should have a holistic approach to the Bible in forming our theology. In this case, it is only Matthew, in Matt 16:18–19, who is of help in reconciling the seemingly disparate pneumatologies of Luke and Paul.*

We learned earlier that Luke likely was a co-worker with Paul on some of his missionary travels. Many NT scholars view Paul as a leading apostle comparable to the twelve apostles, and they rightly assert that Luke would have subordinated himself to Paul on important theological matters. Many make this argument against Pentecostals who base their doctrine of subsequence solely on Luke's book of Acts. I think it is inconceivable that Luke and Paul had varying views on important matters such as the relationship of conversion and Spirit baptism.

---

16. Stronstad, "Forty Years On," 7.

So, Pentecostals are right about Luke's subsequence in Acts 8, and Dunn is right about Paul's simultaneity in his letters. Yet Luke and Paul do not conflict if the reconciling factor between them is Peter using his keys to open kingdom doors. After he finished this role in Acts 10, Paul's simultaneity prevails just as Dunn trumpets. And after Acts 19, Gordon Fee is right in saying the Holy Spirit is "the chief element of the Christian life, from beginning to end."[17]

THE LAW, THE FLESH, AND THE SPIRIT

The Apostle Paul's life was so permeated with the Holy Spirit that it made him an authority par excellence on this subject. We don't have space to examine all that he says about it, but we will now look at his primary texts that relate to the Dunn Debate. And we will do so according to the order of placement of his letters in the NT, which turns out to be the order of his texts that are most important to this debate.

Paul's usual language is "receiving the (Holy) Spirit" and never being "baptized with/in the (Holy) Spirit," as in Acts. Yet for Paul, as for Luke and Peter in Acts, "receiving the Spirit" is synonymous with "baptized with/in the Spirit."

Paul's letter that appears first in the standard order of NT documents is his Epistle to the Romans, which is often called a "book." It immediately follows Luke-Acts, which represents a little over one-fourth of the NT. And Paul's letters are one-fourth of the NT. Thus, Luke and Paul wrote barely over half of the NT.

The most soteriological (from Gr. *soter*="savior") book in the Bible is unquestionably Paul's Epistle to the Romans. He addresses this letter, "To all God's beloved in Rome, who are called to be saints" (Rom 1:7). In his first mention of the Holy Spirit he says, "God's love has been poured into our hearts through the Holy Spirit that has been given to us" (5:5). He clearly means that the Holy Spirit has been given to all genuine believers in Jesus.

Paul teaches extensively about the Holy Spirit in Romans 8 by first laying a foundation for it in Romans 7. So, to properly understand Romans 8 it helps to rightly understand Romans 7.

In Romans 7, Paul presents the inner struggle that is common to all people, not just Christians, which exists due to the law and the flesh. By law, Paul means especially a Jew under the law of Moses. By flesh, Paul refers to

---

17. Fee, *Gospel and Spirit*, 98.

Paul's Teaching on the Holy Spirit and Spiritual Gifts

the inbred nature to sin. Of this Paul writes, "I do not do what I want, but I do the very thing I hate" (Rom 7:15). Christians often say of this text, "I can relate to *that*!" I sympathize. But is that what Paul means?

Christians have long debated whether Paul refers to his Christian life or pre-Christian life in most of Romans 7.[18] Jimmy Dunn observes, "The function of Rom. 7.7–25 is one of the most disputed issues in NT studies."[19] I am inclined to agree with the modern, scholarly consensus of this difficult text, with which Jimmy differs.[20]

Paul introduces this subject by saying, "I am speaking to those who know the law" (Rom 7:1), thus Jews. He writes, "My friends, you have died to the law" (v. 4). He means Jewish Christians are no longer under its authority. Paul says earlier, "You are not under law but under grace" (6:14). When he says, "But now we are discharged from the law" (7:6), he refers to conversion. All of this becomes clear when Paul asks, "Who will rescue me?" and then answers, "Jesus Christ my Lord" (v. 25). Paul means this rescue occurs at conversion and the resurrection.

Gordon Fee adopts this modern consensus of Romans 7 as well.[21] He says, "The questions as Paul himself puts them forward, and to which he offers a response, have to do with Torah [law], and therefore life under Torah, *not with life in Christ*, which for Paul is decidedly *not under Torah*."[22]

To our relief and exulting joy Paul next exclaims, "There is therefore now no condemnation for those who are in Christ Jesus," who "has set you free from the law of sin and of death" (Rom 8:1–2). Then Paul exhorts those who are "in Christ"—his favorite label for Christians—"walk not according to the flesh but according to the Spirit" (v. 4). He adds, "Those who are in the flesh cannot please God. But you are not in the flesh" (vv. 8–9).

So far in Romans 8, Paul says that anyone who lives a lifestyle mostly according to the flesh does not belong to God and Christ, thus is not a genuine Christian. The counterpart is that Christians do not constantly live their lives according to the flesh, since they have been set free from it. Fee explains, "Paul is not . . . dealing with a flesh/Spirit tension in the life of

---

18. This debate was extensive in the Protestant Reformation. See *The Works of James Arminius*, 2:471–683.

19. Dunn, *The Theology of Paul the Apostle*, 472.

20. Dunn, *Jesus and the Spirit*, 313–16; Dunn, *The Theology of Paul the Apostle*, 472–77; Dunn, *Romans 1–8*, 374–412.

21. Fee, *God's Empowering Presence*, 503–15.

22. Ibid., 511. Emphasis his.

the believer, but is spelling out in its starkest form the difference between two kinds of existence: life in the Spirit and life in the flesh, the life of the believer and the life of the unbeliever."[23]

THE SPIRIT OF GOD INDWELLS ALL BELIEVERS

What Paul says next, in Rom 8:9, is his most important text relating to the Dunn Debate. He says, "You are in the Spirit, since the Spirit of God dwells in you. Anyone who does not have the Spirit of Christ does not belong to him" (Rom 8:9). Paul herein interchanges "Spirit of God" and "Spirit of Christ." He says believers live their lives to some extent by the influence of the Spirit since the Spirit indwells them.

Thus, Paul's teaching in Rom 8:9—that all Christians both possess, and live by, the Holy Spirit—militates strongly against the Pentecostals' doctrine of subsequence since, in contrast to most Pentecostals, being given the Spirit and being baptized with the Spirit are the same for Paul. If the Spirit permanently indwells a person, he or she has been baptized with the Spirit. For Paul, this Spirit indwelling begins at conversion.

Yet some Pentecostals distinguish between Spirit indwelling and Spirit baptism. They say Spirit indwelling happens at conversion, but Spirit baptism occurs subsequently. For instance, Howard Ervin says Rom 8:9 "is not the Pentecostal baptism in the Holy Spirit. . . . Rom. 8:9 is concerned with the first experience of conversion and new birth by the Holy Spirit. It does not refer to the subsequent experience of the baptism in the Spirit for power-in-mission."[24] I think Ervin flounders as he subsequently tries to prove this assertion.[25]

Paul's teaching about the universal indwelling of the Holy Spirit in all believers echoes Jesus' teaching on this subject. Recall that he said of the Holy Spirit, "Out of the believer's heart shall flow rivers of living water," thus all believers (John 7:38; cf. 4:14). The Fourth Evangelist then explains, "Now he said this about the Spirit, which believers in him were to receive" (7:39). And recall that at the Last Supper Jesus spoke of "the Holy Spirit" as "another Advocate" for his disciples (14:16, 26), adding, "he abides with you, and he will be in you" (v. 17).

---

23. Ibid., 547.

24. E.g., Ervin, *Conversion-Initiation*, 26.

25. Ibid., 26–27, 115–16.

Paul's Teaching on the Holy Spirit and Spiritual Gifts

Paul also teaches that calling upon God as "Father" is evidence of possessing the Spirit. He says, "For all who are led by the Spirit of God are children of God. For you did not receive a spirit of slavery to fall back into fear, but you have received a spirit of adoption. When we cry, 'Abba! Father!' it is that very Spirit bearing witness with our spirit that we are children of God" (Rom 8:14–16; cf. Gal 4:6). So, Paul says all who sincerely call God their "Father" are his children, which proves that they have his Spirit.

Paul also teaches that the believer's body is a temple of the indwelling Holy Spirit. He asks the Corinthians, "Do you not know that you are God's temple and that God's Spirit dwells in you?" (1 Cor 3:16). He later repeats, "Or do you not know that your body is a temple of the Holy Spirit within you, which you have from God, and that you are not your own?" (6:19). Paul herein tells the Corinthian believers that they all have the Holy Spirit.

"IN ONE SPIRIT WE WERE ALL BAPTIZED INTO ONE BODY"

Paul's primary teaching on spiritual gifts is in his First Corinthians. Non-Pentecostal scholars often cite it where Paul assesses this church as spiritually immature partly due to having an undue focus on the gift of tongues. Then they connect this Pauline teaching to Pentecostalism due to its over-emphasis on tongues. We have seen that Paul tells of divisions in this church over personalities (1 Cor 1:10–16). Then he concludes, "And so, brothers and sisters, I could not speak to you as spiritual people, but rather as people of the flesh, as infants in Christ" (3:1).

Paul also writes in 1 Corinthians, "No one can say 'Jesus is Lord' except by the Holy Spirit" (1 Cor 12:3). He means all who genuinely claim Jesus as their Lord have the Holy Spirit. This text, however, must be tempered with Jesus' teaching on true Lordship in his Sermon on the Mount, "Not everyone who says to me, 'Lord, Lord,' will enter the kingdom of heaven, but only the one who does the will of my Father in heaven" (Matt 7:21).

Due to Rom 8:9, 1 Cor 12:3, and other Pauline texts,[26] Pentecostals admit all believers have "received," or have an association with, the Spirit; but they insist it is not the same as being baptized with the Spirit.

Paul also says, "For in one Spirit we were all baptized into one body— Jews or Greeks, slaves or free—and we were all made to drink of one Spirit"

---

26. E.g., Rom 5:5; 8:9, 11, 14, 16; Gal 4:6; Eph 2:18; 4:4.

(1 Cor 12:13). Some English versions begin by saying, "by one Spirit,"[27] as if the Spirit does the baptizing. On the contrary, Jesus does the baptizing, and he does it *with* the Holy Spirit. The word in the Greek text translated "by" in such versions is *en*, which usually means "in" or "with." Paul comes closest to the language "baptized in/with the (Holy) Spirit" here in 1 Cor 12:13.

What does Paul mean in 1 Cor 12:13 about being "baptized into one body?" He does not refer to water baptism, as some think. Rather, he means at conversion the new believer is metaphorically *baptized into*, that is, *put into*, the body of Christ, which is the church, by means of the Spirit. And the phrase, "made to drink of one Spirit," corresponds to Jesus' declaration we have considered numerous times—"Let the one who believes in me drink. As the scripture has said, 'Out of the believer's heart shall flow rivers of living water'" (John 7:38–39). So, both Jesus and Paul seem to say that all who believe in Jesus will then metaphorically drink of the Spirit.

As we might expect, Jimmy Dunn adopts this interpretation. He explains, "The most popular view of I Cor. 12.13 is that Paul is describing Christian water-baptism which conveys the Spirit. . . . Paul is thinking of baptism in the Spirit; he is not speaking about water at all."[28] Jimmy later repeats most assuredly, "There is no thought of water baptism here whatsoever."[29]

When it comes to critiquing the Pentecostals' doctrine of subsequence and deciding if it is in 1 Corinthians, there is none better to inform us than Gordon Fee. It is largely because of his being Pentecostal and having a best-selling commentary on this Pauline epistle (with an upcoming second edition). Fee agrees with Dunn about 1 Cor 12:13 by saying, "Paul refers to their common reception of the Spirit, presumably at the beginning of their Christian experience," of "whom all alike have received."[30] Fee informs that some scholars distinguish a difference between the two clauses in 1 Cor 12:13 that read, "In one Spirit we were all baptized . . . we were all made to drink of one Spirit." He says they agree that the first clause refers to conversion, but they disagree about the second clause. Fee relates that John Calvin, Martin Luther, and other early Protestant leaders viewed the second clause as a reference to the Lord's Supper, but some Pentecostals refer it to Spirit

---

27. E.g., KJV, NASB, and NIV. The NRSV and ESV have "in one Spirit." The NIV note says, "Or *with*; or *in*." The NASB note says, "Or *in*."

28. Dunn, *Baptism in the Holy Spirit*, 129.

29. Ibid., 131.

30. Fee, *God's Empowering Presence*, 178.

baptism. Fee rejects both interpretations. He argues, convincingly I think, that the second clause repeats the first clause as a parallel.[31]

Also like Dunn, Fee says 1 Cor 12:13 reveals that for Paul, "The Spirit is what essentially distinguishes the believer from the nonbeliever (2:10–14); the Spirit is what especially marks the beginning of Christian life (Gal. 3:2–3); the Spirit above all is what makes a person a child of God (Rom. 8:14–17). . . . The Spirit, whom all [believers] alike have received."[32]

So, we have seen that Gordon Fee is one of the few Pentecostal scholars who reject the Pentecostals' doctrine of subsequence. Instead, he insists that all believers since Pentecost have received the Spirit at conversion. Yet, we have seen that the Samaritans in Acts 8 were an exception, which Gordon admits.

Pentecostal scholar Douglas A. Oss says 1 Cor 12:13 does not refer to Spirit baptism but being baptized into the body of Christ, the church.[33] Thus, Oss distinguishes between these two concepts. He admits, "The only case that could possibly be built from 1 Corinthians 12:13 against the Pentecostal view of the Spirit's empowering work (although not persuasively, in my opinion) is that Pentecostals have used the wrong label in adopting 'baptism in the Holy Spirit.' . . . Many arguments against the Pentecostal doctrine of Spirit baptism militate only against the label; . . . focusing instead merely on the label as the rationale for dismissing the Pentecostal view."[34]

Yes, I think Pentecostals mislabel their post-conversion experience as baptism in the Holy Spirit. But Oss, in criticizing non-Pentecostal Christians for dismissing this Pentecostal distinctive, does not mention why they do. It is mostly because Pentecostals include *glossolalia* as necessary evidence of Spirit baptism. This, not labeling, is what divides them from most Christians. That is why most other Christians disagree with Pentecostals and agree more with Charismatics. They believe in *glossolalia*, but most don't require it as evidence of Spirit baptism.

Oss then cites portions of Acts to support the Pentecostal doctrine of subsequence. He rightly complains that some non-Pentecostal scholars argue against it by claiming Luke narrates experiences and that Christian

---

31. Ibid., 180, 180n370. So also Storms, "A Third Wave View," 178.
32. Fee, *The First Epistle to the Corinthians*, 603.
33. Oss, "A Pentecostal/Charismatic View," 257–60.
34. Ibid., 259–60.

theology should not be based on that, but on didactic teaching as in Paul's letters.[35] But as stated earlier, practice should coincide with instruction.

We have already considered Merrill Unger's objection to using episodes in Acts as a paradigm for others. He further alleges, "The Pentecostal concept of the baptism of the Spirit . . . is based upon experience rather than doctrine. . . . It erects its teaching on these historical and experiential portions, at the same time construing them in a vacuum and failing to reconcile their conclusions with the great doctrinal epistles of the New Testament."[36]

Unger is right in saying that when Pentecostals support their distinctive doctrine by appealing to certain narratives in Acts, they need to try to reconcile these with Paul's didactic teaching on the Spirit. But Unger is not right if he means Luke's narratives in Acts are not based on correct teaching about the Spirit. This brings us back to a repeated conclusion: pneumatology based on the Bible must reconcile Luke's book of Acts and Paul's epistles.

HOW DID THE GALATIANS RECEIVE THE SPIRIT?

Paul wrote his epistle to "the churches of Galatia" because he tells them, "I am astonished that you are so quickly deserting the one who called you in the grace of Christ and turning to a different gospel" (Gal 1:2, 6). He means the false doctrine of the Judaizers. They required Gentile Christians "to live like Jews" (Gal 2:14). Paul counters, "we know that a person is justified not by the works of the law but through faith in Jesus Christ" (v. 16). Does Paul mean the moral precepts of the Mosaic Law?

One of the primary theological advances of NT scholarship in recent decades is called "the new perspective on Paul," an expression Jimmy Dunn coined. It alleges that Lutherans and Reformers misunderstood Paul's "works of the law" as the keeping of the moral precepts of the Law of Moses. But the new perspective on Paul says he only means by "the works of the law" a Jew being "observant." That refers to obeying the Jewish dietary laws, males being circumcised, keeping the Sabbath holy, and "observing special days, and months, and seasons, and years" (Gal 4:10; cf. 5:2).[37]

---

35. Ibid., 260.

36. Unger, *The Baptism and the Gifts of the Holy Spirit*, 14.

37. Besides Jewish scholars, the most prominent writers on "the new perspective on Paul" have been, first, Lutheran scholar Krister Stendahl, then E. P. Sanders, and more recently James D. G. Dunn and N. T. Wright. Both the old and new perspectives agree

Paul's Teaching on the Holy Spirit and Spiritual Gifts

So, Paul chastises these Galatians for turning away from the truth as he delivered it to them. He poses the question, "Did you receive the Spirit by doing the works of the law or by believing what you heard" (Gal 3:2, cf. v. 5). Applying the new perspective on Paul to this statement, it can be paraphrased: "Did you receive the Spirit by keeping the Mosaic Law or by believing what you heard when I preached Jesus to you?" The answer is the latter. And Paul says, effectively, that they received the Spirit by believing in Jesus, thus at conversion.

Paul continues this theme about Spirit reception through faith by saying, "Christ redeemed us from the curse of the law . . . so that we might receive the promise of the Spirit through faith" (Gal 3:13–14). Paul here connects receiving the Spirit with the promise of the Spirit as predicted by John the Baptist and Jesus.[38] These prophecies show that all of the following expressions mean the same: given the Spirit, receiving the Spirit, and being baptized with the Spirit.

"MARKED WITH THE SEAL OF THE PROMISED HOLY SPIRIT"

Continuing through Paul's NT letters, after Galatians comes Ephesians. Its first half is deeply theological. Paul informs, "In Christ we have also obtained an inheritance. . . . In him you also, when you had heard the word of truth, the gospel of your salvation, and had believed in him, were marked with the seal of the promised Holy Spirit; this is the pledge of our inheritance toward redemption as God's own people" (Eph 1:11, 13–14; cf. 4:30; 2 Cor 1:21–22). Paul may have intended this metaphor of Spirit sealing to be synonymous with Spirit baptism.

Regardless, Paul makes it clear that this Spirit sealing occurs at conversion. So, receiving the Spirit (Spirit baptism) is commensurate with being sealed with the Spirit. Yet classical Pentecostals differentiate Spirit sealing and Spirit baptism. Dunn states, "Eph. 1.13 is one of the few Pauline (?) verses much used by Pentecostals in defending their theology of Spirit-baptism:'. . . after that ye believed, ye were sealed with that Holy Spirit of promise' (AV—with the 'after' emphasized). But this sort of exegesis, . . . is based on a fundamental misunderstanding of Greek grammar." Dunn explains the grammar and concludes, "It was when they believed that God

---

that we don't merit salvation.

38. Matt 3:11; Mark 1:8; Luke 3:16; 24:49; John 7:39; Acts 1:5, 8; 2:33; 11:16; Gal 3:14.

sealed them with the Spirit. As in Gal. 3.2, the step of faith is met by the gift of the Spirit."[39] All modern Bible versions serve as a correction of the KJV (AV) here, thus agreeing with Dunn.

Dunn insists, "The Spirit is poured out upon us which brings about our regeneration."[40] In chapter 3, I said God gives his Spirit as the result, not the cause, of being born again. Yet Jesus says in John 3:5 that the Spirit accomplishes the new birth, and it happens by faith as Jesus makes clear in vv. 14–15. But that is not the same as giving the Spirit as a gift. That is why the disciples mentioned in Acts 2, 8, and 19 could be born again prior to being given the Spirit.

But I think Dunn is right in arguing, "Most Pentecostals recognize the force of Rom. 8.9 and agree that to be a Christian one must have received the Spirit in some sense. But for them the focus of attention falls on a *second* reception of the Spirit which they attempt to find as often as possible in Paul, identifying it with such terms as anointing, sealing, and promise. Our study has shown: that Paul knows of only one reception of the Spirit, not two; that the concepts of anointing, sealing, outpouring, promise, gift, etc., all refer to that one coming of the Spirit."[41] Yes indeed, but I think Paul is being existential and thus not considering the past, actually before his own conversion, when the believers in Acts 2 and Acts 8 had a post-conversion Spirit baptism.

"BE FILLED WITH THE SPIRIT"

In chapter 3, we learned from the OT, thus the old covenant, that God's Spirit came and went. The Spirit came upon select individuals temporarily and soon departed. But under the new covenant inaugurated at Pentecost, the Spirit came to stay. That is, the Spirit fell upon believers at Pentecost, the equivalent of being baptized in the Spirit, and indwelt them thereafter.

We have seen the NT never commands being baptized with the Spirit. At Pentecost Peter said, "Repent, and be baptized every one of you in the name of Jesus Christ for the forgiveness of your sins; and *you will receive* the gift of the Holy Spirit" (Acts 2:38 ESV, similarly KJV, NASB; emphasis mine). So, if these Jews repent and are water baptized, symbolizing God's forgiveness of their sins due to Jesus' atoning death and resurrection, they

---

39. Dunn, *Baptism in the Holy Spirit*, 158–59.
40. Ibid., 168.
41. Ibid., 170.

Paul's Teaching on the Holy Spirit and Spiritual Gifts

would receive the Spirit, which is being Spirit baptized. They didn't need to seek it by prayer after conversion, as Pentecostals insist.

After Acts, the NT *does* command believers to be constantly *available* for the indwelling Spirit to fill their lives. Paul writes, "Do not get drunk with wine, . . . but be filled with the Spirit" (Eph 5:18). He means this Spirit-filling is for individuals to manifest the fruits of the Spirit in church meetings as they "sing psalms and hymns and spiritual songs . . . giving thanks to God the Father . . . in the name of our Lord Jesus Christ" (vv. 19–20).

This command by Paul to be Spirit-filled is similar to Jesus' directive, "Ask, and it will be given you; . . . how much more will your heavenly Father give the Holy Spirit to those who ask him!" (Luke 11:9, 13). And David prays in his penitent psalm, "Create in me a clean heart, O God, . . . and do not take your holy spirit from me" (Ps 51:11). So, although the Bible never commands people to be baptized with the Holy Spirit, it exhorts them to pray and be filled with the Spirit (e.g., Acts 4:29–31).

We also learned in chapter 3 that some Pentecostal scholars reject the common dictum of Evangelicals—"one baptism, many fillings." If Howard Ervin is right, Paul contradicts himself in Eph 5:18 by telling people whom he believes have been baptized with the Spirit to "be filled with the Spirit." Ervin contends that the baptizing and filling of the Spirit are the same, and he thereby does not seem to account for sin in the believer's life.[42]

Contrary to some assertions by John Wesley and my dear, blessed Grandmother Zarley, all Christians sin. King Solomon wrote, "There is no one on earth so righteous as to do good without ever sinning" (Eccle 7:20). When the righteous sin, they need to confess their sins to God, ask for his forgiveness, and thereby be restored to fellowship with him (1 John 1:9). Yet all along they retain his Holy Spirit (Rom 8:9).

Ervin also asserts, "The biblical pattern and provision is a state of constant fullness with the Holy Spirit." He says the present imperative of *pleroo* ("be filled") in Eph 5:18 in the Greek NT should be treated as a continuous present—"be continuously filled."[43] This exhortation is similar to Paul's "pray without ceasing" (1 Thess 5:17), and perhaps Jesus' statement, "Be perfect, therefore, as your heavenly Father is perfect" (Matt 5:48).

Ervin supports his idea of constant Spirit-filling as normality by citing the disciples who Luke describes as "full of the (Holy) Spirit" (Acts 6:3, 5;

---

42. Ervin, *Spirit Baptism*, 42–61.
43. Ibid., 45, 58–59.

11:24). But Luke likely is describing their general lifestyle instead of being full of the Spirit at every moment of their lives.

Recall that when the 120 disciples spoke in foreign languages on the day of Pentecost, some folks alleged, "They are filled with new wine" (Acts 2:13). Peter replied, "These are not drunk, as you suppose" (v. 15). Likewise, Paul compares being "filled with the Spirit" with being "drunk with wine" (Eph 5:18). As with drunkenness, so it is with Spirit-filling: when a person gets drunk, their inebriation slowly dissipates as they return to sobriety. Yet (too much?) alcohol remains available for more drinking. So it is with Spirit-filling. After a Spirit-filled experience, a believer returns to normalcy. Yet the Spirit remains available, indwelling a person for future filling.

This comparison corroborates with Jesus' saying at the Feast of Booths. He used the metaphor of drinking by saying, "Let anyone who is thirsty come to me, and let the one who believes in me drink. As the scripture has said, 'Out of the believer's heart shall flow rivers of living water" (John 7:37–38). And in his Sermon on the Mount Jesus said, "Blessed are those who hunger and thirst for righteousness, for they will be filled" (Matt 5:6).

So, being filled with the Spirit is not a constant process; rather, it is similar to hunger and thirst and then fulfilling these needs by eating and drinking. D. A. Carson explains:

> Although all true believers have received the Holy Spirit and have been baptized in the Holy Spirit, nevertheless the Holy Spirit is not necessarily poured out on each individual Christian in precisely equivalent quantities . . . there are degrees of unction, blessing, service, and holy joy, along with some more currently celebrated gifts, associated with those whose hearts have been specially touched by the sovereign God. Although I think it extremely dangerous to pursue a second blessing attested by tongues, I think it no less dangerous not to pant after God at all, and to be satisfied with a merely creedal Christianity that is kosher but complacent, orthodox but ossified, sound but soundly asleep.[44]

WHAT DOES PAUL TEACH ABOUT SPIRITUAL GIFTS, ESPECIALLY GLOSSOLALIA?

What are spiritual gifts and what are their purposes? *Spiritual gifts are extraordinary abilities God gives his people through his Spirit.* For instance,

---

44. Carson, *Showing the Spirit*, 160.

Paul's Teaching on the Holy Spirit and Spiritual Gifts

consider the gift of knowledge. All believers have some knowledge about God, but only some believers have an extraordinary knowledge of God. He gives his people such special abilities to help the church mature in Christ during this evil age and thereby be a shining light in a dark world.

I think Luke and Paul likely do not differ about the gift of *glossolalia*. Luke, as a historian, reports three incidents of *glossolalia* in his book of Acts (Acts 2:3–4, 11; 10:46; 19:6); yet therein he does not provide didactic teaching on the subject. In contrast, Paul teaches at length about *glossolalia* in 1 Corinthians 12–14.

The church at Corinth had submitted some questions to Paul that are first detected in his remark, "Now the matters about which you wrote . . . " (1 Cor 7:1). These questions are revealed in markers that follow.[45] One of them is Paul's statement, "Now concerning spiritual gifts, brothers and sisters, I do not want you to be uninformed" (1 Cor 12:1). Paul then teaches about various spiritual gifts and singles out the gift of tongues. He sometimes compares it to the gift of prophecy that he repeatedly depicts as a greater gift.

So, what does Paul mean in 1 Cor 12:10 by "various kinds of tongues?" As stated in chapter 8, scholars debate about whether or not "tongues" in such passages can mean no more than ecstatic gibberish. Obviously, "other tongues" (Gr. *heterais glossais*) in Acts 2:4 refers to human languages, which Diaspora Jews verified (vv. 5–12). But *glossolalia* in other contexts, such as in 1 Corinthians 12–14, may not refer to languages. Jannes Reiling says of tongues-speaking, "In 1 Cor 12 and 14 Paul attempts to tone down an overestimation of the phenomenon by comparing it to prophecy: speaking in tongues is an individual experience of prayer in incomprehensible words."[46] Some practitioners call it their "prayer language."

As stated above, Pentecostals sometimes cite Martyn Lloyd-Jones in support of post-conversion Spirit baptism. Yet he rightly said, "Some friends would confine this only to certain gifts of the Spirit and they say the one and only proof that we have received the Spirit is that we manifest these gifts. They would base that on 1 Corinthians 12, but that very chapter itself teaches that all do not have the same gifts, one person has one gift and one another. So we must never say unless we have one particular gift we have

---

45. E.g., 1Cor 7:10, 25; 8:1; 11:2–3, 17–20; 12:1; 15:12; 16:1.
46. Reiling, "Holy Spirit," 423.

never been baptized with the Holy Spirit or have never received the Spirit. That very chapter denies that."[47]

Also, many Pentecostal scholars regard Hermann Gunkel highly due to his keen insight about the Holy Spirit. Yet Gunkel states, "In 1 Cor. 12–14 . . . Paul disparages glossolalia, . . . it is entirely conceivable that glossolalia . . . dominated in the gatherings of the community. . . . the Corinthians incurred the apostle's displeasure. . . . the purpose of the community's coming together is the mutual edification of all its members. . . . Where this chief purpose is not achieved, grave errors exist. For that reason, whatever does not serve the community does not belong in the gathering. Because of this, Paul almost totally excludes glossolalia."[48]

So, Paul teaches in 1 Corinthians 12–14 the opposite of what most Pentecostals say—that all Christians should speak in tongues. In 1 Cor 12:4–11, Paul refers to human body parts as metaphors depicting spiritual gifts in the church, which he calls the body of Christ, as follows:

> 4Now there are varieties of gifts, but the same Spirit; 5and there are varieties of services, but the same Lord [Jesus]; 6and there are varieties of activities, but it is the same God [the Father] who activates all of them in everyone. 7To each is given the manifestation of the Spirit for the common good. 8To one is given through the Spirit the utterance of wisdom, and to another the utterance of knowledge according to the same Spirit, 9to another faith by the same Spirit, to another gifts of healing by the one Spirit, 10to another the working of miracles, to another prophecy, to another the discernment of spirits, to another various kinds of tongues, to another the interpretation of tongues. 11All these are activated by one and the same Spirit, who allots to each one individually just as the Spirit chooses.

So far in 1 Corinthians 12, Paul's main point is that God gives people different spiritual gifts by means of his Spirit. Thus, he gives a person *glossolalia*, and he gives another person the gift of wisdom. Paul adds, "For just as the body is one and has many members, and all the members of the body, though many, are one body, so it is with Christ. . . . Indeed, the body does not consist of one member but of many" (1 Cor 12:12, 14). Paul then singles out certain members of the body, such as a hand, an ear, an eye, and a foot

---

47. Lloyd-Jones, *Great Doctrines of the Bible*, 2:238. He teaches about miracles, healings, prophecy, discerning of spirits, and tongues (2:270–74). He says, "These gifts did cease after the days of the apostles" (2:270).

48. Gunkel, *The Influence of the Holy Spirit*, 85–86.

Paul's Teaching on the Holy Spirit and Spiritual Gifts

(vv. 15–21). He means that God's people do not all have the same spiritual gift or gifts, just as the human body is not one member, such as a hand.

Paul continues in 1 Cor 12:27–30, "Now you are the body of Christ and individually members of it. And God has appointed in the church first apostles, second prophets, third teachers; then deeds of power, then gifts of healing, forms of assistance, forms of leadership, various kinds of tongues. Are all apostles? Are all prophets? Are all teachers? Do all work miracles? Do all possess gifts of healing? Do all speak in tongues? Do all interpret?" Paul presents this teaching in question form with his obvious intention being that the correct answer to each question is a resounding "NO." That is, most of us are not like Billy Graham with his gift of evangelism or Oral Roberts with his gifts of healing. *Thus, neither do we all speak in tongues.* And Paul certainly would say this situation is not because God's people don't have enough faith or they all would be Billy Grahams and Oral Roberts. Rather, it is because God has decided this, just as he decided to create the human body so that it would not be only a hand.

Paul concludes this teaching by saying, "But strive for the greater gifts" (1 Cor 12:31). He says it again and adds, "especially that you may prophesy" (14:1). Paul does not mean, as some insist, that each believer should strive to possess and use all spiritual gifts. As stated earlier, that idea clashes with 1 Corinthians 12. Instead, Paul means it *corporately* since that is his context. That is, when the church meets it should strive to have the best gifts exercised most prominently since they produce the greater edification of the church.

This idea in 1 Corinthians that Paul teaches a framework for church meetings becomes increasingly evident with his repeated expression, "when you come together (as a church)" (1 Cor 11:17–18, 20, 33–34).

So, some spiritual gifts are better than others. This is evident wherein Paul lists spiritual gifts by saying, "God has appointed in the church first apostles, second prophets, third teachers" (1 Cor 12:28). Enumerating first, second, and third indicates Paul lists these gifts according to their importance, thus their usefulness. So, apostleship is the greatest gift, and prophecy is the second best gift. These gifts are "greater" than others because they bless the church the most when it comes together, building it up in faith and love. Gunkel says of Paul here, "He maintains that the better a gift serves a community the more valuable that gift is. This shows why Paul declares glossolalia to be inferior—which is clear from the position this gift assumes in his enumeration in 1 Cor. 12:8ff., 28ff."[49]

As if to make sure Paul's readers understand he knows what he is talking about, we have seen that he adds an addendum, "I speak in tongues more than all of you" (1 Cor 14:18).

Robert Menzies is typical of classical Pentecostals who say all Christians should and can speak in tongues. Yet in his chapter titled "Evidential Tongues" in his book *Empowered for Witness*, Menzies largely ignores Paul's main teaching on spiritual gifts, much of it on tongues, in 1 Corinthians 12–14. It is obvious why Menzies does so, since it opposes Pentecostals insisting all Christians should speak in tongues. Menzies only says of Paul's question, "Do all speak in tongues?" (1 Cor 12:30), that it "must be reconciled with 14.5."[50] That text says, "Now I would like all of you to speak in tongues, but even more to prophesy. One who prophesies is greater than one who speaks in tongues, unless someone interprets, so that the church may be built up." This first sentence is reminiscent of Moses wanting all of God's people to be prophets (Num 11:29). But none of this was in God's plan, nor does it fit Paul's teaching in 1 Corinthians 12.

In Menzies' *Empowered for Witness*, he pays much tribute to Gunkel and Schweizer as foremost scholars from whom he learned much about the Spirit. But Gunkel says of 1 Corinthians 12, "Paul next graphically described this thought in the glorious figure (outlined in vv. 12ff.) of the Christian community as the body of Christ, members of which all Christians have become through the gift of the Spirit in baptism."[51]

Much of Paul's teaching on tongues in 1 Corinthians 14 is self-explanatory. And contrary to some Evangelicals, I think Paul says it is proper for Christian tongues-speakers to mostly use their gift privately for self-edification, as in prayer (1 Cor 14:2).[52] So, I disagree with those who contend that spiritual gifts are not for self-edification. Yes, spiritual gifts are mostly for building up the church (vv. 3, 5, 26c); but they also are for personal edification such as encouragement (v. 4). Paul concludes concerning church services, "Do not forbid speaking in tongues" (v. 39). But he cautions that it must be done according to his guidelines just given (vv. 37–40).

---

49. Ibid., 87.
50. Menzies, *Empowered for Witness*, 248.
51. Gunkel, *The Influence of the Holy Spirit*, 89.
52. Dunn, *Jesus and the Spirit*, 231.

Paul's Teaching on the Holy Spirit and Spiritual Gifts

DOES PAUL TEACH CESSATIONISM?

Does Paul teach the cessation of *glossolalia* or any other "supernatural" or "miraculous" gifts of the Spirit? No and yes. That is, not in this age; but in the eschaton—yes.

In chapter 2, I related that early in my theological education I was taught that Paul says in 1 Cor 13:10 that the "supernatural" gifts of the Spirit—healing, miracles, prophesy, and tongues—*ceased* with the completion of the canon of Scripture, that is, the Bible. Some teach an alternative, that these ceased when all of the twelve apostles died. But the result is the same since both are believed to have occurred in the 90s, near the end of the first century. I also related that a few years after I was taught this cessationism, which came from Dallas Theological Seminary, I decided from the Bible it was wrong. Ever since, I have believed that God can give any gifts of his Spirit at any time he chooses. Thus, there is nothing in holy writ that disallows tongue-speakings in this age.

In the middle of Paul's primary teaching on spiritual gifts he pens what is often called "the love chapter," in 1 Corinthians 13. In this poetic masterpiece Paul defines true love. He says love is the greatest of all virtues, even superior to *any* spiritual gift. The latter portion of this brief treatise reads as follows in 1 Cor 13:8–13:

> 8Love never ends. But as for prophecies, they will come to an end; as for tongues, they will cease; as for knowledge, it will come to an end. 9For we know only in part, and we prophesy only in part; 10but when the complete comes, the partial will come to an end. 11When I was a child, I spoke like a child, I thought like a child, I reasoned like a child; when I became an adult, I put an end to childish ways. 12For now we see in a mirror, dimly, but then we will see face to face. Now I know only in part; then I will know fully, even as I have been fully known. 13And now faith, hope, and love abide, these three; and the greatest of these is love.

So, Paul herein teaches that there will come a time when all spiritual gifts—not just healing, prophesy, tongues, and knowledge—will cease. When? And what does Paul mean by saying, "when the complete comes, the partial will come to an end?" Everything is partial in this life. No one knows perfectly about God. No one can prophesy all about the future. That is what Paul means when he adds, "Now we see in a mirror dimly."

So, what does "the complete" (Gr. *to teleion*; "the perfect" in KJV) mean in 1 Cor 13:10? It certainly *does not* mean the completed canon of

Scripture, or the completed apostolic age, because that is not the context in which Paul is writing. "The complete" refers to the glorious kingdom of God that Jesus will bring with him at his second coming. Then Jesus' kingdom will be complete (cf. Acts 3:19–21 with Rom 11:25–27). Gordon Fee explains:

> It is 'partial' because it belongs only to this age. . . . the term 'the perfect' has to do with the Eschaton itself, not some form of perfection in the present age. It is not so much that the End itself is 'the perfect,' language that does not make tolerably good sense; rather, it is what happens at the End, when the goal has been reached . . . At the coming of Christ the final purpose of God's saving work in Christ will have been reached; at that point those gifts now necessary for the building up of the church in the present age disappear, because 'the complete' will have come. To cite Barth's marvelous imagery: '*Because* the *sun* rises all lights are extinguished.[53]

So, all spiritual gifts—special abilities to do things—will cease when Jesus returns with his kingdom since they will no longer be necessary, actually obsolete. They are partial now, but in the eschaton there won't be anything partial. For instance, no one will then have a gift of knowledge since Paul says all believers then will "know fully."

But what does Paul mean, to "see face to face," and "I will know fully, even as I have been fully known"? For the answer, we can appeal again to none better than Assemblies of God member Gordon Fee as we come to the end of this chapter about Paul's teaching on the Holy Spirit and spiritual gifts:

> What is not clear is the exact nuance of the final clause that expresses the nature of that final knowing, "even as I am fully known." . . . God's knowledge of us is immediate—full and direct, "face to face," as it were; at the Eschaton, Paul seems to be saying, we too shall know in this way, with no more need for the kinds of mediation that the mirror illustrates or that "prophecy" and the "utterance of knowledge" exemplify in reality. . . . Most likely the purpose of all this is simply to reinforce what was said in vv. 1–3, that the Corinthians' emphasis on tongues as evidence for spirituality is wrong because it is wrongheaded, especially from people who do not otherwise exhibit the one truly essential expression of the Spirit's presence, Christian love. Good as spiritual gifts are, they are only for the present; Christian love, which the

---

53. Fee, *The First Epistle to the Corinthians*, 645–46. Emphasis his.

Corinthians currently lack, is the "more excellent way" in part because it belongs to eternity as well as to the present.[54]

---

54. Ibid., 648–49.

CHAPTER 11

Roman Catholicism

Although this book is about Peter's kingdom keys and whether or not Pentecostals rightly assert that Spirit baptism occurs after conversion, it would be remiss not to briefly address what Roman Catholics say about it. They constitute half of all 2.4 billion professing Christians in the world, and these two subjects are very important to them. And Catholics agree with Pentecostals about post-conversion Spirit baptism. One of their sacraments has been about this teaching long before Pentecostalism existed. Dunn presents a good, brief history about the development of the relationship of conversion and Spirit baptism in Christian theology as follows:

> Within Christianity down through the centuries there has always been a strain of teaching which holds that salvation, so far as it may be known in this life, is experienced in two stages: first the event of becoming a Christian; then, as a later and distinct event, some special and distinctive operation or gift of the Holy Spirit. In the history of Christian thought this disjointedness was first clearly formulated in the Catholic sacraments of Baptism and Confirmation. According to A. J. Macdonald, the idea that Confirmation confers the gift of the Spirit was held without question until the time of Wyclif. And today in anglo-catholic tradition, although the episcopal laying on of hands is commonly thought of as bestowing a strengthening gift of the Spirit, some continue to speak as though the Spirit is first received at that time. Indeed, since the question was reopened by F. W. Puller in 1880, it has been regularly argued, often with great weight, though not infrequently

Roman Catholicism

with greater ingenuity, that far greater significance (in terms of the Spirit) should be attributed to Confirmation than to Baptism.

With the Reformation's rejection of Confirmation as a sacrament and its switch in emphasis from sacraments to preaching and Scripture, the two-stage view of salvation disappeared below the surface for a time. It began to emerge again with the Puritans, some of whom believed that the experience of assurance was a second and subsequent work of the Spirit in the Christian. But it was John Wesley who raised it again to doctrinal status. In Wesley's view, what the Christian initially received was only justification and partial sanctification, a change primarily in his *relations* with God. Only as a distinct and subsequent experience did he receive the divine gift of entire sanctification or Christian perfection, a change primarily in *himself*.

A direct line of influence can be drawn from Puritan teaching on the Spirit through early Methodism to the nineteenth-century Holiness Movement with its "Higher Life" teaching in which justification by faith (deliverance from the *penalty* of sin) was distinguished from the second divine work of sanctification, also received by faith (deliverance from the *power* of sin).[1]

Dunn adds, "It was the Holiness Movement which brought belief in Spirit-baptism into prominence as a distinct doctrine." He provides more history of this movement, mentioning the Church of the Nazarene, and then states, "It was directly from this context that Pentecostalism sprang." Dunn then provides some history about Pentecostalism and concludes, "On the negative side, one must reject the Pentecostal attempt to split the converting-initiating work of the Spirit into two neatly distinct stages. Of course, as we have seen, they are not alone in this; a high doctrine of Confirmation results in a very similar disjointedness. It is presumably because they [Pentecostals] hold such a doctrine that not a few Roman and anglo-Catholics have found the Pentecostal doctrine of Spirit-baptism so congenial."[2] This congeniality has allowed the Charismatic Movement to have a profound impact on the Roman Catholic Church, resulting in decades of dialogue between their leaders.

Forty years after *Baptism*, Dunn refers to this anglo-Roman Catholic agreement as "the other debate in which *Baptism* was engaged with the more sacramentalist traditions of mainstream Christianity. But that's

---

1. Dunn, *The Christ and the Spirit*, 81–82. Emphasis his. This excerpt was first published in "Spirit-Baptism and Pentecostalism," 397–407.

2. Ibid., 83, 84, 88.

another story and another debate for another day, which I continue to await, though with fading anticipation!"[3]

Due to this history, in this chapter we will first examine briefly the Roman Catholic Church's sacraments of Baptism and Confirmation as it relates to Spirit baptism. Then we will turn our attention to the Church's core teaching on how Peter's kingdom keys are the foundation of its doctrine of the papacy.

BAPTISM

Until recently, if you asked Roman Catholics how to become a Christian they usually replied, "be baptized in the Catholic Church." If you asked about being "born again," informed Catholics said, "that's baptism." They meant water baptism.

The Roman Catholic Church teaches that when Jesus told Nicodemus he needed to be "born again . . . of water and the Spirit" (John 3:3, 5 NIV), he meant water baptism imparts spiritual life to the soul. So, Roman Catholics understand the reception of salvation as conversion-initiation into their church by means of water baptism. This teaching is called "baptismal regeneration," and Roman Catholics are not the only Christians who believe in it.

In chapter 2, I related that in my youth I became a born again Christian at age thirteen, not by being water baptized but by believing in Jesus as my Lord and Savior.[4] Five years later, when I went to college in Houston at age eighteen, for the first time I began to learn the Bible theologically and grow spiritually in my Christian life. But my church pastor de-emphasized water baptism even though he baptized congregants. He was reacting to the three largest church denominations in Texas. Southern Baptists often bragged about how many people they baptized, and the Church of Christ and the Roman Catholic Church espoused baptismal regeneration, which my pastor strongly rejected.

Consequently, it was not until I was about thirty-five years old that I became convinced from reading the Bible that I needed to, and wanted

---

3. Dunn, "Baptism in the Holy Spirit: Yet Once More—Again," 43. Also in Dunn, *Baptism in the Holy Spirit*, 2nd ed., xviii.

4. John 3:3–15 indicates all genuine Christians are "born again" whether they know it or not. Thus, "born again Christian" is a redundancy. But it is useful terminology due to belief in baptismal regeneration.

to, be water baptized. I had co-founded the PGA Tour Bible Study eleven years prior and was by this time its senior leader. I told fellow believers in our group about this recent conviction of mine and that I wanted to be baptized with our fellowship present rather than at home in my church in metro-Houston. It was because the pro golfers and their wives in our study group were my closest Christian friends.

The PGA Tour Bible Study had never had a baptism, though occasionally we had conducted a communion service. So, during the Bob Hope Dessert Classic in Palm Springs, California, fellow Tour player Rik Massengale, his wife Cindy, and I were baptized in a swimming pool at a private home where our fellowship met that week. Jim Hiskey and Mike Smith baptized us. Thus, *I was water baptized for the first time twenty-two years after I became a born again Christian.* Since then, I have believed it is proper for Christian converts to soon be baptized as a testimony to their new life of faith in their Lord and Savior Jesus Christ.

Some readers might question if I was a genuine Christian all of that time before I was water baptized. Believe me, if you knew me well when I was in my twenties and early thirties, you wouldn't have thought that.

Now, as I stated previously, Peter's proclamation in Acts 2:38 is very important for Christian theology. I explained earlier that baptismal regeneration means people become Christians by God forgiving them of their sins as they are water baptized. But I think, as do most Evangelicals and all Pentecostals, that Peter meant water baptism in that text *only as a symbol* of a person's inner repentance and faith in having his or her sins metaphorically washed away by believing in Jesus' atoning death for those sins.

Soon after that blessed day of Pentecost, Peter preached his next sermon in Acts without mentioning water baptism. He said, "Repent therefore, and turn to God so that your sins may be wiped out" (Acts 3:19). Why didn't Peter mention baptism if that's how people are saved?

Furthermore, right after Peter preached to Gentiles in Acts 10, and they simultaneously were saved, he went to Jerusalem to defend his association with them. He related to his fellow Jewish apostles that an angel had told Cornelius, "Send to Joppa and bring Simon, who is called Peter; he will give you a message by which you and your entire household will be saved" (Acts 11:13–14). So, believing in Peter's message was enough for them to be saved.

Requiring people to be water baptized to be saved does not seem to me to be of grace (cf. Eph 2:8–9). And I think proclaiming baptismal regeneration can be compared to those Pharisaic believers who caused dissention at the first apostolic church council at Jerusalem by declaring of Cornelius and those other Gentile men, "Unless you are circumcised according to the custom of Moses, you cannot be saved" (Acts 15:1, cf. v. 5). Peter then explained that when the Cornelius household believed his message, God was "cleansing their hearts by faith" (Acts 15:9). Peter meant that those men didn't need to be circumcised to be saved, and again, neither did he mention water baptism as if it was necessary to be saved.

John the Baptist did not recognize his rite of water baptism as any more than an outward symbol of inner penitence. He commanded the baptizand, "Bear fruits worthy of repentance. . . . Every tree therefore that does not bear good fruit is cut down and thrown into the fire" (Matt 3:8, 10; Luke 3:8–9). Similarly, the primary mark of a Christian is not water baptism but confession of Jesus as Savior and Lord and living a life that demonstrates it. Circumcision for Jewish men and water baptism for Christians were intended as outer signs of inner, saving faith.

If Peter meant baptismal regeneration in Acts 2:38, it raises a serious question about him, the twelve, and the rest of the 120 disciples. Why doesn't the NT ever say they were water baptized as Christians? John likely baptized some of them, but that wasn't Christian baptism.

Luke later relates that when Paul and Silas were in jail in Philippi, the jailer asked them, "'Sirs, what must I do to be saved?' They answered, 'Believe on the Lord Jesus, and you will be saved, you and your household'" (Acts 16:30–31). Though Luke says, "He and his entire family were baptized without delay" (v. 33), Luke gives no indication it saved them.

If Paul believed in baptismal regeneration, he was a sorry evangelist who hardly saved anyone! Why? He wrote to the church at Corinth, "I thank God that I baptized none of you except Crispus and Gaius" (1 Cor 1:14). In saying this, Paul obviously didn't believe people were saved by believing in Jesus plus being water baptized. Instead, Paul said, "Christ did not send me to baptize but to proclaim the gospel" (v. 17). In his speeches in Acts and his NT letters, Paul never says people must be baptized to be forgiven of their sins, saved, or justified.

CONFIRMATION

Some of the most perplexing soteriological problems in church history have concerned the relation of initial faith in Jesus with water baptism,

Roman Catholicism

Spirit baptism, and what the church came to call "confirmation." In the second and third centuries, church fathers taught baptismal regeneration and Spirit reception at water baptism.

By the fifth century in the West, Catholic Church officials began to separate the rite of water baptism from a post-baptismal ceremony for new church members. In this new rite, a bishop would lay his hands on a recipient or multiple recipients as "confirmation" of their previous water baptism and recognition of their reception of the Holy Spirit at that time. This separation occurred partly due to infant baptism, in which those baptized as infants could in adulthood confirm their faith in a separate rite. This ritual is still one of the three "sacraments" of initiation into the Roman Catholic Church, and it is called Confirmation. Those three sacraments are Baptism, Confirmation, and First Communion. Eastern Orthodox churches also practice Confirmation, but they combine it with Baptism in a single ceremony. And in the Roman Catholic Church, Confirmation follows Baptism with an intervening educational program for both children and adults called Catechism. After Catechism, and at the conclusion of Confirmation, Roman Catholic recipients partake of their First Communion.

For many centuries, the Roman Catholic Church has observed a total of seven sacraments. These are in the following order of importance: Baptism, Confirmation, Holy Communion, Confession, Marriage, Holy Orders, and the Anointing of the Sick. When the Protestant Reformation began in the early sixteenth century, it insisted that there were only two sacraments: Baptism and Communion.

How is Roman Catholic Confirmation practiced today? A bishop prepares this ritual by consecrating some aromatic oil by means of prayer. Next, he or a priest begins the Confirmation ceremony by typically delivering a brief homily. Then the bishop lays his hands on each candidate separately, utters the recipient's name, and says, "Receive the gift of the Holy Spirit." He may add, "Be sealed with the Holy Spirit." He then dips his finger in the oil and touches the candidate's forehead with it or pours the oil on his or her forehead. The bishop or priest then concludes the ceremony with the sign of the cross and pronounces a blessing on the recipient(s).

The Catholic Church teaches that in Confirmation recipients receive, that is, are baptized with, the Holy Spirit to strengthen them in faith, spiritually safeguard them in the future, and prepare them for service and mission. The *New Catholic Encyclopedia* states, "Confirmation is a gift of the Holy Spirit that orients the baptized toward mission."[5] Catholics are not considered fully initiated into the Church until they have undergone Confirmation.

So, Catholic officials describe Confirmation as "the descent of the Holy Spirit." They equate it with the four episodes of Spirit baptism in Acts that we have examined. But they cite primarily Acts 8:14–17 and 19:5–6. Recall that Peter and John, and later Paul, laid hands on people and they immediately received the Spirit days or years *after* they were water baptized. In contrast, we learned of the Cornelius household that "the Holy Spirit fell upon all who heard the word," and they were "baptized in the name of Jesus Christ" (Acts 10:44, 48). Since it was apostles who did the laying on of hands in Acts 8:17 and 19:6, the Roman Catholic Church used to insist that this rite must be administered by one of its bishops as a supposed successor of the twelve apostles. But in recent times, the Church has done as Eastern Orthodox churches do by allowing priests to perform Confirmation. Thus, all Catholics, both East and West, believe that only the episcopate can impart the Holy Spirit by the imposition of hands.

The Roman Catholic Church cites church fathers distinguishing Confirmation and Baptism by defining them differently. In contrast, G. W. H. Lampe claims, "The Fathers had no consistent doctrine on the matter. . . . It is extremely difficult for any of the Fathers to define by what means the Christian enters into the possession of the Spirit."[6]

The Catholic Church hails Thomas Aquinas as the best post-apostolic theologian. He says, "So therefore does man receive spiritual life in Baptism, which is a spiritual regeneration: while in Confirmation man arrives at the perfect age, as it were, of spiritual life. Hence Pope Melchiades: 'The Holy Ghost, Who comes down on the waters of Baptism bearing salvation in His flight, bestows at the font, the fullness of innocence; but in Confirmation He confers an increase of grace. In Baptism we are born again unto life; after Baptism we are strengthened.'"[7]

Yet Lampe says again of earlier church history, "The Apostolic Fathers and the Apologists have little to say about the doctrine of Baptism in relation to the Spirit." And he alleges "a deep theological confusion which has persisted down through the centuries" as to whether or not Confirmation should be a separate sacrament from Baptism and to which of these two

---

5. *NCE*, 4:90.

6. Lampe, *The Seal of the Spirit*, ix, 193.

7. Thomas Aquinas, *Summa Theologica*, III, q. 72, Art. 1.

Roman Catholicism

concepts belongs union with Christ and the sealing of the Spirit, both taught by Paul.[8] Also, Lampe objects to his own Anglican Church in modern times practicing Baptism and Confirmation separately as do Roman Catholics.

Paul wrote to the Corinthians, "It is God who establishes us with you in Christ and has anointed us, by putting his seal on us and giving us his Spirit" (2 Cor 1:21–22). He wrote to the Ephesians, "When you had heard the word of truth, the gospel of your salvation, and had believed in him, were marked with the seal of the promised Holy Spirit" (Eph 1:13). Paul adds, "the Holy Spirit of God, with which you were marked with a seal for the day of redemption" (4:30).

Contrary to Roman Catholics, Dunn is right in saying of these texts, "It was when they believed that God sealed them with the Spirit." And Jimmy accuses some Pentecostals of "a fundamental misunderstanding of Greek grammar" in their claim that subsequence is supported in the KJV of Eph 1:13 which reads, "After that ye believed, ye were sealed with that Holy Spirit."[9] Like Dunn, modern versions place the sealing at initial faith.

Thus, Roman Catholic sacraments of Baptism and Confirmation establish a subsequence similar to that claimed by Pentecostals. The Anglican Church makes a similar claim since it practices Baptism and Confirmation as separate rites, too. F. D. Bruner observes that there "is the exact parallel between the high-liturgical and the popular-experiential doctrines of the Holy Spirit as represented respectively in a type of Anglo-Catholicism and in Pentecostalism."[10] Recall that Dunn likewise says that "Acts 8" has been "long the chief stronghold of Pentecostal (baptism in the Spirit) and Catholic (Confirmation) alike."[11]

Contemporary church historians claim that this commonality about subsequence between Roman Catholics and Pentecostals was an important factor in the rise of the Charismatic movement within the Catholic Church. This agreement led Dr. Howard Ervin of Oral Roberts University to become the leading Pentecostal pioneer in Roman Catholic-Pentecostal dialogue. That is why some Pentecostals called him "the father of Catholic Charismatics."

---

8. Lampe, *The Seal of the Spirit*, 103. In Paul, see especially 2 Cor 1:21–22; Eph 1:13–14; 4:30.

9. Dunn, *Baptism in the Holy Spirit*, 158–59.

10. Bruner, *A Theology of the Holy Spirit*, 187.

11. Dunn, *Baptism in the Holy Spirit*, 55.

SOLVING THE SAMARITAN RIDDLE

DOES CONVERSION-INITIATION MEAN BAPTISMAL REGENERATION?

I related in chapter 3 that in Dunn's *Baptism* he equates salvation with his coined term "conversion-initiation." He explains "conversion" as the "inner transformation" and "initiation" as "the ritual, external acts" such as water baptism. He concludes, "The total event of becoming a Christian embraces both 'conversion' and 'initiation.'" He says of this term, "My sole purpose here is clarity of thought."[12] He doesn't achieve it for me. Jimmy even has a chapter in *Baptism* entitled "Conversion-Initiation in the Acts of the Apostles."

Howard Ervin soon became Dunn's primary Pentecostal antagonist. Ervin authored a book, *Conversion-Initiation and the Baptism in the Holy Spirit*, in which he attempts to rebut Dunn's *Baptism* book. Ervin refers to Dunn's "conversion-initiation" term as the name of Jimmy's entire "hypothesis" in *Baptism*.

Does Dunn believe, as Anglo-Catholics do, in baptismal regeneration? This question touches on "the other debate" he awaits "with fading anticipation." Earlier in his *Baptism*, he seems to treat water baptism only as a symbol and thereby disavow baptismal regeneration. He explains, "Man's act in conversion is to repent, to turn and to believe. . . . Baptism gives expression to faith, but without faith baptism is meaningless, an empty symbol. It is false to say that water-baptism conveys, confers or effects forgiveness of sins. . . . receiving forgiveness" occurs due to "repentance or faith as the sole prerequisite. . . . In other words, water-baptism is neither the sole preliminary nor in itself an essential preliminary to receiving forgiveness."[13]

Most Evangelicals and all Pentecostals would agree wholeheartedly with this. They equate God's initial forgiveness of sins with conversion-salvation and insist that subsequent water baptism is a symbol of salvation that has no saving efficacy. Yet Dunn, a moderate Evangelical, also says in *Baptism*, "Baptism was the necessary expression of commitment, without which they could not be said to have truly 'believed.'" He later adds, "The popular idea that conversion precedes baptism, and that baptism is a confession of a commitment made some time previously is not to be found in

---

12. Ibid., 7.
13. Ibid., 96–97.

the NT."[14] Here, Jimmy seems very close to endorsing baptismal regeneration. He continues,

> The second mistake of the Pentecostal is that he has followed the Protestant in his separation of faith from water-baptism. Conversion is for him Spirit-engendered faith reaching out to "receive or accept Jesus," so that a man is a Christian before his water-baptism and the latter is little more than a confession of a past commitment. This may well accord with present Baptist practice, but it is not the NT pattern. . . . putting the act of faith prior to baptism, thereby reducing baptism to mere symbol, . . . Baptism properly performed is for the NT essentially the act of faith and repentance—the actualization of saving faith without which, usually, commitment to Jesus as Lord does not come to its necessary expression. As the Spirit is the vehicle of saving grace, so baptism is the vehicle of saving faith.[15]

In chapter 2 and here, I have related my conversion and water baptism experience, and they conflict with what Dunn says here. Yet he qualifies this statement with the word "usually."

Jimmy seems to have maintained this later viewpoint in some subsequent writings. For instance, he says of Paul's teaching, "Justification is the effect of baptism; the means of union with Christ is baptism."[16] Most Evangelicals and Pentecostals would question this. For they contend that Paul says God justifies people and simultaneously unites them with Jesus Christ when they believe in him, not when they are water baptized. Paul says essentially three times in Rom 3:26–30 that "a person is justified by faith" (v. 28; cf. 5:1; Gal 2:16).

Dunn, however, gives his most thorough treatment of the relation between water baptism and faith in his book *Unity and Diversity in the New Testament*. In ten pages he seems to clarify his position by describing water baptism seven times as the "expression/expressing" of faith.[17] He says plainly and no more therein, "Baptism was an *expression of repentance and faith*."[18]

---

14. Ibid., 96, 214.
15. Ibid., 226–27.
16. Dunn, *The Theology of Paul the Apostle*, 443.
17. Dunn, *Unity and Diversity in the New Testament*, 2nd ed., 155–61.
18. Ibid., 155. Emphasis his.

THE PAPACY

Catholic officials credit church father Cyprian as the first to attribute principal authority in the Church to all of its bishops, thus not only the bishop of Rome. The Church has called this structure "apostolic succession." The bishop at Rome eventually was recognized as the supreme "father" among the other bishops. He was called "pope" since the Latin word for "father" is *papa*, from which Catholics get their term "papacy." The Church says of this hierarchical authority of the papacy that *the pope is to the bishops what Jesus was to his apostles.*

The Catholic Church founded its papacy dogma primarily on two Scriptures, both of them sayings of Jesus. The primary one is Matt 16:19, wherein Jesus promised to give Peter "the keys of the kingdom of heaven." The other text is John 21:15–17, in which the risen Jesus told Peter three times in slightly varied forms, "feed my sheep." So, the Church says the pope is Peter's successor and that he has the primary teaching authority in the Church.

Catholic officials also have reasoned that if the gates of Hell are not to prevail against the Church, as Jesus says in Matt 16:18, it must have a system of authority to protect it from error, that is, from false doctrine. So, *for Roman Catholics, submission to their hierarchical system of authority is submission to Jesus Christ.*[19]

Interestingly, the Roman Catholic Church's papacy dogma was never prominent until right before and during the Protestant Reformation. Ulrich Luz relates that it can be traced back to as early as the third century CE. Yet he further informs:

> Occurrences in the 4th and 5th centuries are sparse. . . . Karlfried Frohlich surmises that throughout the Middle Ages the interpretation of Matt. 16:17–19 in terms of the Pope was extremely rare and was almost exclusively found in legal texts whose sole purpose was to legitimate papal authority against the Eastern patriarchs or the Emperor. It was thus an instrument used to legitimate power. My examination of numerous medieval commentaries confirms this. Thomas Aquinas is one of the very few who even mentions this interpretation, as one possibility among others. In Catholic exegesis it came to the fore in the 16th century, when Catholics had to resist Protestants laying claim to the traditional interpretations.

---

19. Pelikan, *The Riddle of Roman Catholicism*, 80–81.

Indirectly, the triumph of the hitherto quite marginal "papal" interpretation of Matt. 16:18 is a product of the Reformation.[20]

In 1869–1870, the Roman Catholic Church held a council it called Vatican I. It produced a document entitled "First dogmatic constitution on the church of Christ." This official statement repeatedly pronounces anathema (curse) upon those who disagree with any of its declarations. Session 4 of this document consists of four chapters that define the Church's dogma of papal infallibity. An introduction says Jesus "set blessed Peter over the rest of the apostles and instituted in him the permanent principle . . . apostolic primacy." Chapter excerpts in this document are as follows under titles that I have slightly edited for simplicity and clarity, yet italics in these excerpts are not mine:

> Chapter 1: Apostolic Primacy of Peter: We teach and declare that, according to the gospel evidence, a primacy of jurisdiction over the whole church of God was immediately and directly promised to the blessed apostle Peter and conferred on him by Christ the lord. . . . saying: *Feed my lambs, feed my sheep.* . . . Therefore, if anyone says that blessed Peter the apostle was not appointed . . . visible head of the whole church militant; . . . let him be anathema.
>
> Chapter 2: Permanence of Peter's Primacy: That which our lord Jesus Christ, . . . established in the blessed apostle Peter, . . . must of necessity remain for ever, . . . the holy and most blessed Peter, prince and head of the apostles, . . . received the keys of the kingdom from our lord Jesus Christ, . . . Therefore whoever succeeds to the chair of Peter obtains, . . . the primacy of Peter over the whole church. . . . Therefore, if anyone says that it is not by the institution of Christ . . . that blessed Peter should have perpetual successors in the primacy over the whole church; or that the Roman pontiff is not the successor of blessed Peter in this primacy: let him be anathema.
>
> Chapter 3: Apostolic Succession of the Papacy: the Roman pontiff is the successor of blessed Peter, the prince of the apostles, true vicar of Christ, head of the whole church and father and teacher of all christian people. . . . to tend, rule and govern the universal church. . . . the Roman church possesses a pre-eminence of ordinary power over every other church, . . . if anyone says that the Roman pontiff has merely an office of supervision and guidance, and not the supreme power of jurisdiction over the whole church, . . . let him be anathema.

---

20. Luz, *Studies in Matthew*, 168–69.

> Chapter 4: Infallible Teaching Authority of the Papacy: The apostolic primacy which the Roman pontiff possesses as successor of Peter, the prince of the apostles, includes also the supreme power of teaching.... The Roman pontiff is the true vicar of Christ, the head of the whole church, ... this see of St Peter always remains unblemished by any error, in accordance with the divine promise of our Lord and Savior to the prince of his disciples: *I have prayed for you that your faith may not fail; and when you have turned again, strengthen your brethren.* ... This gift of truth and never-failing faith was therefore divinely conferred on Peter and his successors in this see ... We teach and define as a divinely revealed dogma that when the Roman pontiff speaks *ex cathedra*, ... he possesses ... that infallibility ... in defining doctrine concerning faith and morals.... So then, should anyone, which God forbid, have the temerity to reject this definition of ours: let him be anathema.

Vatican II was held in 1962-1965, and it issued a series of extensive documents entitled "Constitutions," "Declarations," and "Decrees." It declares, "Whosoever, therefore, knowing that the Catholic Church was made necessary by God through Jesus Christ, would refuse to enter her or to remain in her could not be saved (Ad Gentes 7)." Its *Dogmatic Constitution on the Church* includes the following excerpts:

> This Sacred Council, following closely in the footsteps of the First Vatican Council, with that Council teaches and declares that Jesus Christ, the eternal Shepherd, established His holy Church, having sent forth the apostles as He Himself had been sent by the Father (Jn. 20:21); and He willed that their successors, namely the bishops, should be shepherds in His Church even to the consummation of the world. And in order that the episcopate itself might be one and undivided, He placed Blessed Peter over the other apostles, and instituted in him a permanent and visible source and foundation of unity of faith and communion.... And just as the office granted individually to Peter, the first among the apostles, is permanent and is to be transmitted to his successors, so also the apostles' office of nurturing the Church is permanent, and is to be exercised without interruption by the sacred order of bishops.... This power can be exercised only with the consent of the Roman Pontiff. For our Lord placed Simon *alone* as the rock and the bearer of the keys of the Church (Mt. 16:18–19), and made him shepherd of the whole flock (cf. Jn. 21:15 ff); it is evident, however, that the power of binding and loosing, which was given to Peter (Mt. 16:19), was granted also to the college of apostles, joined with their head (Mt.

18:18; 28:16–20).... The Roman Pontiff, as the successor of Peter, is the perpetual and visible principle and foundation of unity of both the bishops and of the faithful.

So, the Roman Catholic Church claims Peter was the visible head of the Church and that his office, signified by his keys, is "permanent" and transferred to his successors, namely, the Roman pontiffs. The above quotations from these important Church documents show that the Church still holds to the following declarations: (1) Peter was the first pope because Jesus gave him the keys of the kingdom, (2) these keys represent metaphorically Peter's Church office of teaching authority which is supreme and permanent, and (3) this authority is passed down to Peter's successors in the Church, namely, the popes. The Church deems the present Pope Francis the 266th "successor of St. Peter" and "vicar of Christ." And Vatican I says three times that the pope is the "head of the whole church."

On the contrary, what Jesus said to Peter in Matt 16:19 and John 21:15–17 *does not* mean that Jesus gave Peter a supreme authority in the church to be transferred to others in succeeding generations. Luke has several episodes in Acts about Peter preaching, and three times the Holy Spirit came upon new disciples in Peter's presence, yet Peter is not mentioned in the remainder of the book, that is, in Acts 16–28. This silence suggests that Peter had finished using his keys to initially open kingdom doors that resulted in the Spirit's empowerment of those believers. If so, *Peter's keys of the kingdom of heaven were not permanent but temporary.*

Many Evangelical commentators agree. D. A. Carson well explains about Matt 16:17–19, "The text says nothing about Peter's successors, infallibility, or exclusive authority. These later interpretations entail insuperable exegetical and historical problems—e.g., after Peter's death, his 'successor' would have authority over a surviving apostle, John. What the NT does show is that Peter is the first to make this formal confession and that his prominence continues in the earliest years of the church (Acts 1–12)."[21]

A portion of Michael J. Wilkins' comment about Matt 16:19 is worth repeating here. He states, "All that is directed to Peter is temporarily limited to his lifetime. It is therefore right for us to give due regard to this blessed apostle as one used in a special way in opening the doors of the kingdom of God and in the establishment of the church. But nowhere does Jesus indicate that Peter will play a perpetual role through successors."[22]

---

21. Carson, *Matthew*, 368.
22. Wilkins, *Matthew*, 580.

Craig L. Blomberg further elaborates regarding Matt 16:19, "Peter's primacy is more chronological, in the unfolding events of early Christianity, than hierarchical. . . . At any rate, there is obviously nothing in these verses of the distinctively Catholic doctrines of the papacy, apostolic succession, or Petrine infallibility."[23]

PAPAL COAT OF ARMS

During the Middle Ages, European militaries developed artistic insignia that soldiers painted on their shields to herald their identity. Called "heraldry," their designs could include crossed swords with some background, such as a warrior's helmet. Some families and secular organizations afterwards took up this practice, developing their own colored insignia as a badge worn on clothing and called "coat of arms."

Eventually, Catholic Church bishops created their own insignia, calling it "ecclesiastical heraldry." These included a "papal coat of arms." It typically portrays two crossed keys depicting Peter's kingdom keys and indicating the Church's doctrine of the papacy. So, these crossed keys replaced the crossed swords of secular heraldry; a crown symbolizing papal authority and worn by the pope replaced the helmet of warriors; a cross on top of the crown referred to Jesus' cross. Its highest position on the insignia meant that Jesus is the head of the Church.

Similarly, Peter is often portrayed in Roman Catholic and Eastern Orthodox art as holding a key or a set of keys. And since the sixteenth century, each pope at death has been buried with a set of keys signifying this imagery. A Roman Catholic document says of Peter, "Behold he received the keys of the kingdom of heaven, the power of binding and loosing is committed to him, the care of the whole Church and its government is given to him."[24]

HOW MANY KEYS DID JESUS GIVE PETER?

Luke's book of Acts seems to indicate that Jesus gave Peter three keys of the kingdom of heaven. For we have seen in Acts that Peter opened three kingdom doors for the Bible's three divisions of humanity: Jews in Acts 2,

---

23. Blomberg, *Matthew*, 255–56.
24. Epist., lib, V, ep. Xx, in P.L., LXXVII, 745

Roman Catholicism

Samaritans in Acts 8, and Gentiles in Acts 10. It appears that those doors stay open and Peter's mission is finished. If true, the Roman Catholic Church's assertion that Peter's kingdom keys are permanent is incorrect.

Furthermore, Peter opening three kingdom doors may relate to three incidents: (1) Jesus' prediction that Peter would deny him three times, (2) Peter's three denials, and (3) the three times Jesus spiritually restored Peter. Regarding the third episode, the NT relates that the risen Jesus appeared to his disciples about ten times over a period of forty days before he ascended to heaven. One of these times was when seven of Jesus' disciples returned briefly to Galilee after their Lord's death and resurrection, and one night they went fishing on Lake Tiberias/Galilee (John 21:1–3). At daybreak, and while still in the boat, they saw Jesus on the shore without recognizing him. He shouted to them to cast their net on the other side of the boat. When they did, they caught a net full of fish. Upon realizing it was Jesus, they rushed ashore and ate breakfast with him. Then "Jesus said to Simon Peter, 'Simon son of John, do you love me more than these?'" (John 21:15). What did Jesus mean by the word "these?"

Some scholars claim the word "these" in John 21:15 refers to the fish. That implies Peter was discouraged and thinking of returning to his previous life as a commercial fisherman. But this word more likely refers to *why* Peter denied Jesus three times during the night of his arrest. Earlier that night, Jesus said to his disciples, "'You will all become deserters because of me this night;' . . . Peter said to him, 'Though all become deserters because of you, I will never desert you.' Jesus said to him, 'Truly I tell you, this very night, before the cock crows, you will deny me three times.' Peter said to him, 'Even though I must die with you, I will not deny you'" (Matt 26:31, 33–35). So, God tested Peter since he boasted he was stronger in faith and love toward Jesus than his fellow apostles were. On that seemingly fateful night, Peter denied Jesus three times and immediately wept bitterly as he recalled Jesus' prediction (Matt 26:75 par.).

The later dialogue between the risen Jesus and Peter in John 21:15–19 is as follows:

> 15When they had finished breakfast, Jesus said to Simon Peter, "Simon son of John, do you love me more than these?" He said to him, "Yes, Lord; you know that I love you." Jesus said to him, "Feed my lambs." 16A second time he said to him, "Simon son of John, do you love me?" He said to him, "Yes, Lord; you know that I love you." Jesus said to him, "Tend my sheep." 17He said to him the third time, "Simon son of John, do you love me?" Peter

> felt hurt because he said to him the third time, "Do you love me?" And he said to him, "Lord, you know everything; you know that I love you." Jesus said to him, "Feed my sheep. 18Very truly, I tell you, when you were younger, you used to fasten your own belt and to go wherever you wished. But when you grow old, you will stretch out your hands, and someone else will fasten a belt around you and take you where you do not wish to go." 19(He said this to indicate the kind of death by which he would glorify God.) After this he said to him, "Follow me."

When Jesus asked Peter three times if he loved him, he likely did it to cause Peter to recall three things: (1) Jesus' prediction that Peter would deny him three times, (3) Peter's boastful reply that he would not, implying he loved Jesus more than his fellow apostles did, and (2) Peter's three denials. So, John 21:17 says "Peter felt hurt" because he was convicted by it.

It is difficult to tell what Jesus meant by his word "these" in John 21:15, whether the other disciples or the fish. If the disciples, that would seem to encourage rivalry which conflicts with Jesus' words, "what is that to you" (v. 22), and his earlier rebukes about this (Mark 9:33–37; 10:41–45 par.). If the fish or tackle, Jesus would have been dissuading Peter from returning to his fishing occupation and challenging him to become fishers of men. Regardless, Jesus surely questioned Peter in order to forgive him and restore him to spiritual health. Then Jesus predicted the manner Peter would glorify God in death. Tradition says the Roman state executed Peter, probably in CE 67, for not renouncing his Christian faith. Tradition also says Peter was crucified upside down upon request.

So, what do Peter's three denials and his three-fold spiritual restoration have to do with the number of his kingdom keys? My speculative answer is that Jesus may have predicted Peter's three denials, not some other number, since he would subsequently use three metaphorical keys to do the exact opposite by opening three doors to the kingdom for people to enter and for Jesus to baptize them in the Holy Spirit by means of Peter's presence. If this connection is correct, it seems to be more evidence that Peter's kingdom keys were not permanent, but temporary.

CHAPTER 12

Conclusions

SUMMARIZING SPIRIT BAPTISM IN LUKE'S BOOK OF ACTS

This final chapter consists of review, tying up loose ends, and offering some conclusions.

We have examined all four episodes that Luke narrates in his book of Acts about being baptized with/in the Holy Spirit that are recorded in Acts 2, 8, 10, and 19. And we have learned that Luke uses various expressions to describe this Spirit baptism, which are as follows:

- "You will be baptized with the Holy Spirit" (Acts 1:5; 11:16)
- "You will receive power when the Holy Spirit has come upon you" (Acts 1:8)
- "(They might/may) receive(d) the Holy Spirit" (Acts 8:15, 17, 19; 10:47; 19:2; cf. 2:38)
- "Giving them the Holy Spirit" (Acts 15:8)
- "The Holy Spirit fell upon all who heard the word" (Acts 10:44)
- "The Holy Spirit fell upon them just as it had upon us at the beginning" (Acts 11:15)
- "(Receive) the gift of the Holy Spirit" (Acts 2:38; 10:45; cf. 8:20; 11:17)

- "The promise of the Holy Spirit" (Acts 2:33; cf. 1:4; 2:39)

It was concluded that all of these expressions mean the same thing—being baptized in/with the Holy Spirit.

One of the main things we have learned is that *Luke's book of Acts provides no uniform relationship between conversion and Spirit baptism*. And after Peter finished his role in using kingdom keys, in Acts 10, with the exception of the Ephesians anomaly in Acts 19, Luke provides several incidents in which people believed and some of them were water baptized;[1] yet Luke does not mention that they were Spirit baptized. This silence suggests that, whether Luke understood it or not, it was no longer necessary to inform about Spirit baptism in such cases since it always occurred simultaneously at conversion. This silence further suggests that it was no longer necessary to experience, and thus report, any unusual behavior to verify Spirit baptism such as tongues-speaking.

In major English Bible versions, the noun "baptism" never appears in Acts or the entire NT for that matter when referring to Spirit baptism. So, the clause "baptism of/in/with the (Holy) Spirit" does not appear in the NT. What does appear is "baptize/baptized you/baptizes in/with the Holy Spirit." These expressions are in the Greek NT with the words *baptizo* and *en pneumati agio*.[2] The preposition *en* can be translated "in" or "with." Most English versions in these texts render it "with."

The expression "baptism *of* the Holy Spirit" can convey a false impression, as if the Holy Spirit does the baptizing. Instead, the Spirit is a passive agent. John the Baptist said of Jesus, "He will baptize you with the Holy Spirit and fire" (Matt 3:11/Luke 3:16; cf. John 1:33). And Jesus said to his disciples about the Spirit, "I am sending upon you what my Father promised" (Luke 24:49). So, just as John baptized *with* water, so Jesus baptizes *with* the Holy Spirit.

We also have learned that the NT says believers experience one Spirit baptism but many Spirit fillings. Hermann Gunkel states, "In the New Testament age all Christians are generally regarded as filled with the Spirit. This is the characteristic difference between the New Testament and ancient Israel as well as Judaism, which recognized possession of the Spirit only on the part of individuals. . . . The Holy Spirit fills a person as water

---

1. "Believed"/"believers:" Acts 11:21 (cf. v. 24); 13:12, 48; 14:1; 17:12, 34; 19:18. "Believed" and water "baptized:" Acts 16:14–15, 25–34; 18:8.

2. See Matt 3:11; Luke 3:16; John 1:33; Acts 1:5; 11:16; cf. Mark 1:8.

Conclusions

fills a container and that as much of the Holy Spirit is given as a person can hold, until he is 'full of the Holy Spirit.'"[3]

And we have seen that *Luke's book of Acts provides no uniform relation between Spirit baptism and the laying on of hands, water baptism, or tongues-speaking.* Yet we can summarize this data and make some conclusions about it.

Regarding the laying of hands, in Acts 8 and 19 it was done to impart Spirit baptism; but Acts 2 does not mention it for the 3,000 Jews; and in Acts 10, Spirit baptism occurred without the imposition of hands.

Regarding tongues-speaking, in Acts 10 and 19 the recipients of Spirit baptism then spoke in tongues; but concerning the 3,000 new believers in Acts 2, there is no mention of either. And regarding the Samaritans in Acts 8, there is no mention of them speaking in tongues when they were Spirit baptized.

Regarding water baptism, the Samaritans in Acts 8 were water baptized a few days before they were Spirit baptized; but in Acts 10, the Cornelius household was converted and Spirit baptized at the same moment and water baptized soon afterwards. Consequently, water baptism is not a prerequisite for Spirit baptism, yet this generally has been presupposed throughout church history. And in Acts 19, when the Ephesians were rebaptized they also were Spirit baptized and spoke in tongues.

The following incidents in Acts show that there is no prescribed order for faith and water baptism in relation to Spirit baptism, although faith always occurs first:

- The 3,000 Jews' order in Acts 2:38: repentance-faith, water baptism, and Spirit baptism
- The Samaritans' order in Acts 8: faith, water baptism, and Spirit baptism days later
- The Gentiles' order in Acts 10: faith and Spirit baptism together, then water baptism
- The Ephesians' order in Acts 19: faith and a later rebaptism with Spirit baptism

Regardless of their order, what is the relation between water baptism and Spirit baptism? This is a difficult question that has been much debated in church history. Moreover, what does Paul mean by "one baptism" when

---

3. Gunkel, *The Influence of the Holy Spirit*, 42–43. Luke pens the expression "full of the (Holy) Spirit" in Luke 4:1; Acts 6:3; 11:24; cf. 6:5.

he writes that there is "one Lord, one faith, one baptism" (Eph 4:5)? Does he mean water baptism and Spirit baptism are one, as F. D. Bruner claims. He says of church fathers, "The baptism with the Holy Spirit and [water] baptism, they knew belonged together in such a way as to form the 'one baptism' of the church (Eph. 4:5; cf. 1 Cor. 12:13; John 3:5; Tit. 3:5)."[4]

To conclude, *there is no uniformity in Acts about tongues-speaking in relation to Spirit baptism.* The 120 disciples spoke foreign languages at Pentecost, but Luke does not say the 3,000 Jewish converts were Spirit baptized and spoke in foreign languages. It is the same for the many more thousands of Jewish converts mentioned in Acts 4:4 and 5:14. But due to Peter's words in Acts 2:38 and 5:32, it must be assumed that the 3,000 Jewish converts received the Spirit at Pentecost. Again, Luke doesn't say anything about them speaking in tongues.

And we have seen that Luke doesn't even say the Samaritans in Acts 8:17–18 spoke in tongues when they received the Spirit. He only implies that they manifested some kind of outward evidence when they were Spirit baptized. And when Luke first relates Paul's conversion he quotes Ananias telling Paul he would "be filled with the Holy Spirit" (Acts 9:17). Yet Luke doesn't say Paul was then Spirit filled or Spirit baptized and spoke in tongues. While Luke says the Gentiles in Acts 10 and the Ephesians in Acts 19 were Spirit baptized and simultaneously spoke in tongues, in similar, prior incidents Luke doesn't report tongues-speaking. So, contrary to classical Pentecostalism, *it should be concluded that Luke does not provide a paradigm in his book of Acts for Spirit baptism with evidential tongues.*

Again, from Acts 19 to the end of the book of Acts there is no mention of anyone being Spirit baptized, let alone it being evidenced by tongues-speaking. Why? *When Peter finished his role of using kingdom keys in Acts 10, and Paul corrected the anomaly in Acts 19, Spirit baptism thereafter always occurred at conversion without any necessity to prove it with glossolalia or any other outward manifestation of the Spirit.*

Interestingly, Pentecostals claim that when they are Spirit baptized and simultaneously speak in tongues, they afterwards never lose that ability. Yet Luke doesn't say anything like this in Acts, and neither does he say people were taught *how* to speak in tongues, as Pentecostals often do with candidates. Once Moses "gathered seventy elders," and "when the spirit rested upon them they prophesied. But they did not do so again" (Num 11:25).

---

4. Bruner, *A Theology of the Holy Spirit*, 193–94.

Conclusions

Thus, we have examined all of the incidents in Acts regarding whether or not Spirit baptism occurred simultaneously with conversion, as Evangelicals insist, or subsequent to conversion, as Pentecostals contend. And we have found that *there is no uniformity in Acts, and thus no pattern for all believers, regarding the timing of Spirit baptism in relation to conversion during this early period of church history. The only uniformity in Acts is that Peter was present when the three racial classifications of people were Spirit baptized for the first time.* Presumably, the 3,000 Jews in Acts 2, and certainly the Gentiles in Acts 10, received the Spirit *when* they believed in Jesus and thus *when* they were converted. In contrast, the Samaritans in Acts 8 and Ephesians in Acts 19 received the Spirit sometime *after* they were converted. At the least, *the Samaritans' experience supports the Pentecostal doctrine of separability and subsequence, but only for this early period; yet the Gentiles' experience in Acts 10 militates against it.*

Robert Menzies claims, "This problem is resolved, however, when we recognize the distinctive character of Luke's prophetic pneumatology: the internal contradictions disappear and Luke's is seen to be remarkably consistent."[5] Again, I think Menzies' proposal to resolve this lack of uniformity in Acts, and his contention that the pneumatologies of Luke and Paul differ, results in Luke and Paul disagreeing no matter how much Menzies insists otherwise. That should be unacceptable to both Evangelicals and Pentecostals because of their conservative view of the inspiration of the Bible. And if Luke was primarily a theologian specializing in pneumatology in his book of Acts, as Menzies and others insist, Luke was not a very good one. For, due to this alleged incongruity, Luke has left some pneumatological questions unanswered for us moderns who regard them as very important.

So, for Luke's literary integrity to be vouchsafed in Acts, he should be viewed mostly as a historian whose primary purpose was to report historical facts involving the growth in size and geographical spread of the Jesus movement. As Ben Witherington says of Luke on Acts, "He is writing in the main as a historian, not primarily as a theologian." And Ben well states concerning the varying order of Spirit baptism and water baptism incidents in Acts, "One can only conclude from this that Luke was not trying to teach his audience some sort of normative order to be followed in later church practice.... Without neglecting or disparaging Luke's theological acumen

---

5. Menzies, *Empowered for Witness*, 211.

one must say that his interests lie primarily in the realm of history, albeit a theological sort of history—salvation history."[6]

Yet there is no incongruity in Luke's accounts in Acts 2, 8, and 10 if we realize that those new believers were baptized with the Spirit only when Peter was present, exercising his role in using kingdom keys. That is why there was subsequence for the Samaritans in Acts 8 and presumably no subsequence, but simultaneity, for the 3,000 Jews in Acts 2 and certainly for the Gentiles in Acts 10. *It all had to do with Peter's presence*, with him undertaking his role as the leader among the apostles in beginning to fulfill Jesus' prophecy in Acts 1:8: "You will be my witnesses in Jerusalem, in all Judea and Samaria, and to the ends of the earth."

WILL JESUS RETURN "SOON?"

Early Pentecostal leaders strongly asserted that Jesus would return soon and establish his earthly kingdom that he would rule for a thousand years, called premillennialism (Rev 20). Many of them thought it would happen in their lifetimes. Their two main reasons for this assertion were their belief about Spirit baptism and Peter's quotation of Joel 2:28–32 at Pentecost, about the Spirit being poured out in "the last days" (Acts 2:17; cf. Joel 2:28). Although this conviction of Jesus' soon return may have been an impetus for Pentecostals to evangelize, this belief always subjects the biblical prediction about Jesus' return to sharp criticism. Arguably, the chief criticism that skeptics have lodged against Jesus, his early disciples, and later Christianity itself is the claim that Jesus would return soon.[7] And I am surprised that so many distinguished NT scholars, some of them my friends, think this is what the NT says. It has now been over 100 years since modern Pentecostalism began, and Jesus has not returned. Moreover, nearly two millennia have transpired since Jesus was here, and he still has not come back.

Regarding Peter's "last days" in Acts 2:17, the Hebrew text of Joel 2:28 has *acheri-chen*. This word is there translated "then" or "and afterwards" in English versions. The LXX translates it similarly as *meta tauta*, meaning "after these things." But it is rendered *en tais eschatais emerais* in the Greek text of Acts 2:17, meaning "in the last days." Did Peter mean by these words that Jesus would return soon, at least during the first century?

---

6. Witherington, *The Acts of the Apostles*, 147, 154.

7. German, Lutheran, theologian Hermann Samuel Reimarus first made this criticism in his *Fragments*, published posthumously in 1778.

Conclusions

After the Romans' destruction of the temple at Jerusalem, in CE 70, Jesus clearly could not have returned soon. The book of Daniel predicts, and Jesus affirmed, that the temple, with its animal sacrificial system, will exist at Jerusalem in the end times.[8] So, the Jews must rebuild their temple and institute its sacrificial system prior to Jesus' return. Thus, Jesus cannot return soon because these and many other Bible prophecies must first be fulfilled.

Most Dispensationalists have taught that some of these unfulfilled Bible prophecies will be fulfilled during a seven-year period they call "the tribulation." So, they teach a two-stage second coming, with the tribulation occurring between them. In the first stage, Jesus comes into the earth's atmosphere, which they call "the rapture," and then he raptures (catches up) his church into the air and takes it to heaven. In the second stage, following the tribulation, Jesus returns with his church to earth. Dispensationalists also claim there are no unfulfilled biblical prophecies that must be fulfilled prior to the rapture. They usually fit the building of Jerusalem's temple into the early portion of this seven-year tribulation. So, they say Jesus can return during our age "at any moment" to rapture his church, which they call "the doctrine of imminency."

It is ironic that modern Pentecostalism began with the belief that Jesus would return soon and that much of it, especially the Assemblies of God (AOG) church denomination, adopted this Dispensational scheme called "pretribulationism." It seems that these Pentecostals did so because of its concomitant doctrine of imminency, thus expecting that Jesus could return soon to rapture his church. This is ironic because of what Dispensationalists have always taught with equal conviction about the gift of speaking in tongues.

Pretribulationism was first taught in 1830 by J. N. Darby (1800–1882), the foremost Plymouth Brethren Bible teacher known as "the father of Dispensationalism." He also taught that "supernatural gifts," which included tongues, ceased at the end of the first century. For the past sixty years, Dallas Theological Seminary (DTS) has been the bastion of Dispensationalism in the world and perhaps the foremost institution that teaches this "cessationism."

Darby and the Plymouth Brethren opposed the contemporary, charismatic London preacher Edward Irving (1792–1834), the chief forerunner

---

8. Daniel 8:11–14; 9:27; 11:31; 12:11; Matt 24:15/Mark 13:14. See also Mal 3:1; Rev 11:1–2.

of modern Pentecostalism. Irving emphasized prophetic utterances and spiritual gifts, and many in his church spoke in tongues. He also preached that Jesus' return was imminent. Some church historians claim Irving and a female member of his congregation, Ms. Margaret MacDonald, originated pretribulationism. They also assert that Darby got it from them.[9] But recent historians have proved this wrong.[10]

When the Pentecostal Movement began, it rightly embraced premillennial faith. But it did not clarify if Jesus would return once or twice, the latter as in pretribulationism. In 1932, a controversy arose within the AOG denomination over this issue. Its Fundamental Truths included two articles about Jesus' return that had affirmed premillennialism, yet they did not clearly set forth pretribulationism. The Executive Presbytery settled the issue by declaring, "We believe in the imminent personal return of our Lord Jesus Christ as the blessed hope of the church, and that we disapprove of any of our ministers teaching that the church must go through the tribulation." Three years later, in 1935, this pretribulationism statement was refined and inserted into the AOG bylaws.

Many Pentecostal church denominations have never adopted pretribulational belief. But it does coincide with some distinctive beliefs of the Pentecostal-Charismatic movement. That is, pretribulationism and some Pentecostal-Charismatic teachings, which have led to the formation of "the health and wealth gospel," represent an escape from trials, tribulations, and suffering. Pentecostal Gerald T. Sheppard informs that early Pentecostal leaders "assumed that a pre-tribulational rapture best preserved their hope in the 'any-moment' return of Jesus Christ." He says it also had the effect of making Pentecostalism more acceptable to the Evangelical-Fundamentalist movement because so many people in it advocated pretribulationism.[11]

In chapter 2, I said I am a former Dispensationalist. My church taught pretribulationism to me from 1959 to 1970. But in 1971, and only due to my personal Bible study, I began to suspect that this pretribulational interpretation, which I had dearly clung to as a devout student of Bible prophecy, was incorrect. So, that winter I went to Mosher Library at DTS and for the next five days, fourteen hours per day, I did an in-depth study of pretribulationism and researched its origin. I then changed to believing

---

9. E.g., Tregelles, *The Hope of Christ's Second Coming*, 35.

10. Dave MacPherson has been the main proponent of this allegation about Ms. MacDonald, but several historians have proved him wrong.

11. Sheppard, "Pentecostals and the Hermeneutics of Dispensationalism," 22.

Conclusions

that the Bible only teaches a single, posttribulational return of Jesus. Since then, I have believed the Bible teaches that when Jesus returns he will exit heaven, resurrect dead saints, descend to earth, deliver Jews from annihilation, destroy the Antichrist and his armies, conduct the judgment, and fully establish his worldwide kingdom of peace on earth—all in one coming. This viewpoint is called "historic premillennialism" because several, early church fathers taught it.[12]

In the last chapter, we learned of Jesus' triple admonition to Peter, recorded in John 21, "feed/tend my sheep." Most recent NT scholars rightly claim that the Gospel of John originally ended at John 20:31. The two primary reasons are that vv. 30–31 are such an appropriate conclusion to the book, and John 21 seems to be an addendum that was added later. If so, why was it added? The answer seems to be hidden in the two primary truths of this addendum that have been held in tension throughout church history: (1) teaching God's people ("feed my sheep") and (2) watching and waiting for Jesus to return. For we read in John 21:20–23:

> 20Peter turned and saw the disciple whom Jesus loved following them; he was the one who had reclined next to Jesus at the supper and had said, "Lord, who is it that is going to betray you?" 21When Peter saw him, he said to Jesus, "Lord, what about him?" 22Jesus said to him, "If it is my will that he remain until I come, what is that to you? Follow me!" 23So the rumor spread in the community that this disciple would not die. Yet Jesus did not say to him that he would not die, but, "If it is my will that he remain until I come, what is that to you?"

So, it seems someone added this addendum to the Gospel of John to correct a false rumor that had spread within at least the Johannine church community. It was about the unidentified disciple mentioned in John 21:20 (cf. 13:23; 20:2; 21:7). Scholars call him "the beloved disciple." Although they have had no consensus about his identity, church fathers unanimously regarded him as the Apostle John. The rumor was that Jesus would return during this disciple's lifetime. Scholars generally believe John lived the longest of the twelve apostles. Legend says he was the only member of the original twelve apostles who did not suffer martyrdom.

The author of John 21 says the rumor about his decease was based on a misunderstanding of what Jesus had said. That is, Jesus did not say

---

12. In my STILL HERE book series on eschatology, a planned volume is on posttribulationism v. pretribulationism.

he would return during that disciple's lifetime, but that's what some people later thought he meant.

So, not only have some Christians in church history since the apostolic era erroneously believed that Jesus would return soon, and many thought it would happen in their lifetimes, according to John 21 some Christians during the apostolic era believed this as well.

In a future volume in my book series on eschatology entitled STILL HERE,[13] I intend to show that the Bible does not teach that Jesus will return soon, or at any moment, even though some English Bibles say it is "soon."[14]

HAVE PENTECOSTALS MISLABELED A POST-CONVERSION EXPERIENCE?

We have seen that Pentecostals rightly insist that the 120 disciples on the day of Pentecost in Acts 2 and the Samaritans in Acts 8 were converted and subsequently baptized with the Holy Spirit at a later time in their lives. But Pentecostals have erred in treating these episodes as normative, and thus a paradigm, for all believers thereafter. And regarding the Acts 2 episode, subsequence happened to the 120 disciples merely because there had to be a starting point in time when the Spirit would come upon God's people. Thus, that was a one-time event never to be repeated. The Samaritans experienced subsequence due to Peter using his kingdom keys when he came into their presence. And in the Acts 10 episode, those Gentiles believed and were Spirit baptized simultaneously because Peter was doing the preaching. But after that, Luke says no more about Peter doing such things. Why? Peter had finished his temporary role of using his kingdom keys to unleash Spirit baptism presumably on the 3,000 Jews in Acts 2, the Samaritans in Acts 8, and the Gentiles in Acts 10. Then he was finished using his keys.

Howard Ervin says concerning the Pentecostals' distinctive doctrine of subsequence evidenced by tongues, "If the Pentecostal doctrine is to be proven wrong, the Pentecostal experience must also be discredited."[15] How

---

13. The tagline of my STILL HERE series is "A Nonfiction Alternative to *Left Behind* Theology." *Left Behind*, written by Tim LaHaye and Jerry Jenkins, is the bestselling, Christian, fiction book series of all time. It is Dispensational and thus pretribulational.

14. The NIV, NRSV, and ESV translate *erchomai tachu* as "I am coming soon" in Rev 3:11; 22:7, 12, 20, cf. 2:16. But the KJV has "I come quickly," and the NASB has "I am coming quickly." *Tachu* can be translated "soon," "quickly," or "swiftly." Context is the determining factor.

15. Ervin, *Conversion-Initiation*, 74.

Conclusions

is that logical? I believe the Pentecostal doctrine of subsequence is wrong after Peter finished using his kingdom keys; but I don't discredit spiritual experiences Pentecostals have had upon which they base their distinctive doctrine. Rather, I think *Pentecostals have mislabeled ecstatic experiences they have had following conversion by improperly labeling them the baptism with/in/of the Holy Spirit.*

Regardless, Pentecostals should be respected for their sincerity and earnestness in worshipping God and serving him. I especially admire them for their zeal in evangelism and missions by spreading the gospel worldwide. And they deserve much credit for emphasizing spiritual gifts and the Spirit-filled life. Wayne Grudem informs in his best-selling book entitled *Systematic Theology,* "Systematic theology books have not traditionally included a chapter on baptism in the Holy Spirit," but he says it has been occurring recently "with the spread of Pentecostalism."[16]

Yet concerning labels, I think Christians ought not quibble much over terminology. Paul wrote, "The kingdom of God does not consist in words but in power" as a "demonstration of the Spirit" (1 Cor 4:20; 2:4 NASB).

Roger Stronstad is a Canadian Pentecostal NT scholar involved in this Dunn Debate who believes in post-conversion Spirit baptism; yet he does not believe it must be accompanied with *glossolalia*. He explains:

> The literature of the New Testament reveals three primary dimensions of the activity of the Holy Spirit: 1) salvation, 2) sanctification, and 3) service. These dimensions are interdependent and complementary. However, in the development of Protestant theology, the Reformed tradition has emphasized the activity of the Spirit in initiation-conversion, the Wesleyan tradition has subsequently emphasized the activity of the Spirit in holiness and sanctification, and the Pentecostal tradition has finally emphasized the charismatic activity of the Spirit in worship and service.[17]

So, let us strive to be earnest, well-balanced Christians who experience all of these activities of the Holy Spirit.

---

16. Grudem, *Systematic Theology*, 763.
17. Stronstad, *The Charismatic Theology of St. Luke*, 83.

SOLVING THE SAMARITAN RIDDLE

CHRISTIAN UNITY AND THE FUTURE OF THE DUNN DEBATE

Even though Dunn in *Baptism* argues against Pentecostals regarding subsequence, he pays much tribute to them in it in various ways. For instance, he explains positively regarding the three waves of Christianity that Catholicism has focused on the church, Protestantism has centered on the Bible, and Pentecostalism has highlighted the Holy Spirit. Concerning these first two waves he observes, "Pentecostals have reacted against both these extremes. Against the mechanical sacramentalism of extreme Catholicism and the dead biblicist orthodoxy of extreme Protestantism they have shifted the focus of attention to the *experience* of the Spirit. Our examination of the NT evidence has shown that they were wholly justified in this."[18]

Although Jimmy employs some polemics against Pentecostals in *Baptism*, in the Dunn Debate various scholars, including Pentecostals, acknowledged his humility in it. An example of his attitude is that forty years after *Baptism* was published Jimmy concluded, "I am somewhat disappointed that the debate which my *Baptism* book seems to have occasioned has not revealed more inadequacies of my thesis than it has." He says of future "discussion and debate" about this topic, "which is what I hope for, my own perception of the issue will be clarified and deepened in the process . . . at least in terms of the debate with classic Pentecostalism's understanding of Sprit baptism."[19] That's humility. That's vintage Jimmy Dunn!

So, this Dunn Debate is largely between Evangelicals and Pentecostals. So far, there has been no consensus between them. Yet Pentecostal scholar Robert Menzies is optimistic about this debate's future. He says, "I see the assimilation of the modern Pentecostal movement into the broader Evangelical world as an exciting and positive event."[20] For that to happen, I think Pentecostals will have to make the change that some Charismatics and all Third Wavers have, that it is unnecessary for tongues to accompany Spirit baptism.

Unity between classical Pentecostals and so many other Christians has been hindered due to Pentecostals asserting their doctrine of subsequence, but especially with evidential tongues. Due to this distinctive, Pentecostals

---

18. Dunn, *Baptism in the Holy Spirit*, 225. Emphasis his.

19. Dunn, "Yet Once More—Again," 43; Dunn, *Baptism in the Holy Spirit*, 2nd ed., xvii.

20. Menzies and Menzies, *Spirit and Power*, 63.

Conclusions

generally have viewed themselves as more advanced and more spiritual, thus having a higher degree of communion with God. It presents them as first-class Christians, thus relegating all other Christians to a second-class status. But many other Christians perceive this Pentecostal attitude as an arrogant super-elitism. Dunn says of this phenomenon, "Many Pentecostals have gone much too far in ... demonstrating a painfully smug spiritual superiority-complex."[21]

Wayne Grudem well explains this Pentecostal hindrance to unity with other Christians:

> What is the problem with viewing Christians as existing in two categories like this? The problem is that it contributes to a "we-they" mentality in churches, and leads to jealousy, pride, and divisiveness. No matter how much these people who have received this special empowering of the Holy Spirit try to be thoughtful and considerate of those who have not, if they genuinely love their fellow brothers and sisters in Christ, and if this has been a very helpful experience in their own Christian lives, they cannot help but give the impression that they would like others to share this experience as well. Even if they are not proud in their hearts (and it seems to me that most are not) with respect to this experience, such a conviction that there is a second category of Christians will inevitably give an impression of pride or spiritual superiority. Yet there will very likely be a sense of jealousy on the part of those who have not had such an experience. In this way, a view of two groups within the church is fostered, and the repeated charge of divisiveness that is made against the charismatic movement is given some credibility ...
>
> We must understand first what is commonly taught [by Pentecostals] about the need to prepare for baptism in the Holy Spirit. Very often people will be taught that they should confess all known sins, repent of any remaining sin in their lives, trust Christ to forgive those sins, commit every area of their lives to the Lord's service, yield themselves fully to him, and believe that Christ is going to empower them in a new way and equip them with new gifts for ministry. Then after that preparation, they are encouraged to ask Jesus in prayer to baptize them in the Holy Spirit. But what does this preparation do? It is a guaranteed prescription for significant growth in the Christian life! ...
>
> If Pentecostal and charismatic Christians would be willing to teach on these things without the additional baggage of two-level

---

21. Dunn, *The Christ and the Spirit*, 90.

Christianity that is implied by the term "baptism in the Holy Spirit," they might find a new era of greatly increased effectiveness in bringing teaching on these other areas of the Christian life to evangelicals generally.[22]

So, Grudem suggests that if Pentecostals would abandon labeling their post-conversion experience as a "baptism in the Holy Spirit," yet continue forward with their ministry, they might realize a greater effectiveness. But many Pentecostals are of the opposite mindset. They fear that abandoning their distinctive doctrine of subsequence with evidential tongues will cause their ministry to drastically decline.

Pentecostal scholar Martin William Mittelstadt is an authority on scholarly Pentecostal literature about the NT. He admits, "As a people of the Spirit, Pentecostals are at times rightly accused of triumphalism" and that they "easily become susceptible to an uncritical sense of invincibility."[23] He surprisingly informs about their distinctive doctrine, "Certain Pentecostal leaders have narrowed and/or reduced emphasis on Spirit baptism for at least two reasons: 1) many are disgruntled and/or wounded due to abusive teaching and experience; 2) others find the message condescending and cite Pentecostal pride and exclusivism, particularly a zealous overemphasis on tongues."[24]

To assert that so many great Christians in the past have been devoid of Spirit baptism because they did not speak in tongues does not make any sense. This allegation goes against such godly Christians as William Tyndale, William Carey, William Wilberforce, John Wesley, Mother Teresa, and Billy Graham just to name a few. And since many Pentecostal scholars claim that Spirit baptism is mostly or solely for service, especially evangelism, does that mean Billy Graham needed to get baptized with the Holy Spirit and thus speak in tongues to be adequately empowered to evangelize? Ex-Pentecostal Max Turner writes mildly, but truly, of this problem by saying of Pentecostals:

> Those who apply the analogy of the Samaritan converts to traditional Protestantism are usually sufficiently charitable to recognize renowned spiritual leaders and pastors, powerful preachers and

---

22. Grudem, *Systematic Theology*, 777, 779, 783.

23. Mittlestadt, *Reading Luke-Acts in the Pentecostal Tradition*, 126.

24. Mittlestadt, "Academic and Pentecostal: An Appreciation of Roger Stronstad," 43. Accessed on June 26, 2014 at https://journal.twu.ca/index.php/CJPC/article/viewFile/20/6.

Conclusions

expositors, effective missionaries, and great men and women of prayer and of obedient discipleship in those other traditions (people who nevertheless disagree with classical Pentecostal or other 'Charismatic' expositions of the Spirit). But is it coherent to claim such men and women of God do these things *without* what Luke means by the Pentecostal gift of the Spirit? . . . It does not make Lukan sense to claim that the effective spiritual preachers, missionaries and evangelists outside the Pentecostal/Charismatic stream have yet to receive the Pentecostal 'Spirit of prophecy.'[25]

Because of all this, I think classical Pentecostals should be able to figure out that something is not right about the core distinctive of their tradition. In chapter 2, I revealed that early in my theological education I was taught that tongues-speaking Pentecostals are of the devil. I eventually realized that that is dead wrong! Pentecostals are my brothers and sisters in Christ, and I accept their cherished tongues-speaking as biblical. Yet I think they should acknowledge that other Christians have the Holy Spirit just as much as they do, even though nearly all of us do not speak in tongues. If my hypothesis in this book is correct—that Peter's role of using kingdom keys helps explain the relation between conversion and Spirit baptism in the NT—maybe it will help some Pentecostals and other Christians to increase the unity in the body of Christ as we strive together for a shared testimony to the world about God our Father, our Lord and Savior Jesus Christ, and Jesus baptizing his people with the Holy Spirit.

---

25. Turner, *Power from on High*, 451–52. Emphasis his.

Works Cited

Albright, W. F., and C. S. Mann. *Matthew: Introduction, Translation, and Notes.* New York: Doubleday, 1971.
Arminius, James. *The Works of James Arminius: The London Edition.* Translated by James Nichols and William Nichols. 3 vols. Vol. 1:1825. Vol. 2:1828. Vol. 3:1875. Reprint, Grand Rapids: Baker, 1986.
Barrett, C. K. "Apollos and the Twelve Disciples." In *The New Testament Age: Essays in Honor of Bo Reicke.* Edited by William C. Weinrich. 2 vols. Macon, GA: Mercer, 1984.
Bauckham, Richard. *The Theology of the Book of Revelation.* Cambridge, UK: Cambridge University Press, 1993.
Beasley-Murray, G. R. *Baptism in the New Testament.* Exeter, England: Paternoster, 1962.
Blomberg, Craig L. *Matthew.* Nashville: Broadman, 1992.
Bock, Darrell L. *Acts.* Grand Rapids: Baker Academic, 2007.
Brown, Raymond E. *The Gospel According to John (xiii–xxi): An Introduction, Translation, and Notes.* New York: Doubleday, 1970.
Bruce, F. F. *The Book of Acts.* Grand Rapids: Eerdmans, 1954.
———. *Commentary on the Book of Acts: The English Text with Introduction, Exposition and Notes.* Grand Rapids: Eerdmans, n.d.
Bruner, Frederick Dale. *Matthew: A Commentary: Volume 2: The Churchbook Matthew 13–28.* Revised and expanded ed. Original 1990. Grand Rapids: Eerdmans, 2004.
———. *A Theology of the Holy Spirit: The Pentecostal Experience and the New Testament Witness.* London: Hodder & Stoughton/Grand Rapids: Eerdmans, 1970.
Carson, D. A. *Matthew.* Grand Rapids: Zondervan, 1984.
———. *Showing the Spirit: A Theological Exposition of 1 Corinthians 12–14.* Grand Rapids: Baker, 1987.
Cathcart, Kevin J., and Robert P. Gordon. *Targum of the Minor Prophets* (Aramaic Bible, vol. 14). Wilmington, Delaware: Michael Glazier, 1989.
Cho, Youngmo. *Spirit and Kingdom in the Writings of Luke and Paul: An Attempt to Reconcile these Concepts.* Milton Keynes, England: Paternoster, 2005.
Davies, W. D. and Dale C. Allison, Jr. *The Gospel According to Saint Matthew,* 3 vols. London: T&T Clark, 1991.
Delling, Gerhard. "*hemera* (day)." *TDNT* 2 948–53.

Works Cited

Dunn, James D. G. *The Acts of the Apostles*. Petersborough, England: Epworth/Valley Forge, PA: Trinity, 1996.

———. *Baptism in the Holy Spirit: A Re-examination of the New Testament Teaching on the Gift of the Spirit in Relation to Pentecostalism Today*. London: SCM Philadelphia: Westminster, 1970.

———. *Baptism in the Holy Spirit: A Re-examination of the New Testament Teaching on the Gift of the Spirit in Relation to Pentecostalism Today*, 2nd ed. London: SCM, 2010.

———. "Baptism in the Holy Spirit—yet once more." *JEPTA* 18 (1998) 3–25.

———. "Baptism in the Holy Spirit—yet once more, again." *JPT* 19 (2010) 32–43.

———. "Baptism in the Spirit: A Response to Pentecostal Scholarship in Luke-Acts." *JPT* 3 (1993) 3–27.

———. *The Christ and the Spirit: Volume 2: Pneumatology*. Edinburgh, Scotland: T&T Clark, 1998.

———. *Christology in the Making: A New Testament Inquiry Into the Origins of the Doctrine of the Incarnation*. Philadelphia: Westminster, 1980.

———. *Jesus and the Spirit: A Study of the Religious and Charismatic Experience of Jesus and the First Christians as Reflected in the New Testament*. London: SCM, 1975.

———. *Romans 1–8*. Dallas, TX: Word, 1988.

———. "Spirit-Baptism and Pentecostalism." *SJT* 23 (1970) 397–407.

———. *The Theology of Paul the Apostle*. Grand Rapids: Eerdmans, 1998.

———. "They Believed Philip's Preaching (Ac 8.12): A Reply." *IBS* 1 (1979) 173–83.

Ervin, Howard M. *Conversion-Initiation and the Baptism in the Holy Spirit: An Engaging Critique of James D. G. Dunn's Baptism in the Holy Spirit*. Peabody, MA: Hendrickson, 1984.

———. *Spirit-Baptism: A Biblical Investigation*. Peabody, MA: Hendrickson, 1987.

Fee, Gordon D. "Baptism in the Holy Spirit: The Issue of Separability and Subsequence." *Pneuma* 7:2 (Fall, 1985) 87–99.

———. *God's Empowering Presence: The Holy Spirit in the Letters of Paul*. Peabody, MA: Hendrickson, 1994.

———. *Gospel and Spirit: Issues in New Testament Hermeneutics*. Peabody, MA: Hendrickson, 1991.

———. *The First Epistle to the Corinthians*. Grand Rapids: Eerdmans, 1987.

Finney, Charles G. *Lectures on Systematic Theology*. Edited by J. H. Fairchild. Original 1847. Southgate, CA: Colporter Kemp, 1948.

———. *Memoirs of Rev. Charles G. Finney*. New York: Fleming H. Revell, 1876.

Fitzmyer, Joseph A. *The Acts of the Apostles: A New Translation with Introduction and Commentary*. New York: Doubleday, 1997.

———. *The Gospel According to Luke X-XXIV: A New Translation with Introduction and Commentary*. New York: Doubleday, 1985.

France, R. T. *The Gospel of Matthew*. Grand Rapids: Eerdmans, 2007.

Gaebelein, Arno C. *The Gospel of Matthew: An Exposition*. Neptune, NJ: Loizeaux Brothers, 1910.

Grudem, Wayne A. *Are Miraculous Gifts for Today? Four Views*. General editor. Grand Rapids: Zondervan, 1996.

———. *Systematic Theology: An Introduction to Biblical Doctrine*. Grand Rapids: Zondervan, 1994.

Works Cited

Gunkel, Hermann. *The Influence of the Holy Spirit: A Popular View of the Apostolic Age and the Teaching of the Apostle Paul*. Translated by Roy A. Harrisville and Philip A. Quanbeck II. Ger. original 1888. Philadelphia: Fortress, 1979.

Hawthorne, Gerald. *The Presence and the Power: The Significance of the Holy Spirit in the Life of Jesus*. Dallas: Word, 1991.

Hoekema, Anthony A. *Holy Spirit Baptism*. Grand Rapids: Eerdmans, 1972.

Johnson, Luke Timothy. *The Acts of the Apostles*. Edited by Daniel J. Harrington. Collegeville, MN: Liturgical, 1992.

Keener, Craig S. *Acts: An Exegetical Commentary: Volume 1: Introduction and 1:1—2:47*. Grand Rapids: Baker, 2012.

———. *Acts: An Exegetical Commentary: Volume 2: 3:1—14:28*. Grand Rapids: Baker, 2013.

———. *A Commentary on the Gospel of Matthew*. Grand Rapids: Eerdmans, 1999.

———. *Crucial Questions about the Holy Spirit*. Grand Rapids: Baker, 1996.

Kistemaker, Simon J. *Exposition of the Acts of the Apostles*. Grand Rapids: Baker, 1990.

Kuyper, Abraham. *The Work of the Holy Spirit*. Translated by Heiligen Geest. New York: Funk & Wagnalls, 1900.

Lampe, G. W. H. *God as Spirit: The Bampton Lectures, 1976*. Oxford: Clarendon, 1977.

———. *The Seal of the Spirit: A Study in the Doctrine of Baptism and Confirmation in the New Testament and the Fathers*. Original 1951. Reprint, Eugene, OR: Wipf and Stock, 2004.

Law, William. *A Practical Treatise on Christian Perfection*. 1726.

———. *A Serious Call to a Devout and Holy Life*. 1729.

Lloyd-Jones, Martyn. *Great Doctrines of the Bible: Volume I: God the Father, God the Son: Volume II: God the Holy Spirit: Volume III: The Church and the Last Things*. Wheaton, IL: Crossway Books, 2003. Originally published as three volumes: *God the Father, God the Son; God the Holy Spirit; The Church and the Last Things*.

Luther, Martin. *Luther's Works*. Edited by Hilton C. Oswald. 55 vols. St. Louis, MO: Concordia, 1975.

Luz, Ulrich. *Studies in Matthew*. Translated by Rosemary Selle. Grand Rapids: Eerdmans, 2005.

McArthur, Harvey K. "On the Third Day." *NTS* 18 (1971–70) 81–86.

Menzies, Robert P. *The Development of Early Christian Pneumatology with Special Reference to Luke-Acts*. Sheffield, England: Sheffield Academic, 1991.

———. *Empowered for Witness: The Spirit in Luke-Acts*. Sheffield, England: Sheffield Academic, 1994.

Menzies, William W., and Robert P. Menzies. *Spirit and Power: Foundations of Pentecostal Experience*. Grand Rapids: Zondervan, 2000.

Metzger, Bruce M. *A Textual Commentary on the Greek New Testament*. United Bible Societies, 1971.

Mittlestadt, Martin William. "Academic and Pentecostal: An Appreciation of Roger Stronstad." *CJPCC* 1 (2010) 31–64.

———. *Reading Luke-Acts in the Pentecostal Tradition*. Cleveland, TN: CPT, 2010.

Morris, Leon. *The Gospel according to Matthew*. Grand Rapids: Eerdmans/Leicester, UK: Inter-Varsity, 1992.

Nolland, John. *The Gospel of Matthew: A Commentary on the Greek Text*. Grand Rapids: Eerdmans, 2005.

Osborne, Grant L. *Matthew*, ZECNT. Grand Rapids: Zondervan, 2010.

Works Cited

Oss, Douglas A. "A Pentecostal/Charismatic View." In *Are Miraculous Gifts for Today? Four Views*. Edited by Wayne A. Grudem. Grand Rapids: Zondervan, 1996. Pages 237–308.
Packer, J. I. *Keep in Step with the Spirit*. Old Tappan, NJ: Revell, 1984.
Pelikan, Jaroslav. *The Riddle of Roman Catholicism*. New York: Abingdon, 1959.
Pervo, Richard I. *Acts: A Commentary*. Edited by Harold W. Attridge. Hermenia. Minneapolis: Fortress, 2009.
Peterson, David G. *The Acts of the Apostles*. Pillar New Testament Commentary. Grand Rapids: Eerdmans, 2009.
Petts, David. "The Baptism in the Holy Spirit in Relation to Christian Initiation." MTh thesis; Nottingham, England: Nottingham University Press, n.d.
Polhill, John B. *Acts*, NAC 26. Nashville: Broadman, 1992.
Reiling, Jannes. "Holy Spirit." In *DDD*, 418–24.
Schleiermacher, Friedrich. *The Christian Faith*. Original 1821. ET of 2nd Ger. ed. Philadelphia: Fortress, 1928.
Schweitzer, Albert. *The Quest of the Historical Jesus: A Critical Study of Its Progress from Reimarus to Wrede*. Ger. original 1906
Schweizer, Eduard. *The Holy Spirit*. Translated by Reginald H. and Ilse Fuller. Ger. original 1978. Philadelphia: Fortress, 1980.
Shelton, James B. *Mighty in Word and Deed: The Role of the Holy Spirit in Luke-Acts*. Peabody, MA: Hendrickson, 1991.
Sheppard, Gerald T. "Pentecostals and the Hermeneutics of Dispensationalism: The Anatomy of an Uneasy Relationship." *Pneuma* 6 (Fall 1984) 5–33.
Smith, Dennis E., and Joseph B. Tyson. *Acts and Christian Beginnings: The Acts Seminar Report*. Salem, OR: Poleridge, 2013.
Smith, Timothy L. *Called unto Holiness: The Story of the Nazarenes: The Formative Years*. Kansas City: Nazarene, 1962.
———. *Revivalism and Social Reform in Mid-Nineteenth Century-America*. New York: Abington, 1957.
Storms, C. S. "A Third Wave View." In *Are Miraculous Gifts for Today? Four Views*. General editor Wayne A. Grudem. Grand Rapids: Zondervan, 1996. Pages 175–223.
Stott, John R. W. *Baptism & Fullness: The Work of the Holy Spirit Today*, 2nd ed. Downers Grove, IL: InterVarsity, 1975.
Stronstad, Roger. J. *The Charismatic Theology of St. Luke*. Peabody, MA: Hendrickson, 1984.
———. "Forty years On: An Appreciation and Assessment of *Baptism in the Holy Spirit* by James D. G. Dunn." *JPT* 19 (2010) 3–11.
———. *Spirit, Scripture and Theology: A Pentecostal Perspective*. Baguio City, Philippines: Asia Pacific Theological Seminary, 1995.
Stuart, Douglas. *Hosea-Jonah*. WBC. Waco, TX: Word, 1987.
Synan, Vinson. *The Century of the Holy Spirit: 100 Years of Pentecostal and Charismatic Renewal, 1901–2001*. Nashville: Thomas Nelson, 2001.
———. *The Holiness-Pentecostal Tradition: Charismatic Movements in the Twentieth Century*. Grand Rapids: Eerdmans/Cambridge: U.K., 1971.
Thomas, John Christopher. "A Celebration of and Engagement with James D. G. Dunn's *Baptism in the Holy Spirit* Forty Years On." *JPT* 19 (2010) 19–24.
Torrey, R. A. *The Baptism with the Holy Spirit*. New York: Fleming H. Revell, 1875.

Works Cited

Tregelles, S. P. *The Hope of Christ's Second Coming: How Is It Taught in Scripture? And Why?* 6th ed. Chelmsford, England: The Sovereign Grace Advent Testimony, 1886.

Turner, Max. *Power from on High: The Spirit in Israel's Restoration and Witness in Luke-Acts.* Sheffield, England: Sheffield Academic, 2000.

Turner, M. M. B. "Luke and the Spirit: Studies in the Significance of Receiving the Spirit in Luke-Acts." PhD diss., Cambridge University, 1980.

Unger, Merrill F. *The Baptism and Gifts of the Holy Spirit.* Chicago: Moody, 1974.

Wesley, John. *A Plain Account of Christian Perfection.* Original 1726.

———. *A Plain Account of Christian Perfection: As Believed and Taught by The Rev. Mr. John Wesley, From the year 1725, to the year 1777.* N.d.

Wilkins, Michael J. *Matthew* in the NIV Application Commentary. Grand Rapids: Zondervan, 2004.

Witherington III, Ben. *The Acts of the Apostles: A Socio-Rhetorical Commentary.* Grand Rapids: Eerdmans, 1998.

Zarley, Kermit. *The Gospels Interwoven.* Original 1987. Reprint, Eugene, OR: Wipf and Stock, 2001.

———. *The Restitution of Jesus Christ.* Self-published, 2008.

———. *The Third Day Bible Code.* Austin, TX: Synergy, 2006.

———. *Warrior from Heaven.* Austin, TX: Synergy, 2009.

Index of Authors

Albright, W. F., and C. S. Mann, 61
Arminius, James, 161

Barrett, C. K., 144
Beasley-Murray, G. R., 105, 144
Blomberg, Craig L., 69, 192
Bock, Darrell L., 150
Brown, Raymond E., 47–49
Bruce, F.F., 114, 144, 149–50
Bruner, Frederick Dale, ix, 64, 67, 79, 89, 110, 113, 140, 185, 198

Carson, D. A., 26, 58, 63, 100, 107, 150–51, 154, 170, 191
Cathcart, Kevin J., and Robert P. Gordon, 129
Cho, Youngmo, 157

Davies, W.D., and Dale C. Allison, Jr., 65–66
Delling, Gerhard, 125, 129
Dunn, James D. G., iv, vii–xi, 27, 35–36, 38, 40, 42, 46, 48, 80, 82, 86–90, 98–103, 105–06, 108–10, 113–16, 122–24, 126, 137–40, 146–50, 152–53, 155–57, 159–62, 164–68, 178–80, 185–87, 206–07

Ervin, Howard M., ix, 24–25, 45, 92–93, 112, 117, 121–22, 140, 147–48, 157, 162, 169, 185–86, 204

Fee, Gordon D., ix, 27–28, 30, 72, 100, 102, 104, 115, 148, 152–53, 160–61, 164–65, 176
Finney, Charles G., 22
Fitzmyer, Joseph A., 65, 86, 101, 143–44, 150
France, R. T., 58–59

Gaebelein, Arno C., 66–67
Grudem, Wayne A., 205, 207–08
Gunkel, Hermann, 108, 157, 172–74, 196

Hawthorne, Gerald, 35–36
Hoekema, Anthony A., ix, 99, 104, 153

Jeremias, Joachim, 63, 65, 68
Johnson, Luke Timothy, 106, 150

Keener, Craig S., 57, 81, 84–85, 105–06, 122–23, 132–33
Kuyper, Abraham, 35
Kistemaker, Simon J., 123

Lampe, G. W. H., 35, 156, 184–85
Law, William, 19
Lloyd-Jones, Martyn, 79, 89, 171
Luther, Martin, 64, 129, 164
Luz, Ulrich, 188

McArthur, Harvey K., 129

Index of Authors

Menzies, Robert P., ix, 40–41, 103–04, 112, 140–41, 144, 156–58, 174, 199, 206
Menzies, William W., and Robert P. Menzies, 158, 206
Metzger, Bruce M., 49, 117
Mittelstadt, Martin William, 27, 155–56, 208
Morris, Leon, 70

Nolland, John, 64

Osborne, Grant L., 69, 111
Oss, Douglas A., 165

Packer, J. I., 87, 153
Pelikan, Jaroslav, 188
Pervo, Richard I., 116
Peterson, David G., 74, 81, 101, 119, 132, 149
Petts, David, 108
Polhill, John B., 80, 147

Reiling, Jannes, 171

Schleiermacher, Friedrich, 37–38
Schweizer, Eduard, 35, 37, 157, 174
Schweitzer, Albert, 37
Shelton, James B., ix, 40, 87, 104, 156–57

Sheppard, Gerald T., 202
Smith, Dennis E., and Joseph B. Tyson, 74
Smith, Timothy L., 19, 21
Storms, C. Samuel, 32, 165
Stott, John R. W., ix, 102–04, 107
Stronstad, Roger. J., ix, 40, 73, 89, 93, 104, 136, 156–57, 159, 205, 208
Stuart, Douglas, 129
Synan, Vinson, 20–22

Thomas, John Christopher, 48–49
Torrey, R. A., 22–23, 30
Tregelles, S. P., 202
Turner, Max, ix, 86, 101, 114, 156, 208

Unger, Merrill F., 84, 88, 90–91, 147, 156, 166

Wesley, John, 18–20, 22, 124, 169, 179, 208
Wilkins, Michael J., 111, 191
Witherington III, Ben, 73–74, 81, 86, 105, 114–15, 123, 136, 147, 151, 199–200

Zarley, Kermit, vii, x, 2, 34, 71, 76, 126, 129

Index of Subjects and Names

A

Abraham, 57, 126–7
Ananias, 94–95, 120–25, 198
Ananias and Sapphira, 113, 116
Angel(s), 52, 60–61, 70, 76, 114, 117, 121, 132, 136–37, 139, 181
Anglican Church/Anglicanism, 19, 185
Apollos, 135, 142–45, 148, 150–51, 154
Aquinas, Thomas, 184, 188
Arminian-Wesleyan theology, 19
Assemblies of God Church: beginning of, 29; Fundamental Truths of, 29–31, 85, 91, 202; size of, 29
Association of Pentecostal Churches of America, 23
Athanasius, 36
Augustine, 58

B

Baptism of John, 142–44
Baptism with/in water. See Water baptism
Berachah Church, 17, 26
Binding, 62, 64–65, 67–71, 94–95, 113–16, 190, 192
Born again. See New birth
Butler, Glenn, 15

C

Calvary Chapel church movement, 31
Calvin, John, 105, 164
Canon within a canon, 72
Campbell, Alexander, 22
Carey, William, 208
Cessationism/Cessationists, 26, 31, 111, 175, 201
Charismatic movement, 23, 31, 85, 179, 185, 207
Christian baptism, 40, 42, 113, 143–44, 146, 148, 151, 182
Christian Church, 13, 15, 22, 29, 33
Christian, origin of word, 86, 146
Christian perfection (-ism), 18–19, 22, 179
Chrysostom, John, 104
Church age, 31, 92
Church of the Nazarene, 15, 19, 21, 23, 179
Cleansing (from sin), 23, 108, 132, 139–40, 182
Confirmation. See Roman Catholic Church
Continuity/Continualists, 31
Conversion, definition of, 120–21
Conversion-initiation, 42, 159, 180, 186
Cornelius, 90, 92, 112, 117, 121, 131–37, 139, 141, 181–82, 184, 197

D

Day of Pentecost. See Pentecost, day of
Discontinuity/Discontinualists, 157

219

Index of Subjects and Names

Dispensationalism, Dispensationalists, 17, 90, 201–02, 204
Dobson, James, 15
Doctrine of subsequence. See Subsequence, doctrine of
Dunn Debate, the, ix–x, 90, 106, 159–60, 162, 205–06
Dunn, James D. G., vii–xi, 27, 35–36, 38, 40–41, 46, 80, 86–89, 98–103, 105–06, 108–10, 113–16, 122–24, 126, 137–40, 146–49, 152–53, 155–57, 159–61, 164–68, 178–79, 185–87, 206

E

Eastern orthodox churches, 183–84, 192
Ellington, Duke, 1–3, 5, 10–12
End times, the, 62, 126, 128–30, 134, 201
Ephesian twelve/Ephesians, 134, 143, 145–54, 159, 185, 196–99
Eschaton, the, 45, 175–76
Evangelism, 46, 68, 102, 156, 173, 205, 208
Exorcism(s)/exorcizing, 38, 54

F

Feast of Pentecost, 79, 83
Feast of Tabernacles/Booths, 44
Feast of Weeks, 83
Fee, Gordon, viii, 26, 28, 30, 72, 100, 102, 104, 148, 152–53, 160–61, 164–65, 176
Finney, Charles G., 22
Fire-Baptized Holiness Church, 21
First church council, 138
First Communion. See Roman Catholic Church
Fletcher, John, 20
Forgiveness, 49, 53, 80, 108, 132–33, 136, 140, 168–69, 186
Free Methodist Church, 5, 8, 11, 15, 17, 19–21
Fundamentalism, 23, 202

G

Glossolalia. See Speaking in tongues
Graham, Billy, 15, 22–25, 173, 208

H

Hades (Hell), gates of, 55, 61, 95
Healing(s), 22, 24, 26, 31, 35, 38, 54, 112, 123, 133, 172–73, 175
Hinn, Benny, 22
Hiskey, Jim, 23–25, 181
Holiness movement, 17, 19–21, 28, 179
Holy Spirit (=Spirit of God): as Advocate/Paraclete, 44, 48, 49, 53, 162; existence of, 149; filled with, x, 19, 32, 35, 49, 76, 78, 92–93, 106, 118, 120–24, 136, 169–70, 196, 198, 205; gift of, 41–42, 78–79, 82, 86, 88–89, 91, 99, 107–09, 133, 139–40, 146, 167–68, 174, 178, 183, 195, 209; indwelling of, 37, 39, 162–63, 169–70; receiving of, 83–84, 86, 97, 99, 108, 153–55, 160, 167; sealed with, 167–68, 183, 185

I

Imminency, doctrine of, 201
Iowa Holiness Association, 21
Irwin, Benjamin Hardin, 21
Isaac, 126–27
Israel's endtimes conversion, 128

J

Jesus: ascension of, 35, 41, 44, 49–50, 83, 88–89, 97; baptism of, 34, 53–54, 145; baptizes with the Holy Spirit, 42, 48, 53, 78, 111, 145, 150, 196; breathed the Holy Spirit on disciples, 45–47, 84; identity of, 54–56, 62, 68, 111; as Lamb of God, 40, 43, 59, 145, 152; as Messiah, 40, 49, 54–55, 57–60, 68, 74, 78, 80, 84, 86–87, 97, 100, 128, 137–38, 143–47, 149; miracles of,

Index of Subjects and Names

34, 36–38, 54; resurrection of, 35, 40–41, 46, 50, 62, 88–89, 125–27, 129–30, 143, 151–52, 154, 168, 193; return of, 26, 74–76, 81, 128, 130, 176, 200–04; Spirit-anointing and empowering of, 34, 36–39, 54
John, the Apostle, 23, 86, 98–99, 104–07, 109–12, 116, 154, 184
John's baptism, 90, 143, 148, 150–52
John the Baptist, 38, 42, 53, 55, 78, 81, 97, 135, 144–45, 150, 154, 167, 182, 196
Judgment, the, 75, 203
Justification, 179, 187
Justin Martyr, 36, 116

K

Kermit Zarley: Blog, x; Lectures, vii
Key of the house of David, 61, 63–64
Keys of the kingdom (of heaven), x, 32, 55, 62, 64, 67, 71, 83–84, 93, 95, 111, 188–89, 191–92
Kingdom of God/Christ, 39, 61, 65–66, 75, 98, 100–11, 176, 191, 205

L

Laying on of hands, 105, 112, 154, 178, 184, 197
Last Supper, 44, 53, 87, 162
Law of Moses. See Torah
Law, William, 19
Loosing, 62, 64–65, 67–71, 95, 114, 131, 190, 192
Lunde, John, viii
Luther, Martin, 64, 129, 164

M

Mary/Jesus' mother, 76, 152
Mary Magdalene, 60
Massengale, Rik and Cindy, 181
McKnight, Scot, vii–viii, x–xi, 27–28
Methodist Church, 20, 33
Miracle(s), 26, 31, 34–39, 54, 79, 98, 104–05, 172–73, 175
Mosaic Law. See Torah

Moses, 41, 45, 54, 58, 82, 127–29, 138, 174, 182, 198
Mother Teresa, 208

N

Nazarene(s), 20, 23–24, 86,
New birth/born again, 16, 18, 29, 39–42, 45–46, 85, 87–88, 91, 109, 121, 124, 139–40, 162, 168, 180–81, 184
New Covenant, 41, 90, 136, 168
New perspective on Paul, 166–67
Nicodemus, 16, 39–41, 43, 180
Nordling, Cherith Fee, 28

O

Old Covenant, 41, 89–90, 136, 168

P

Papacy, doctrine of. See Roman Catholic Church
Parham, Charles F., 21, 29
Pentecostal-Charismatic movement, 28, 31, 202
Pentecostal Church of the Nazarene, 23
Pentecostal movement, 21, 23, 28, 202, 206
Pentecost, day of, 35, 40, 43, 45–49, 65, 76, 78–94, 97, 105, 107–11, 122, 129, 134, 136–38, 143, 148, 150–51, 154, 165, 168–69, 181, 198, 200, 204
Peter, the Apostle: preeminence of, 59–61, 106
PGA Tour Bible Study, 24, 31, 180–81, 183
Philip the Evangelist, 86, 97–102, 104–07, 109, 114–18, 154, 159
Pneumatology/pneumatologies, 85, 104, 156–59, 166, 199
Pope Francis, 191
Pope Melchiades, 184
Posttribulationism, 203
Preaching. See Evangelism
Premillennialism, 200, 202–03
Pretribulationism, 201–04

Index of Subjects and Names

Priscilla and Aquila, 115, 143–44, 151

R

Regeneration, baptismal, 42, 80, 136, 180–83, 186–87
Regeneration, spiritual, 23, 40–42, 46, 80, 84, 86, 89–90, 140, 147, 156, 168, 184
Repentance, 42, 49, 53, 80, 91, 108, 116, 124, 136–37, 139, 143, 151, 181–82, 186–87, 197
Resurrection, the, 26, 62, 129–30, 161
Revivalism, 21
Roberts, Evelyn, 24
Roberts, Oral, 22, 24–25, 112, 173
Roman Catholic Church: Baptism in, 180; Confirmation in, 98, 104, 178–80, 183–85; doctrine of papacy, 58–59, 63, 180, 188–90, 192; First Communion in, 183; Sacrament(s)/sacramentalism of, 178–80, 185, 206

S

Sacrament(s)/sacramentalism. See Roman Catholic Church
Salvation Army, 21
Salvation history, 41, 46, 88, 200
Salvation/saved, 10, 18, 20, 46, 66, 90–91, 99, 104, 107–11, 136–37, 140, 147, 152, 156, 167, 178–80, 186, 205
Sanctification, 18–21, 23, 30, 32, 132, 179, 205
Second blessing, 19, 85, 170
Separability. See Subsequence, doctrine of
Seymour, William J., 28–29
Sheol, 61–62
Simon Magus (the Magician), 97–98, 103, 109, 113–16
Simon Peter. See Peter, the Apostle
Smith, Chuck, 31
Smith, Mike, 181
Society of Biblical Literature, viii, 27

Speaking in tongues, 31, 79, 83, 91, 113, 122, 156, 165, 173–75, 198, 205
Spiritual gifts, xi, 31, 105, 112, 163, 170–76, 202, 205
Steinbeck, John, 6
Stephen, 52–53, 97, 119, 121–22
Stone, Barton, 22
Subsequence (and separability), doctrine of, viii–x, 22, 29, 31–32, 84–86, 91–92, 97, 102–03, 109, 111–12, 117–18, 121–22, 124, 130, 136, 139–41, 146–48, 152, 155–60, 162, 164–65, 185, 199–200, 204–06, 208

T

Tertullian, 62
Theophilus, 73–74
Thieme Jr., Robert B., 17, 26
Third day (three days) motif, 126, 130
Third Wave, 31–32
Thompson family, 15
Thousand-Year Day Principle, 130
Tongues speaking. See Speaking in tongues
Torah, 32, 39–41, 70, 79, 81, 127, 132, 134, 138, 160–61, 166
Torrey, R. A., 22–23, 30
Tribulation, the, 62, 200–02
Tyndale, William, 208
Typology, 127

U

Upper Room, 76

V

Vatican I, 65, 189, 191
Vatican II, 80, 190
Vineyard church movement, 31
Vision(s), 77, 83, 120–21, 132–33, 136

W

Wagner, C. Peter, 31

Index of Subjects and Names

Water baptism, xi, 34, 37–38, 105, 108, 124, 136, 141–42, 151–52, 164, 180–83, 186–87, 197–99
Way, the, 86, 120, 143–44, 148
Wesley, John, 18–20, 22, 124, 169, 179, 205, 208
Westminster Confession, 65
World Assemblies of God Fellowship, 30–31
Wilberforce, William, 208

Wimber, John, 31

Z

Zarley, Barbara/Kermit's mother, 1, 8, 15–17, 21, 33
Zarley, Con, 6
Zarley, Edna, 6, 18, 169
Zarley, Marilyn, 25–26
Zarley, Kermit, Sr./Pop, 1–5, 6–15
Zwingli, Ultricht, 64

Index of Scripture and Other Ancient Writings

OLD TESTAMENT

Genesis
1:1–2	51
1:2	52
6:3	52
11	79
17:5	57
22:4	127, 129
32:28	57

Exodus
19:11	127

Leviticus
11	132
11:44	30
20:7	30
23:17	83

Numbers
11:1–15	45
11:16	45
11:17b	80
11:25	45, 198
11:28–29	45
11:29	82, 174

Deuteronomy
4:27	128
4:29–30	128
10:15–16	41
18:15	54
28:12	128
30:1–5	128
31:17–18	82
32:20–21	82
32:30	82

Joshua
Josh 1:11	127

1 Kings
22:19–22	71

2 Kings
20:5	127

2 Chronicles
10:5	126
10:12	126

Esther
4:15–16	126
5:1	126–27, 129

Psalms
2	57, 152
51:11	149, 169
82:1	71
89:5–7	71
90:4	130
104:29	82
110	152
118:22	59
135:5	71
136:2	71
138:1	71

Isaiah
1:15	82
8:17	82
6:8–10	128
11:2	36
22:20–22	63–64
22:22	64
26:19	129
28:16	59
30:20	82
35:5–6	38

Index of Scripture and Other Ancient Writings

Isaiah (continued)

35:8	82
38:10	62
39:29	79
42:1	36
44:3	44
44:3–4	79
44:4	134
45:15	82
49:5	129
53	117
54:8	82
55:1	44
57	81
57:13	82
57:14	82
57:17	82
57:19	81
58:11	44
59:2	82
59:21	134
61:1	23, 36, 38
62:2	129
62:7–9	129
63:10–11	149
64:7	82
65:9	82

Jeremiah

2:13	44
4:4	41
5:21	128
31:31	41
31:31–33	134
31:33	41
32:40	134
50:4–5	82

Ezekiel

18:30–31	41
36:25–26	41
36:26–27	134
37:14	134
37:26	134
39:23–24	82
39:29	82, 134

Daniel

7:9–10	70
7:13	56
7:13–14	75
7:26	70

Hosea

3:4–5	128
5:15	128
6:1–2	128
6:2	129–30
6:1–3	129–30
5:6	82
5:12—6:1–3	129
5:15	82

Joel

2	134
2–3	134
2:11–17	129
2:28	134, 200
2:28–29	37, 45
2:28–32	79, 83, 134, 200

Micah

5:3–5	129

Zechariah

12:10–14	129

Malachi

3:1	201
4:5–6	129

NEW TESTAMENT

Matthew

1:18	34
1:20	34
3:2	54, 81, 97
3:8	182
3:10	182
3:11	78, 150, 167, 196
3:11–12	42, 152
3:13	145
3:13–17	54
3:16–17	145
4:1	54
4:2	54
4:3–11	54
4:17	54, 81, 97
4:19	46
5:5	82
5:6	170
5:48	19, 169
6:9	88–89
6:10	61
6:24	115
7:11	74
7:13–14	66
7:21	88, 163
7:21–23	115
7:24–27	58
10:1–4	96
10:2	59
10:5–8	96
11:2–3	152
11:2–5	38
12:18	36
12:28	38
12:32	37
12:38–40	152
12:40	62, 125, 127
12:50	88
13:4	66
13:21	115
14:1–2	55
14:3–12	55
14:28	59
14:31	61
14:33	96
15:15	59, 96
15:21	96
15:24	152
16:4	127, 152
16:13–19	133
16:13–20	55, 63
16:15	60
16:16	40

Index of Scripture and Other Ancient Writings

16:16–19	57
16:17–19	x, 58, 71, 188
16:18	66, 95, 188
16:18–19	57
16:19	x, 64–65, 68, 70, 83–84, 93, 95, 115, 131, 188, 190–92,
16:19b	68–70
16:21	61, 125, 152
16:21–22	82
16:22	60
16:23	59, 61
17:1	59
17:4	60
17:22–23	82, 152
17:23	125
17:24	60
18:1	69
18:15	68
18:15–17	67–68
18:15–18	67
18:16	68
18:17	68
18:18	45, 67–70, 191
18:21	60
19:27	60
20:17–19	152
20:18–19	82
20:19	125
21:10	55
21:33—22:14	96
21:42	59
23:2	116
23:5	116
23:13	65
24:15	201
24:36	37
26:6–12	152
26:31	193
26:33–35	193
26:37	59
26:37–41	60
26:63	57
26:69–74	61
26:75	193
27:20–24	80
27:21	80
27:25	81
27:62–64	126
28:19	82

Mark

1:4–5	53
1:7–8	42, 53
1:8	167, 196
1:15	81
5:37	59
8:27–29	56
8:31	125
8:31–32	82
9:31	125
9:31–32	82
9:33–37	194
10:33–34	82
10:34	125
10:41–45	194
11:21	60
13:14	201
13:32	37
15:11	80
16:7	60
16:13	115
16:15	82
16:16	64

Luke

1:1–2	74
1:1–4	73
1:3	73
1:35	34
1:47–53	23
2:42	127
2:46	127
3:8–9	182
3:16	78, 145, 150, 167, 196
3:16–17	42, 152
4:1	197
4:1–2	35
4:14	35
4:16	35
4:18	23, 35, 38
4:21	35, 38
5:5	89
5:21	55
7	73
7:18–22	38
7:19–20	152
7:49	55
8:13	101, 115
8:45	59
9:9	55
9:18–20	56
9:20	89
9:22	82, 125
9:44–45	82
9:51–53	99
9:54	99
10:9	97
10:11	97
10:20	90
10:29–37	107
11:2	88–89
11:9	169
11:13	74, 169
11:14	38
11:15	38
11:20	38
11:52	65
12:41	60
12:48	116
13:24	66
13:25–27	66
18:31–34	82
18:33	125
19:11–12	75
19:13–27	75
22:66	80
24:7	125
24:46	125
24:46–49	49
24:47	82
24:49	43, 83, 167, 196

John

1:14	36
1:16	39
1:29	152
1:29–34	43, 145
1:33	48

Index of Scripture and Other Ancient Writings

John (continued)

1:35–36	145
1:35–49	46
1:40	57
1:40–42	146
1:41	40, 146
1:42	57
1:44–45	146
1:49	40, 146
2:11	34
2:19–22	152
3:1–3	39
3:3	180
3:3–5	16, 109
3:3–15	180
3:5	40, 46, 168, 180, 198
3:5–10	39
3:10	40
3:14	47
3:14–15	168
3:22–23	135
3:28	145
3:30	145
3:34	39
4:1–3	135
4:3–4	43
4:5–8	43
4:7	43
4:8	107
4:9	107
4:13–14	44–45
4:14	162
4:19–26	100
4:20–22	107
4:20	110
4:22	107, 110
4:29	54
5:19	36
5:30	36
6:14	54
6:15	23
6:63	35
6:68	60
6:69	60
7:26	54
7:31	54
7:37–38	170
7:37–39	44, 87
7:38	45, 150, 162
7:38–39	39, 164
7:39	45, 47, 87, 150, 162, 167
7:40–41	54
8:12	54
8:25	55
8:28	47
8:30–32	115
8:53	55
9:5	54
9:39–41	128
10:24	55
12:32	47
12:34	47, 55
12:46	54
13:9	60
13:10	87
13:23	203
13:31–32	47
13:31—14:3	44
14:2–3	44
14:6	144
14:10	37
14:16	48, 162
14:16–17	44, 48, 53
14:17	162
14:17b	48–49
14:21	88
14:23	88
14:26	44, 48, 53, 162
14:33	57
15:3	87
15:22	57
15:26	44
16:6–7	44
16:7	44, 48
16:8	53
16:14–16	48
17:1	47
18:10	60
20:1–2	60
20:1–6	60
20:2	203
20:19	45
20:19–23	47
20:21	46
20:21–23	45, 48
20:21–22	84
20:22	45–48, 84
20:24	45
20:30–31	203
20:31	57, 203
21	203–04
21:1–3	193
21:3	61
21:4–8	61
21:7	203
21:15	193–94
21:15–17	61, 188, 191
21:15–19	193
21:17	194
21:20	203
21:20–23	203
21:22	194

Acts

1—2	87
1–8	159
1–10	81–82, 86, 156
1–12	191
1:1	73–74
1:2	50
1:4	196
1:4–5	43
1:4–9	49
1:5	x, 46, 75, 78–79, 82, 92, 97, 167, 195–96
1:6	75
1:6–7	37
1:7–8	75
1:8	x, 75, 82, 97, 110, 114, 118, 131, 140, 167, 195, 200
1:9	47, 97
1:9–11	76
1:12–13	76
1:14	76
1:15	40, 76
1:15–26	61
1:20–25	76
1:21	89
1:26	76

Index of Scripture and Other Ancient Writings

Reference	Pages
2	x, 43, 46, 78–79, 84, 91–92, 111–12, 121, 131, 134, 140–41, 154, 168, 192, 195, 197, 199–200, 204
2–8	113
2:1–4	46–48, 97
2:1–41	76
2:2–3	78, 91
2:3	78
2:3–4	171
2:4	29, 49, 78, 84, 92, 97, 171
2:4–13	79, 134
2:5–12	171
2:11	79, 171
2:13	170
2:14	81
2:15	170
2:16	83
2:17	200
2:22	35
2:22–49	75
2:23	80
2:29	81, 122
2:33	47, 167, 196
2:36	59, 65, 80–81
2:36–38	80
2:37	122
2:38	79–80, 82, 91–92, 103, 105, 108–10, 168, 181–82, 195, 197–98
2:38–39	81, 101–02
2:38–42	84
2:39	81–82, 196
2:40	74
2:41	97, 112
2:44	86
3—4:22	106
3:1	93
3:1–8	112
3—4:22	106
3:6	93
3:14–15	80
3:17	122
3:18	65
3:18–20	59
3:19	181
3:19–21	75, 81, 128, 176
3:20	65
3:25	81
4:4	79, 93, 97, 101, 112, 198
4:8	49, 92
4:10	59, 65, 80
4:10–12	75
4:11	59
4:12	137
4:13	23, 106
4:29–31	169
4:31	49, 92
4:32	94
4:34–35	94
5	95
5:1–11	95, 113
5:11	95
5:12	95, 112
5:14	97, 112, 198
5:15	93, 112
5:18	91
5:29–32	75
5:30	80
5:31	47, 91
5:31–32	92
5:32	91, 198
5:34	119
6:2–4	136
6:3	169, 197
6:3–6	101
6:5	169, 197
6:5—7:60	97
7:2	122
7:51–52	52, 124
7:52	80
7:58	119
7:59	121
8	x, 81, 86, 98–99, 102–05, 107, 109–13, 121, 131, 136, 140–41, 153–54, 157–60, 165, 168, 185, 193, 195, 197, 199–200, 204
8:1	119
8:1–25	97, 102
8:3	119
8:4–24	101–02
8:4–25	98, 105, 112
8:5	100
8:5–14	100–01, 103
8:8	117
8:9	114
8:10	116
8:12	100–01, 115
8:12–13	115
8:12–17	29, 101, 153
8:13	115
8:14	101, 104
8:14–17	184
8:14–24	106
8:15	105, 195
8:15–17	105, 117
8:16	106
8:16–17	84
8:17	118, 154, 184, 195
8:17–18	198
8:18	106, 110
8:18–19	113
8:19	195
8:20	195
8:20–22	116
8:22	116
8:23	115–16
8:24	114, 116
8:26	117
8:26–40	101
8:27–28	117
8:29–35	106
8:30–35	117
8:36–39	117
8:38–39	117
8:39	117, 147
9	118, 121–23, 126
9:1	147
9:1–7	84, 148
9:1–19	119
9:2	86, 144
9:5	121
9:9	125
9:10–19	123
9:12	112

Index of Scripture and Other Ancient Writings

Acts (continued)

9:17	92, 105, 122, 198	11:14–15	141		159–60, 168, 195–99
9:17–18	112	11:14–16	29	19:1	148
9:18	123	11:15	92, 137, 195	19:1–7	106, 142, 146–47, 149, 151–53
9:19	123, 125	11:16	167, 195–96		
9:20–22	75	11:17	108, 137–38, 195	19:2a	146
9:31	95	11:18	137, 139	19:2b	150
9:33–35	94	11:21	196	19:2	148–49, 195
9:36–42	94	11:24	169, 196–97	19:2–6	153
9:40	112	11:26	86, 146	19:4	151
10	x, 81–82, 86, 92, 108, 110–12, 117–18, 134, 136, 139–41, 148, 154, 159–60, 181, 193, 195–200, 204	13	156	19:5	106, 152
		13:9	49, 92	19:5–6	152, 184
		13:12	196	19:6	84, 105, 134, 153, 171, 184
		13:15	122		
		13:26	122	19:9	86, 144
		13:28–39	75	19:11	112
10:1–2	131	13:38	122	19:16	84
10:2	136	13:48	196	19:18	196
10:2–4	91	13:52	49, 92, 117	19:23	144
10:3–4	121	14:1	196	20:5—21:18	73
10:3–33	132	14:3	112	20:21	75
10:4	136	15:1	182	20:32	132
10:10	132	15:1–2	138	22	121
10:13	132	15:5	138, 182	22:1	122
10:15	132	15:7	138–39	22:1–21	122
10:17–24	132	15:7–8	141	22:3	119
10:22	136	15:7–9	29	22:4	144
10:24	133	15:8	138–39, 195	22:5	122
10:28	133	15:8–9	108	22:8	121
10:33	133	15:9	132, 139, 182	22:13	122
10:34–48	133	16–28	191	22:16	106, 124
10:35	136	16:10–17	73	23:1	122
10:36	65	16:14–15	196	23:5–6	122
10:38	35	16:25–34	196	24:5	86
10:38–43	75	16:30–31	182	24:14	86, 144
10:39	80	16:31	75	24:22	86, 144
10:40	125	16:33	182	26	121
10:43	136	17:11	101	26:1–23	122
10:44	85, 184, 195	17:12	196	26:15	121
10:44–46	29, 92, 105	17:30–31	75	26:17–18	132
10:45	93, 195	17:34	196	26:20–23	75
10:46	134, 171	18:8	196	26:28	86
10:47	138, 195	18:24–28	142	27:1—28:16	73
10:48	135, 184	18:24—19:7	142, 148, 150	28:8	112
11:1	101, 139			28:16	73
11:13–14	181	18:25	144, 148, 150	28:17	122
11:14	139, 147	19	99, 108–09, 112, 121, 134, 153–54,	28:21	122
				28:23	75

Index of Scripture and Other Ancient Writings

28:31	75, 100	4:20	205	1:13	124
		5:6–7	95	2:7	137
Romans		5:7	152	2:14	166
1:7	160	6:9	115	2:16	166, 187
1:11	112	6:19	163	3:2	167–68
3:26–30	187	7:1	171	3:2–3	165
3:28	187	10:1–4	58	3:5	167
5:1	187	11:17–18	173	3:13–14	167
5:5	160, 163	11:20	173	3:14	81, 167
6:4	126	11:33–34	173	4:6	163
6:14	161	12	32, 171–74	4:10	166
7	160–61	12–14	134, 171–74	5:2	166
7:1	161	12:1	171	5:19–21	115
7:4	161	12:3	88, 121, 163	5:22	93, 117
7:6	161	12:4–11	172	5:22–23	24
7:7–25	161	12:10	171		
7:15	161	12:12	172	**Ephesians**	
7:25	161	12:13	32, 83, 89, 99,	1:11	167
8	160–61		164–65, 198	1:13	167, 185
8:1–2	161	12:14	172	1:13–14	167, 185
8:4	161	12:15–21	173	2:8–9	16, 181
8:8–9	161, 163	12:27–30	173	2:18	163
8:9	39, 99, 162–63,	12:28	173	2:19–20	59
	168–69	12:30	174	3:19	39
8:11	163	12:31	173	4:4	163
8:14	163	13	175	4:5	151, 198
8:14–16	163	13:8–10	26	4:30	167, 185
8:14–17	165	13:8–13	175	5:5–6	115
8:16	163	13:10	175	5:18	32, 93, 169–70
9:33	59	13:12	26	5:19–20	169
10:9	87	14	171, 174		
11:25–26	128	14:2	174	**Colossians**	
11:25–27	176	14:3	174	1:19	39
14:17	117	14:4	174	2:9	39
		14:5	174	2:12	126
1 Corinthians		14:18	122, 174	4:12–14	73
1:10–13	144	14:26c	174	4:14	73
1:10–16	163	14:37–40	174		
1:12	135	14:39	174	**1 Thessalonians**	
1:13–15	135	15:4	125, 129	1:6	101
1:14	182			2:13	101
1:17	135, 182	**2 Corinthians**		5:17	169
2:4	205	1:21–22	167, 185		
2:10–14	165			**1 Timothy**	
3:1	163	**Galatians**		4:14	112
3:10–11	59	1:2	166		
3:16	163	1:6	166		

231

Index of Scripture and Other Ancient Writings

1 Timothy (continued)
6:10	115

2 Timothy
1:6	112
4:11	73

Titus
1:16	115
3:6	93

Hebrews
6:4–6	115
10:26–27	115
11:17–19	127

James
1:21	101
2:14	115
2:20–26	115

1 Peter
1:16	30
2:4–8	59

2 Peter
3:8	130

1 John
1:7	19
1:9	18–19, 169
2:4	115
3:6	18
3:6–10	115
3:8	18
3:9	18
4:7–8	115
5:1	40
5:4	115
5:18	18, 115

Revelation
1:18	62
2:16	204
3:7	66
3:11	204
4:1	62
4:4	71
4:10	71
5:6	71
5:8	71
5:11	71
5:14	71
6:16–17	152
11:1–2	201
17:14	152
19:4	71
19:11–21	152
20	200
21:2	64
21:12–15	62
21:14	59
21:21	62
21:25	64
22:7	204
22:12	204
22:20	204

ANCIENT CHRISTIAN WRITINGS

Athanasius
Orations against the Arians — 36

Justin Martyr
Acts of Peter	116
Dialogue with Trypho	36
First Apology	116

Pseudo-Clementine
Homilies	116

Tertullian
The Apology	62

Thomas Aquinas
Summa Theologica	184

www.ingramcontent.com/pod-product-compliance
Lightning Source LLC
Chambersburg PA
CBHW051636230426
43669CB00013B/2322